T0073149

Biological
Language Model
Theory and Application

East China Normal University Scientific Reports
Subseries on Data Science and Engineering

ISSN: 2382-5715

Chief Editor
Weian Zheng
Changjiang Chair Professor
School of Finance and Statistics
East China Normal University, China
Email: financialmaths@gmail.com

Associate Chief Editor
Shanping Wang
Senior Editor
Journal of East China Normal University (Natural Sciences), China
Email: spwang@library.ecnu.edu.cn

This book series reports valuable research results and progress in scientific and related areas. Mainly contributed by the distinguished professors of the East China Normal University, it will cover a number of research areas in pure mathematics, financial mathematics, applied physics, computer science, environmental science, geography, estuarine and coastal science, education information technology, etc.

Published

Vol. 12 *Biological Language Model: Theory and Application*
by Qiwen Dong (East China Normal University, China),
Xiaoyang Jing (Yunnan University, China),
Aoying Zhou (East China Normal University, China) and
Xiuzhen Hu (Inner Mongolia University of Technology, China)

Vol. 11 *Probabilistic Approaches for Social Media Analysis:*
Data, Community and Influence
by Kun Yue (Yunnan University, China), Jin Li (Yunnan University, China), Hao Wu (Yunnan University, China), Weiyi Liu (Yunnan University, China) and Zidu Yin (Yunnan University, China)

Vol. 10 *Clustering and Outlier Detection for Trajectory Stream Data*
by Jiali Mao (East China Normal University, China),
Cheqing Jin (East China Normal University, China) and
Aoying Zhou (East China Normal University, China)

More information on this series can also be found at https://www.worldscientific.com/series/ecnusr

(Continued at end of book)

East China Normal University Scientific Reports | Vol. 12
Subseries on Data Science and Engineering

Biological Language Model

Theory and Application

Qiwen Dong
Xiaoyang Jing
Aoying Zhou
Xiuzhen Hu
East China Normal University, China

World Scientific

NEW JERSEY · LONDON · SINGAPORE · BEIJING · SHANGHAI · HONG KONG · TAIPEI · CHENNAI · TOKYO

Published by

World Scientific Publishing Co. Pte. Ltd.

5 Toh Tuck Link, Singapore 596224

USA office: 27 Warren Street, Suite 401-402, Hackensack, NJ 07601

UK office: 57 Shelton Street, Covent Garden, London WC2H 9HE

Library of Congress Cataloging-in-Publication Data
Names: Dong, Qiwen, author. | Jing, Xiaoyang, 1991–   author. |
    Zhou, Aoying, 1965–   author. | Hu, Xiuzhen, author.
Title: Biological language model : theory and application / Qiwen Dong,
    Xiaoyang Jing, Aoying Zhou, Xiuzhen Hu.
Other titles: East China Normal University scientific reports ; v. 12
Description: Hackensack : World Scientific, [2020] | Series: East China
    Normal University scientific reports, 2382-5715 ; vol. 12. Subseries on
    data science and engineering | Includes bibliographical references and index.
Identifiers: LCCN 2019052135 | ISBN 9789811212949 (hardcover) | ISBN 9789811212956 (ebook) |
    ISBN 9789811212963 (ebook other)
Subjects: MESH: Computational Biology | Sequence Analysis | Natural Language Processing
Classification: LCC QH324.2 | NLM QU 26.5 | DDC 570.285--dc23
LC record available at https://lccn.loc.gov/2019052135

British Library Cataloguing-in-Publication Data
A catalogue record for this book is available from the British Library.

For any available supplementary material, please visit
https://www.worldscientific.com/worldscibooks/10.1142/11629#t=suppl

Desk Editors: Tay Yu Shan/Nur Izdihar Binte Ismail

Typeset by Stallion Press
Email: enquiries@stallionpress.com

East China Normal University Scientific Reports

Shengli Tan (Changjiang Chair Professor, Department of Mathematics, East China Normal University)

Peng Wu (Changjiang Scholar Chair Professor, Department of Chemistry, East China Normal University)

Jianpan Wang (Professor, Department of Mathematics, East China Normal University)

Rongming Wang (Professor, School of Financial and Statistics, East China Normal University)

Wei-Ning Xiang (Zijiang Chair Professor, Department of Environmental Science, East China Normal University; Professor, Department of Geography and Earth Science, University of North Carolina at Charlotte)

Danping Yang (Professor, Department of Mathematics, East China Normal University)

Kai Yang (Professor, Department of Environmental Science, East China Normal University)

Shuyi Zhang (Zijiang Chair Professor, School of Life Sciences, East China Normal University)

Weiping Zhang (Changjiang Chair Professor, Department of Physics, East China Normal University)

Xiangming Zheng(Professor, Department of Geography, East China Normal University)

Aoying Zhou (Changjiang Chair Professor, School of Data Science and Engineering, East China Normal University)

Subseries on Data Science and Engineering

Chief Editor
Aoying Zhou
Changjiang Chair Professor
School of Data Science and Engineering
East China Normal University, China
Email: ayzhou@sei.ecnu.edu.cn

Associate Editors
Rakesh Agrawal (Technical Fellow, Microsoft Research in Silicon Valley)
Michael Franklin (University of California at Berkeley)
H. V, Jagadish (University of Michigan in Ann Arbor)
Christian S. Jensen (University of Aalborg)
Masaru Kitsuregawa (University of Tokyo, National Institute of Informatics (NII))
Volker Markl (Technische Universität Berlin (TUBerlin))
Gerhard Weikum (Max Planck Institute for Informatics)
Ruqian Lu (Academy of Mathematics and Systems Science, Chinese Academy of Sciences)

Preface

Since the end of the 20th century, with the implementation and successful completion of the Human Genome Project, life sciences researchers have obtained a huge amount of biological data, especially with the development of the sequencing technology of biological macromolecules, thus increasing the number of nucleic acid and protein sequences in an explosive manner. How to get valuable information from biological data? This has thus become a new research hotspot to reveal the law of life activities and has contributed to the birth of a new discipline — Bioinformatics.

Bioinformatics is an interdisciplinary subject formed by integrating biology, information science and applied mathematics. There are different definitions of bioinformatics for different researchers. In a broad sense, bioinformatics is a discipline that deals with the collection, management and analysis of a mass of biological data. At present, bioinformatics mainly focuses on nucleic acids and proteins. In a narrow sense, bioinformatics is a subject that uses the tools and methods of biology, computer science and mathematics to obtain, process, manage, analyze and interpret information on biological macromolecules, and then reveals its biological significance. At present, the research focus of bioinformatics is mainly concentrated on genomics and proteomics. Generally, starting from the initial nucleotide or amino acid sequence, the structural and functional information of biological macromolecules contained in the sequence is analyzed by using the theories and methods of computer science, mathematics and statistics.

Proteins play a key role in various basic biological processes. As the material basis of life activities, proteins participate in various life processes, such as catalyzing almost all chemical reactions in biological cells, regulating gene activity and participating in the formation of most cell structures. In view of the key role of proteins in life activities, the study of protein structure and function has always been the focus of life science research.

Protein sequences are similar to sentences in natural language, as they are both linear arrangements of basic units. The mapping of sequences to structures and functions of proteins is conceptually similar to the mapping of words to meanings. This analogy has been studied by a growing body of research, but are there any linguistic features in protein sequences? What are the basic units in protein sequence language? Large amounts of genomic protein sequence data for *Homo sapiens* and other organisms have recently become available together with a growing body of protein structure and function data. The expected exponential increase in the amount of the data in the coming decade creates an opportunity for attacking the sequence–structure–function mapping problem with sophisticated data-driven methods. Such methods have been proven to be immensely successful in the domain of natural language.

The purpose of this book is to introduce the relevant techniques of biological language modeling into bioinformatics and promote the development of protein sequence–structure–function mapping. In view of the above purpose, the linguistic features of protein sequences are analyzed and several amino acid encoding schemes are explored. Then, several research topics including remote homology detection, protein structure prediction and protein function prediction are investigated by using biological language model approaches. Finally, a brief summary and future perspective are proposed. We hope that this book will be helpful for research in the field of bioinformatics, especially the mapping of protein sequences to their structure and function.

Qiwen Dong
Xiuzhen Hu
Xiaoyang Jing
Aoying Zhou

Acknowledgments

This work was supported by the National Key Research and Development Program of China under grant 2016YFB1000905 and the National Natural Science Foundation of China (Grant No. U1401256, U1711262, U1811264, 61672234, 61961032, 31260203, 61402177).

We would like to thank all the people who have made contributions to and given their valuable suggestions regarding this book, especially Bin Liu, Ming Gao, Dingjiang Huang and Daocheng Hong. We would also like to express our sincere thanks and appreciation to the people at University Press, for their generous help throughout the publication preparation process.

Contents

Chapter 1

Introduction

1.1 Background and Motivation

The task of human genome sequencing was completed in 2003, and life science from then on stepped into the post-gene era. The research focuses are gradually shifting from accumulating data to methods to interpret the data, i.e. how to extract structural and functional information from sequence data. Post-genome sequencing research includes comparative genomics, structural genomics, functional genomics, proteomics, holistic biology and pharmacogenomics.

The proteome[1] is a dynamic concept that is not only different in different tissues and different cells of the same organism but is constantly changing throughout the developmental stages of the same organism until the final demise of that organism. The complex pattern of gene expression leads to a variety of complex life activities. In fact, each form of movement in the stages of life is the result of different combinations of specific protein groups that appear at different times and spaces. The sequence of the genetic DNA does not provide this information, so the language of the nucleic acid alone is not sufficient to describe the entire life activity. It can be seen that the research task of both the whole and the dynamic proteome is very heavy and is a follow-up part of the genomic research that is indispensable for elucidating the nature of life activities. Post-genome

1

or -proteome research will undoubtedly become the main task of relay genome research in life science research in the 21st century.

The mapping relationship between a biological sequence and its structure and function is similar to the word-to-semantic mapping relationship in a language.[2] In linguistics, words can be arranged into meaningful sentences; in biology, amino acid arrangement represents the structure and function of proteins. The arrangment of amino acids to form a protein can be regarded as similar to a meaningful arrangement of words, thereby leading to the specific structures and functions of proteins. The words in a document map directly to the semantics and contain relevant information about the topic of the article; similarly, the protein sequence can be regarded as the original text, containing information about structure and function, which can be used to further understand the mutual interaction between proteins.

As protein primary structure sequencing technology matures, the amount of genomic and proteomic sequence data continues to increase, as does the associated structural and functional data. These data will increase exponentially over the next decade, making it possible to use a data-driven approach to solve protein sequence–structure–function mapping problems. Data-driven methods have been successfully applied in many areas of natural language processing, such as speech recognition, text categorization, information extraction and machine translation.[3]

The emergence of a large number of corpora has promoted the development of computational linguistics. Similarly, the emergence of a large amount of protein sequence–structure–function data has enabled computational methods and information techniques to be applied in this field. Computational linguistic tools including statistical language models, text classification techniques, machine learning methods and higher-level language processing methods have been applied to understand the structure and function of proteins in cells. The purpose of this book is to introduce relevant techniques of biological language modeling in bioinformatics and promote the development of protein sequence–structure–function mapping.

1.2 Related Topics

1.2.1 Linguistic feature analysis of protein sequences

Protein sequences are similar to the sentences seen in natural language, as both are made up of linear arrangements of basic units. The mapping of sequences to the structures and functions of proteins is conceptually similar to the mapping of words to meanings. This analogy has been studied by a growing body of research,[4] but are there any linguistic features in protein sequences? What are the basic units in protein sequence language?

1.2.2 Amino acid encoding for protein sequence

In general, protein sequences are represented by using twenty letters of the amino acid alphabet. Since such a representation cannot be directly processed before it is converted to digital representation, obtaining the digital representation for an amino acid[5, 6] is the first step of machine-learning-based protein structure and function prediction methods, and effective digital representation[7] is crucial to the final success of these methods.

1.2.3 Remote homology detection

With the rapid development of completely sequenced genomes, a large amount of sequence data has been deposited in databases, and now their structure and function need to be elucidated. In general, the easiest way to annotate newly sequenced proteins is to transfer annotations from well-characterized homologous proteins.[8] Therefore, the development of a novel algorithm for protein homology detection is of great importance.[9, 10] This is especially so since remote homology detection — the detection of homologous relationship with low sequence identities — remains a challenging problem in computational biology.[11, 12]

1.2.4 Structure prediction

With the success of a series of genome-sequencing projects, the number of known protein sequences has grown exponentially. The amount of sequence data in the current molecular database far exceeds the amount of structural data, and the acquisition of structural information is very important to reveal the biological function of proteins. However, due to technical difficulties and the laborious nature of structural biology experiments, the speed of protein structure determination lags far behind the increase in the number of sequences. Studying protein structure prediction[13] has great theoretical and practical value. In theory, it is beneficial for people to systematically and completely understand the whole process of transferring biological information from DNA to biologically active proteins as well as to clarify the central law more completely.[14] Having a deeper understanding of the various phenomena in the life process ultimately promotes the rapid development of life sciences.[15] As regards application, it is beneficial for people to analyze disease pathogenesis and find treatment methods, and design proteins with novel biological functions, thereby promoting the rapid development of medicine, agriculture and animal husbandry. Thus, developing efficient computer-based algorithms to predict high-resolution 3D protein structures from their sequences becomes increasingly important.[16, 17]

1.2.5 Function prediction

Proteins are one of the most important molecules in biology as they have a role in many life processes, such as transcription, metabolism and regulation. It is thus of great importance to perform function analysis on proteins to help understand the processes of life.[18] Due to the huge amount of proteins present, it is difficult to verify the function of each and every protein. Computational approaches for function prediction are necessary to assist in the functional identification of the proteome.[19] The related research[9] includes such aspects as interaction prediction and ontology-based function prediction. Since proteins perform their function by binding with other ligands, including proteins, metal ions, DNA, RNA, etc., it is essential to predict the binding sites of proteins to further explore in detail the function of proteins.[20]

1.3 Organization of the Book Content

The structure of this book is organized as follows. First, it begins by providing an introduction to the proteome, the biological language model and its application. Then, several research topics of the biological language model are proposed, with detailed introductions on the background and a description of the methods, i.e. linguistic feature analysis of protein sequences, amino acid encoding for protein sequences, protein remote homology detection, protein structure prediction and protein function prediction. For the topic of linguistic feature analysis of protein sequences, the n-grams of whole genome protein sequences from 20 organisms were extracted to obtain statistical sequence analysis results for a large number of genomic and proteomic sequences available for different organisms. Their linguistic features were analyzed by two tests — Zipf's power law and Shannon's entropy — developed for analysis of natural languages and symbolic sequences. As regards amino acid encoding, a comprehensive review of the available methods for this is proposed, and these methods are grouped into five categories according to their information sources and information extraction methodologies, which are as follows: binary encoding, physicochemical properties encoding, evolution-based encoding, structure-based encoding and machine-learning encoding. For protein remote homology detection, latent semantic analysis is used to extract and represent the contextual-usage meaning of words of protein sequences by statistical computations, and the auto-cross covariance transformation is introduced to transform protein sequences into fixed-length vectors. For the protein structure prediction topic, a novel index at the profile level is presented for protein domain linker prediction, a building-block library-based method has been presented to predict the local structures and the folding fragments of proteins, conformational entropy is used as an indicator of protein flexibility and a class of novel nonlinear knowledge-based mean force potentials is presented. For the protein function prediction topic, profile-level interface propensities are used for binding site prediction, sequence composition information is used for gene ontology-based protein function prediction and the n-gram biological language model from natural language processing has been used to filter the missing proteins. Finally, the conclusion and future perspectives are proposed.

References

[1] Wasinger V.C. Progress with gene-product mapping of the mollicutes: Mycoplasma genitalium. *Electrophresis*, 1995, 16(7): 1090–1094.

[2] Ganapathiraju M., Balakrishnan N., Reddy R., Klein-Seetharaman J. Computational biology and language. Ambient intelligence for scientific discovery. *LNAI*, 2005, 3345: 25–47.

[3] Manning C.D., Schütze H. *Foundations of Statistical Natural Language Processing.* 1999. Cambridge, MA: MIT Press.

[4] Ganpathiraju M., Weisser D., Rosenfeld R., Carbonell J., Reddy R., Klein-Seetharaman J. Comparative n-gram analysis of whole-genome protein sequences. In *Proceedings of the Human Language Technologies Conference*, San Diego, 2002, pp. 1367–1375.

[5] Tanaka S., Scheraga H.A. Medium- and long-range interaction parameters between amino acids for predicting three-dimensional structures of proteins. *Macromolecules*, 1976, 9(6): 945–950.

[6] Yang K.K., Wu Z., Bedbrook C.N., Arnold F.H. Learned protein embeddings for machine learning. *Bioinformatics*, 2018, 34(15): 2642–2648.

[7] Asgari E., McHardy A.C., Mofrad M.R. Probabilistic variable-length segmentation of protein sequences for discriminative motif discovery (DiMotif) and sequence embedding (ProtVecX). *Sci Rep*, 2019, 9(1): 3577.

[8] Moult J., Fidelis K., Kryshtafovych A., Schwede T., Tramontano A. Critical assessment of methods of protein structure prediction (CASP) — Round XII. Proteins: Structure, Function, and Bioinformatics, 2018, 86: 7–15.

[9] Guo Y., Yu L., Wen Z., Li M. Using support vector machine combined with auto covariance to predict protein-protein interactions from protein sequences. *Nucleic Acids Res*, 2008, 36(9): 3025–3030.

[10] Haandstad T., Hestnes A.J., Saetrom P. Motif kernel generated by genetic programming improves remote homology and fold detection. *BMC Bioinformatics*, 2007, 8(1): 23.

[11] Lingner T., Meinicke P. Remote homology detection based on oligomer distances. *Bioinformatics*, 2006, 22(18): 2224–2231.

[12] Yang Y., Tantoso E., Li K.B. Remote protein homology detection using recurrence quantification analysis and amino acid physicochemical properties. *J Theor Biol*, 2008, 252(1): 145–154.

[13] Li J., Cai J., Su H., Du H., Zhang J., Ding S., Liu G., Tang Y., Li W. Effects of protein flexibility and active site water molecules on the prediction of sites of metabolism for cytochrome P450 2C19 substrates. *Mol Biosyst*, 2016, 12(3): 868–878.

[14] Manoharan P., Chennoju K., Ghoshal N. Target specific proteochemometric model development for BACE1 — Protein flexibility and structural water are critical in virtual screening. *Mol Biosyst*, 2015, 11(7): 1955–1972.

[15] Antunes D.A., Devaurs D., Kavraki L.E. Understanding the challenges of protein flexibility in drug design. *Expert Opin Drug Discov*, 2015, 10(12): 1301–1313.

[16] Yang J., Wang Y., Zhang Y. ResQ: An approach to unified estimation of B-Factor and residue-specific error in protein structure prediction. *J Mol Biol*, 2016, 428(4): 693–701.

[17] Sharma A., Manolakos E.S. Efficient multicriteria protein structure comparison on modern processor architectures. *Bio Med Res Int*, 2015, 2015: 13.

[18] Tetko I.V., Rodchenkov I.V., Walter M.C., Rattei T., Mewes H.W. Beyond the 'best' match: Machine learning annotation of protein sequences by integration of different sources of information. *Bioinformatics*, 2008, 24(5): 621–628.

[19] Kim M.-S., Pinto S.M., Getnet D., Nirujogi R.S., Manda S.S., Chaerkady R., Madugundu A.K., Kelkar D.S., Isserlin R., Jain S. A draft map of the human proteome. *Nature*, 2014, 509(7502): 575–581.

[20] Nanni L., Lumini A. An ensemble of K-local hyperplanes for predicting protein-protein interactions. *Bioinformatics*, 2006, 22(10): 1207–1210.

Chapter 2

Linguistic Feature Analysis of Protein Sequences

2.1 Motivation and Basic Idea

Proteins play an important role in the function of complex biological systems. But the relationship between primary sequences, three-dimensional structures and functions of proteins is one of the most important unanswered questions in biology. With the completion of the Human Genome Project and all kinds of work in assessing biological sequences accurately, a large number of genomic and proteomic sequences are available for different organisms at present. The exponential increase of these data provides an opportunity for us to attack the sequence–structure–function mapping problem with sophisticated data-driven methods. Such methods have been successfully used in the domain of natural language processing. There are analogies between biological sequences and natural language. In linguistics, some words and phrases can form a meaningful sentence, while in biology, some tactic nucleotides denote genes and some fixed protein sequences can determine the structure and function of the protein.[1] But is there a "language" in biological sequences?

Mantegna[2] analyzed the linguistic features of noncoding DNA and emphasized that there exists a "language" in noncoding DNA. Although there are some insufficiencies in the work,[3-5] many methods used in natural language processing have been used in biological sequences. N-grams of DNA[6] and protein[7] have been extracted. A bio-dictionary has been built and used to annotate proteins.[8]

Latent semantic analysis has been used to characterize the secondary structure of proteins.[9] Probabilistic models from speech recognition have been used to enhance the protein domain discovery.[10]

The n-gram analysis method is one of the most frequently used techniques in computational linguistics. It takes the assumption that only the previous $n - 1$ words in a sentence have an effect on the probabilities for the next word.[11] It has been successfully used in automatic speech recognition, document classification, information extraction, statistical machine translation and other challenging tasks in natural language. In this chapter, the n-grams of whole genome protein sequences have been extracted, their Zipf's law has been analyzed and some statistical features have been extracted from the n-grams.

2.2   Comparative n-gram Analysis

Amino acids are treated as words, since each amino acid carries a chemical "meaning". In order to extract the n-gram from whole genome protein sequences, all the proteins of the same organism were arranged in series and split by blank, e.g. protein1 protein2 protein3 etc. Due to the large size of the genomic data, the suffix array[12, 13] was used to reduce the computational cost. To extract the n-gram statistical data, we developed a toolkit that can carry out the following functions:

1. Count protein number and length.
2. Count n-grams and most frequent n-grams.
3. Count n-grams of specified length.
4. Determine relative frequencies of specific n-grams across organisms.
5. Assess the distribution of n-gram frequencies in a specific organism.

The method was applied to protein sequences derived from whole genome sequences of 20 organisms. The protein sequence data was downloaded from the Swiss-prot database.[14] The number of proteins varies from 484 (Mycoplasma_genitalium) to 25612 (Human).

We developed a modification of Zipf-like analysis that could reveal differences between word usage in different organisms. First, the amino acid n-grams of a given length were sorted in descending order by frequency for the organism of choice. The comparative n-gram plots comparing the n-grams of one organism to those of other organisms were drawn using the top 20 n-grams. Figure 2-1 shows the comparative n-gram analysis of Human (A) for $n = 3$ and R_norvegicus (B) for $n = 4$. The x-axis represents the ranked n-grams of a specific organism. The y-axis represents the corresponding frequency. The sorted n-grams of the organism of choice are shown as the bold line. Thick lines indicate the frequencies of n-grams with given rank in other organisms. Table 2-1 shows the 20 organisms used in this book.

In natural language, there are some words that are used frequently and some rarely; similarly in proteins, the frequencies of usage of the 20 amino acids are different. From the uni-gram plot of 20 organisms, Leucine was found to be one of the most frequent amino acids, ranked among the top three. Tryptophan and Cysteine, on the other hand, are the most rare amino acids, and their ranks occupy the last three spots. In language, frequent words are usually not closely related to the actual meaning of the sentence, whereas the rare words often are. So too is the case with the rare amino acids, which may be important for the structure and function of the protein.

Another statistical feature of n-grams is that there are organism-specific "phrases" in the protein sequences. Examples are shown

Table 2-1   Organism names used in the plot.

Organism	Organism
A_thaliana	Human
Aeropyrum_pernix	Methanopyrus_kandleri
arabidopsis	Streptomyces_avermitilis
Archaeoglobus_fulgidus	Mycoplasma_genitalium
Bacillus_anthracis_Ames	Neisseria_meningitidis_MC58
Bifidobacterium_longum	Pasteurella_multocida
Borrelia_burgdorferi	R_norvegicus
Buchnera_aphidicola_Sg	s_pombe
Encephalitozoon_cuniculi	Worm
Fusobacterium_nucleatum	Yeastpom

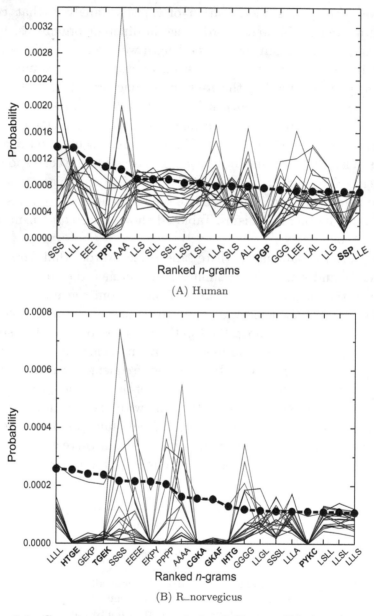

(A) Human

(B) R_norvegicus

Figure 2-1 Comparative *n*-gram analysis of Human (A) for $n = 3$ and R_norvegicus (B) for $n = 4$.

in Fig. 2-1. In Human (Fig. 2-1(A)), the phrases "PPP" "PGP" and "SSP" are among the top 20 most frequently used 3-grams, but they are used in other organisms with very low frequencies. Also in R_norvegicus (Fig. 2-1(B)), similar phrases are "HTGE", "GEKP", "CGKA", "GKAF", "IHTG" and "PYKC". These highly idiosyncratic n-grams suggest that there are organism-specific usages of "phrases" in protein sequences.

2.3 The Zipf Law Analysis

Claiming Zipf's law in a data set seems to be simple enough: if n values, x_i ($i = 1, 2 \ldots n$), are ranked by $x_1 \geq x_2 \geq \ldots x_r \ldots \geq x_n$, Zipf's law[15] states that

$$x_r = \frac{C}{r^\alpha} \qquad (2\text{-}1)$$

where x_r is in the data set whose rank is r, and C and α are constants which denote features of Zipf's law. It can be rewritten as

$$\log x_r = c - \alpha \log(r) \qquad (2\text{-}2)$$

This equation implies that the x_r versus r plot on a log–log scale will be a straight line.

In natural language, the words' frequency and their ranks follow Zipf's law. Especially in English, Zipf's law can be applicable to words, parts of speech, sentences and so on.

Zipf's law of n-grams has been analyzed using the results of n-gram statistics. Figure 2-2 shows the log–log plot of n-gram frequency versus their rank for A_thaliana (A) and Human (B). When n is larger than 4, the plot is similar to a straight line and the value of α is close to 0.5. We can claim that the n-grams of whole genome protein sequences approximately follow Zipf's law when n is larger than 4.

A statistical measure giving partial information about the degree of complexity of a symbolic sequence is obtainable by calculating the n-gram entropy of the analyzed text. The Shannon n-gram entropy is defined as

$$H(n) = -\sum_{i=1}^{\lambda^n} P_i \log_2 P_i \qquad (2\text{-}3)$$

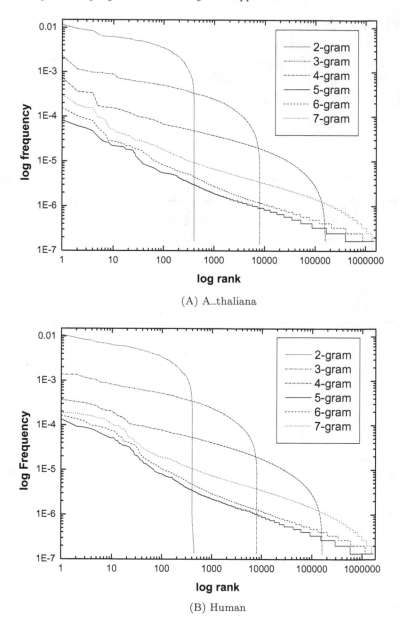

(A) A_thaliana

(B) Human

Figure 2-2   Zipf's Law analysis for A_thaliana (A) and Human (B).

where P_i is the frequency of the n-gram and λ is the number of letters of the alphabet.

From the n-gram entropy, one can obtain the redundancy R represented in any text. The redundancy is given as

$$R = 1 - \lim_{n \to \infty} \frac{H(n)}{Kn} \qquad (2\text{-}4)$$

where $K = \log_2 \lambda$. The redundancy is a manifestation of the flexibility of the underlying language.

To test whether the n-gram Zipf law could be explained by chance sampling, random genome protein sequences have been generated that have the same sequence length and frequency of amino acids as the natural genome. The process used to generate such random genome sequences is the same as the one used by Chatzidimitriou.[3]

The n-gram redundancy of natural and artificial genome protein sequences have been calculated for different values of n (see Fig. 2-3); n-gram redundancy can be approximately expressed as

$$R(n) = 1 - \frac{H(n)}{K * n} \qquad (2\text{-}5)$$

Here, the alphabets are amino acids, and so the value of λ is 20.

From Fig. 2-3, one can see that the n-gram redundancy of the natural genome is larger than that of the artificial genome. This means that the n-gram entropy of the natural genome is small and that a "language" may exist in the protein sequence.

2.4 Distinguishing the Organisms by Uni-Gram Model

Here, perplexity is used to distinguish the different organisms. Perplexity represents the predictive ability of a language model on a testing text. Let $W = w[1], w[2] \ldots w[n]$ denote a sequence of words in the testing text. Let $\mathrm{Ck}(i)$ be the context the language model chooses for the prediction of the word $w[i]$. Furthermore $p(w[i] \mid \mathrm{ck}(i))$ denotes the probability assigned to the ith word by the model.

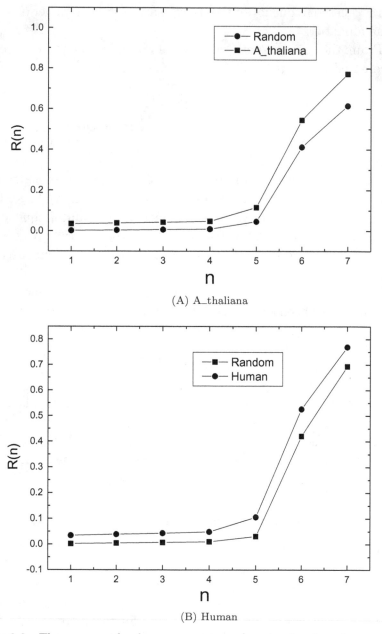

(A) A_thaliana

(B) Human

Figure 2-3   The *n*-gram redundancy comparison of a natural and random genome for A_thaliana (A) and Human (B).

The total probability (TP) of the sequence is

$$\text{TP} = p(W) = p(w[1:n]) = \prod_{i=1}^{i=n} p(w[i] \mid \text{ck}[i]) \qquad (2\text{-}6)$$

Then, the perplexity PP is

$$PP = (TP)^{-1/n} \qquad (2\text{-}7)$$

where n is the length of the total sequences.

A simple uni-gram (context-independent amino acid) model was trained by the 90 percent proteins from Borrelia_burgdorferi. The perplexity of the other 10 percent proteins and proteins from the other 19 organisms were calculated. Table 2-2 provides detailed results. Different organisms have different perplexities, which indicates that the different "dialects" in proteins may be embodied in the organisms. Another important phenomenon is that the perplexity is independent of the size of the testing proteins. To validate this, another experiment was carried out. The proteins of A_thaliana were used to train the uni-gram model, and then the human proteins were split into 10 shares randomly so as to calculate the perplexity. The results obtained were: 18.2049 18.2091 18.153 18.1905 18.2698 18.2101 18.1556 18.1495 18.3173 18.1925. These perplexities change at a small scale. So, the perplexity is related to the uni-gram model

Table 2-2   The perplexities of different organisms.

Organism	Perplexity	Organism	Perplexity
A_thaliana	19.4913	Human	20.6397
Aeropyrum_pernix	19.4739	Methanopyrus_kandleri	19.819
Arabidopsis	19.5059	Streptomyces_avermitilis	21.0707
Archaeoglobus_fulgidus	18.4882	Mycoplasma_genitalium	17.3464
Bacillus_anthracis_Ames	18.3561	Neisseria_meningitidis_MC58	19.4759
Bifidobacterium_longum	20.1821	Pasteurella_multocida	19.1712
Borrelia_burgdorferi	16.003	R_norvegicus	20.5656
Buchnera_aphidicola_Sg	16.924	S_pombe	18.9674
Encephalitozoon_cuniculi	18.7647	Worm	19.6435
Fusobacterium_nucleatum	16.7724	yeastpom	19.0126

and the organism used to test it and has no relation to the size of testing proteins.

2.5 Conclusions

In this chapter, the n-gram and linguistic features of whole genome protein sequences have been analyzed. The results show that (1) the n-grams of whole genome protein sequences approximately follow Zipf's law when n is larger than 4, (2) the Shannon n-gram entropy of the natural genome proteins is lower than that of artificial proteins, (3) a simple uni-gram model can distinguish different organisms, (4) there are organism-specific usages of "phrases" in protein sequences. Further work will aim at detailed identification of these "phrases" and the building of a "biological language" which has special words, phrases and syntaxes to map out the relationship of protein sequence, structure and function.

References

[1] Anfinsen C.B. Principles that govern the folding of protein chains. *Science*, 1973, 181(4096): 223–230.

[2] Mantegna R.N., Buldyrev S.V., Goldberger A.L., Havlin S., Peng C.K., Simons M., Stanley H.E. Systematic analysis of coding and noncoding DNA sequences using methods of statistical linguistics. *Phys Rev E Stat Phys Plasmas Fluids Relat Interdiscip Topics*, 1995, 52(3): 2939–2950.

[3] Chatzidimitriou-Dreismann C.A., Streffer R.M., Larhammar D. Lack of biological significance in the 'linguistic features' of noncoding DNA — A quantitative analysis. *Nucleic Acids Res*, 1996, 24(9): 1676–1681.

[4] Tsonis A.A., Elsner J.B., Tsonis P.A. Is DNA a language? *J Theor Biol*, 1997, 184(1): 25–29.

[5] Voss R.F. Comment on "Linguistic features of noncoding DNA sequences". *Phys Rev Lett*, 1996, 76(11): 1978.

[6] Burge C., Campbell A.M., Karlin S. Over- and under-representation of short oligonucleotides in DNA sequences. *Proc Natl Acad Sci USA*, 1992, 89(4): 1358–1362.

[7] Ganapathiraju M., Weisser D., Rosenfeld R., Carbonell J., Reddy R., Klein-Seetharaman J. Comparative n-gram analysis of whole-genome

protein sequences. In *Proceedings of the Human Language Technologies Conference*, San Diego 2002, pp. 1367–1375.

[8] Rigoutsos I., Huynh T., Floratos A., Parida L., Platt D. Dictionary-driven protein annotation. *Nucleic Acids Res*, 2002, 30(17): 3901–3916.

[9] Ganapathiraju M., Klein-Seetharaman J., Balakrishnan N., Reddy R. Characterization of protein secondary structure — Application of latent semantic analysis using different vocabularies. *IEEE Signal Processing Magazine*, 2004, 21: 78–87.

[10] Coin L., Bateman A., Durbin R. Enhanced protein domain discovery by using language modeling techniques from speech recognition. *Proc Natl Acad Sci USA*, 2003, 100(8): 4516–4520.

[11] Charniak E. *Statistical Language Learning*. 1996. Cambridge, MA: MIT Press, p. 192.

[12] Manber U., Myers G. Suffix arrays: A new method for on-line string searches. *SIAM J Comput*, 1993, 22(5): 935–948.

[13] Kasai T., Lee G., Arimura H., Arikawa S., Park K. Linear-time longest-common-prefix computation in suffix arrays and its applications. In *Proceedings of the 12th Annual Symposium on Combinatorial Pattern Matching*. 2001, Jerusalem, Israel: Springer-Verlag, pp. 181–192.

[14] Boeckmann B., Bairoch A., Apweiler R., Blatter M.C., Estreicher A., Gasteiger E., Martin M.J., Michoud K., O'Donovan C., Phan I., Pilbout S., Schneider M. The SWISS-PROT protein knowledgebase and its supplement TrEMBL in 2003. *Nucleic Acids Res*, 2003, 31(1): 365–370.

[15] Kingsley Zipf G. Human Behavior and the Principle of Least Effort. SERBIULA (sistema Librum 2.0), 1948, II.

Chapter 3

Amino Acid Encoding
for Protein Sequence

3.1 Motivation and Basic Idea

The digital representation of amino acids is usually called feature extraction, the amino acid encoding scheme, the residue encoding scheme, etc. Here, we use amino acid encoding as the terminology of choice. It should be noted that amino acid encoding is different from protein sequence encoding. Protein sequence encoding represents the entire protein sequence by using an n-dimensional vector, such as the n-gram,[1] pseudo amino acid composition,[2,3] etc. Since the amino acid-specific information is lost, protein sequence encoding can be only used to predict sequence-level properties (i.e. protein fold recognition). Amino acid encoding represents each amino acid of a protein sequence by using different n-dimensional vectors; thus, its vector space for a protein sequence is $n*L$ (L denotes the length of the protein sequence). By combining with different machine learning methods, amino acid encoding can be used in protein property prediction both at the residue level and the sequence level (i.e. protein fold recognition, secondary structure prediction, etc). In the past decades, various amino acid encoding methods have been proposed from different perspectives.[4-6] The most widely used encodings are one-hot encoding, position-specific scoring matrix (PSSM) encoding, and some physicochemical property encodings. In addition to those encodings, some other encodings have also been proposed, such as the encoding estimated from interresidue contact energies,[7] the encoding learned from protein structure alignments[8] and the encoding learned from sequence context.[9] These encoding methods explore amino acid encoding from new perspectives, and can be the complement of the above encodings. Kawashima *et al.*[10] have proposed a database of numerical indices of amino acids and amino acid pairs, and this contains information on the physicochemical and biochemical properties of amino acids.

3.2 Related Work

3.2.1 Binary encoding

The binary encoding methods use multidimensional binary digits (0 and 1) to represent amino acids in protein sequences. The most commonly used binary encoding is one-hot encoding, which is also called orthogonal encoding.[5] For one-hot encoding, each of the 20 amino acids is represented by a 20-dimensional binary vector. Specifically, the 20 standard amino acids are fixed in a specific order, and then the ith amino acid type is represented by 20 binary bits with the ith bit set to "1" and others to "0". There is only one bit equal to "1" for each vector; hence, it is called "one-hot". For example, the twenty standard amino acids are sorted as $[A, C, D, E, F, G, H, I, K, L, M, N, P, Q, R, S, T, V, W, Y]$; the one-hot code of "A" is 10000000000000000000, that of "C" is 01000000000000000000, and so on. Since protein sequences may contain some unknown amino acids, it should be noted that one more bit is needed to represent the unknown amino acid type in some cases, and the dimension of its binary vector will be 21.[11]

Because one-hot encoding is a high-dimensional and sparse vector representation, there is a simplified binary encoding method based on conservative replacements through evolution.[12] Deriving from the point accepted mutation (PAM) matrices,[13] the 20 standard amino acids are divided into six groups: $[H, R, K]$, $[D, E, N, Q]$, $[C]$, $[S, T, P, A, G]$, $[M, I, L, V]$ and $[F, Y, W]$. Six dimensional binary vectors are used to represent amino acids based on their groups.

Another low-dimensional binary encoding scheme is the binary 5-bit encoding introduced by White and Seffens.[14] Theoretically, the binary 5-bit code could represent 32 ($2^5 = 32$) possible amino acid types. In order to represent the 20 standard amino acids, the ones encoded by all 0s, the ones encoded by all 1s and those encoded with 1 or 4 ones ($5 + 5 = 10$) are removed, finally leaving 20 encodings ($32 - 1 - 1 - 10 = 20$). This binary 5-bit encoding uses a 5-dimension binary vector to take the place of the 20-dimension vector of one-hot encoding, which may lead to less model complexity.[5]

3.2.2 Physicochemical properties encoding

From the perspective of molecular composition, a typical amino acid generally contains a central carbon atom (C) which is attached with an amino group (NH_2), a hydrogen atom (H), a carboxyl group (COOH) and a side chain (R). The side chains (R) are usually carbon chains or rings (except for proline) which are attached to various functional groups.[5] The physicochemical properties of those components play critical roles in the formation of protein structures and functions; thus, these properties can also be used as features for protein structure and function prediction.[15]

Among various physicochemical properties, the hydrophobicity of the amino acid is believed to play a fundamental role in organizing the self-assembly of a protein.[16] Based on the propensity of the amino acid side chain to be in contact with a polar solvent like water, the 20 amino acids can be classified as either hydrophobic or hydrophilic. The free energy of amino acid side chains transferring from cyclohexane to water can be used to represent its hydrophobicity in a quantifiable manner.[6] If the free energy is a positive value, the amino acid is hydrophobic, while negative values indicate hydrophilic amino acids. Hydrophobic amino acids are usually buried inside the protein core in protein three-dimensional structures, while the hydrophilic amino acids preferentially cover the surface of the protein three-dimensional structures. Furthermore, the hydrophilic amino acids are called polar amino acids. In a typical biological environment, some polar amino acids carry a charge, Lysine (+), Histidine (+), Arginine (+), Aspartate (−) and Glutamate (−), while other polar amino

Table 3-1   The hydrophobic properties of 20 standard acid sides.

Hydrophobicity	Amino acids	3-letter abbreviation	1-letter abbreviation
Hydrophobic	Alanine	Ala	A
	Isoleucine	Ile	I
	Leucine	Leu	L
	Methionine	Met	M
	Phenylalanine	Phe	F
	Valine	Val	V
	Proline	Pro	P
	Glycine	Gly	G
Charged	Lysine (+)	Lys	K
	Histidine (+)	His	H
	Arginine (+)	Arg	R
	Aspartic (−)	Asp	D
	Glutamic (−)	Glu	E
Polar	Glutamine	Gln	Q
	Asparagine	Asn	N
	Serine	Ser	S
	Threonine	Thr	T
	Tyrosine	Tyr	Y
	Cysteine	Cys	C
	Tryptophan	Trp	W

acids, Asparagine, Glutamine, Serine, Threonine and Tyrosine, are neutral.[17] A detailed classification of the hydrophobic properties of the 20 standard acid sides is shown in Table 3-1. Other than hydrophobicity properties, the codon diversity and size of amino acids are also used as features. The codon diversity of an amino acid is reflected by the number of codons coding for the amino acid, and the size of an amino acid denotes its molecular volume.[15]

Some physicochemical property-based amino acid encodings have been proposed in previous studies. Fauchère *et al.*[18] established 15 physicochemical descriptors of side chains for 20 natural and 26 non-coded amino acids which reflect hydrophobic, steric, electronic, and other properties of amino acid side chains. Radzicka and Wolfenden[19] obtained digitized indications of the tendencies of amino acids to leave water and enter a truly nonpolar condensed phase in their experiments. Lohman *et al.*[20] represented amino acids by using seven physicochemical properties to predict transmembrane protein sequences, and the properties are hydrophobicity, hydrophilicity, polarity, volume, surface area, bulkiness and refractivity. Atchley *et al.*[15] used multivariate statistical analyses to produce multi-dimensional patterns of attribute covariation for the 20 standard amino acids, which reflect the polarity, secondary structure, molecular volume, codon diversity and electrostatic charge of amino acids.

3.2.3 Evolution-based encoding

The evolution-based encoding methods extract the evolutionary information of residues from sequence alignments or phylogenetic trees to represent amino acids, mainly by using the amino acid substitution probability. These evolution-based encoding methods can be categorized into two groups based on position relevance: position-independent methods and position-dependent methods.

The position-independent methods encode amino acids by using fixed encodings, regardless of the amino acid position in the sequence and the amino acid composition of the sequence. The most commonly used position-independent encoding methods are the PAM matrices and the BLOSUM matrices, and a common flowchart is shown in Fig. 3-1. The point accepted mutation (PAM) matrices represent the replacement probabilities for change from a single amino acid to another single amino acid in homologous protein sequences,[13] which are focused on the evolutionary process of proteins. The PAM matrices are calculated from protein phylogenetic trees and related protein sequence pairs. The assumption of the PAM matrices is that the accepted mutation is similar in physical and chemical properties to the old one and the likelihood of amino acid X replacing Y is the same as that of Y replacing X; thus, the PAM matrices are $20 * 20$ symmetry matrices where each row and column represents one of the 20 standard amino acids. Corresponding to different lengths of evolution time, different PAM matrices can be generated. The 250 PAMs, which means the amino acid replacements to be found after 250 evolutionary changes, was found by the authors to be an effective scoring matrix for detecting distant relationships,[13] and

1. Target sequences

> SEQ1
RRSPPADAIPKSKKVKVSHRSHSTEPGLVLTLGQGDVGQLGLGENVMERKKPALVSIPEDVVQAEAGGMHTVCLSKSGQV...

>SEQ2
STNLKDVLASLIPKEQARIKTERQQHGNTAVGQITVDMSYGGMRGMKGLIYETSVLDPDEGIRF...

> SEQ3
DSEINIFVSIDKDGTNVISYPELEQYVAENNLDPSMVEKWKQLFDPDNTGSITLETECSKLGLKPAFIIDEREQKGLIIAA

2. Sequence alignments

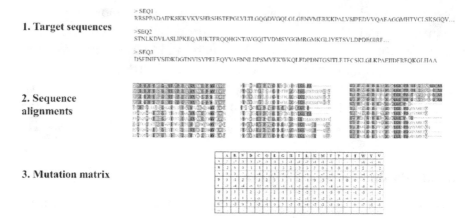

3. Mutation matrix

Figure 3-1   The flowchart of position-independent amino acid encoding methods. First, the target proteins are selected (step 1). Then, the sequence alignments are constructed based on some criteria (step 2). Finally, the mutation matrix is calculated and is regarded as the amino acid encoding (step 3).

it is now widely used in related research.[21, 22] The blocks amino acid substitution matrices (BLOSUM)[23] are amino acid substitution matrices derived based on conserved regions constructed by the PROTOMAT[24] from non-redundant protein groups. The values in the BLOSUM matrices represent the probabilities that amino acid pairs will exchange places with each other. To reduce the contributions of most closely related protein sequences, the sequences are clustered within blocks. Different BLOSUM matrices can be generated by using different identical percentages for clusters, and the BLOSUM62 matrix performed better overall.[23]

Different from position-independent matrices, the position-dependent methods encode amino acids at different positions by using different encodings, even if the amino acid types are the same. The position-dependent encodings are deduced from the multiple sequence alignments (MSAs) of target sequences; the flowchart for this is shown in Fig. 3-2. The position-specific scoring matrix (PSSM) is the most widely used encoding method. The PSSM is also called the position weight matrix (PWM), which represents the log-likelihoods of the occurrence probabilities of all possible molecule types at each location in a given biological sequence.[25]

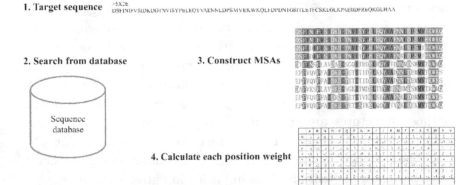

1. **Target sequence**

2. **Search from database**

3. **Construct MSAs**

Sequence
database

4. **Calculate each position weight**

Figure 3-2 The flowchart of position-dependent amino acid encoding methods. First, the target protein sequence is selected (step 1). Then, multiple sequence alignments are constructed by searching the protein sequence database (steps 2 and 3). Finally, the position weight is calculated by columns and is regarded as the corresponding amino acid encodings (step 4).

Generally, the Position-Specific Iterative Basic Local Alignment Search Tool (PSI-BLAST)[26] is used to execute sequence alignment and generate MSA for the target protein sequence. Then the corresponding PSSM is calculated from the MSA. For a protein sequence with length L, its PSSM is an $L * 20$ matrix, in which each row represents the log-likelihoods of the probabilities of 20 amino acids occuring at its corresponding position. Besides the PSI-BLAST, the HMM-HMM alignment algorithm HHblits is also widely used to generate the probabilities profile, which is more sensitive than the sequence-profile alignment algorithm PSI-BLAST, as demonstrated by Remmert *et al.*[27]

3.2.4 Structure-based encoding

The structure-based amino acid encoding methods, which can also be called statistical-based methods, encode amino acids by using structure-related statistical potentials, mainly using the inter-residue contact energies.[28] The basic assumption is, in a large number of native protein structures, the average potentials of inter-residue contacts can reflect the differences of interaction between residue pairs,[29] which play an important role in the formation of protein backbone structures.[28] The inter-residue contact energies of the 20 amino acids are usually estimated based on amino acid pairing frequencies from native protein structures.[28] The typical procedure to calculate the contact energies comprises three steps. First, a protein structure set is constructed from known native protein structures. Then, the inter-residue contacts of the 20 amino acids observed in those structures are counted. Finally, the contact energies are deduced from the amino acid contact frequencies by using the predefined energy function, and different contact energies reflect different contact potentials of amino acids in native structures.

Many previous studies have focused on structure-based encodings. In order to account for medium- and long-range interactions which determine the protein folding conformations, Tanaka and Scheraga[28] evaluated the empirical standard free energies to formulate amino acid contacts from the contact frequencies. By employing the lattice model, Miyazawa and Jernigan[29] estimated contact energies by using quasi-chemical approximation with an approximate treatment of the effects of chain connectivity. Later, they reevaluated the contact energies based on a larger set of protein structures and also estimated an additional repulsive packing energy term to provide an estimate of the overall energies of inter-residue interactions.[30] To investigate the validity of the quasi-chemical approximation, Skolnick *et al.*[31] estimated the expected number of contacts by using two reference states, the first of which treats the protein as a Gaussian random coil polymer and the second of which includes the effects of chain connectivity, secondary structure and chain compactness. The comparison results show that the quasi-chemical approximation is, in general, sufficient for extracting the amino acid pair potentials. To recognize native-like protein structures, Simmons *et al.*[32] used distance-dependent statistical contact potentials to develop energy functions. Zhang and Kim[33] estimated 60 residue contact energies that mainly reflect the hydrophobic interactions and show strong dependence on the three secondary structural states. These energies were found to be effective in threading and three-dimensional contact prediction according to their test results. Later, Cristian *et al.* set up an iterative scheme to extract the optimal interaction potentials between the amino acids.[34]

3.2.5 Machine-learning encoding

Different from earlier manually defined encoding methods, the machine-learning based encoding methods learn amino acid encodings from protein sequence or structure data by using machine learning methods, typically using artificial neural networks. In order to reduce the complexity of the model, the neural network for learning amino acid encodings is weightsharing for 20 amino acids. In general, the neural network contains three layers: the input layer, the hidden layer and the output layer. The input layer corresponds with the original encoding of the target amino acid, which can be one-hot encoding, physicochemical encoding, etc. The output layer also corresponds with the original encoding of the related amino acids. The hidden layer, which represents the new encoding of the target amino acid, usually has a reduced dimension compared with the original encoding.

To our knowledge, the earliest concept of learning-based amino acid encodings was proposed by Riis and Krogh.[35] In order to reduce the redundancy of one-hot encoding, they used a 20 ∗ 3 weightsharing neural network to learn a 3-dimensional real number representation of 20 amino acids from one-hot encoding. Later, Jagla and Schuchhardt[36] also used the weight sharing artificial neural network to learn a 2-dimensional encoding of amino acids for human signal peptide cleavage site recognition. Meiler *et al.*[37] used a symmetric neural network to learn reduced representations of amino acids from amino acid physicochemical and statistical properties. The parameter representations were reduced from five and seven dimensions, respectively, to 1, 2, 3 or 4 dimensions, and then these reduced representations were used for *ab initio* prediction of protein secondary structure. Lin *et al.*[8] used an artificial neural network to derive encoding schemes of amino acids from protein three-dimensional structure alignments, and each amino acid is described using the values taken from the hidden units of the neural network.

In recent years, several new machine-learning-based encoding methods[9, 38, 39] have been proposed with reference to distributed word representation in natural language processing. In natural language processing, the distributed representation of words has been proven to be an effective strategy for use in many tasks.[40] The basic assumption is that words sharing similar contexts will have similar meanings; therefore these methods train the neural network model by using the target word to predict its context words or by predicting the target word from its context words. After training on unlabeled datasets, the weights of the hidden units for each word are used as its distributed representation. In protein-related studies, a similar strategy has been used by assuming that the protein sequences are sentences, and that the amino acids or sub-sequences are words. In previous researches, these distributed representations of amino acids or sub-sequences show potential in protein family classification and disordered protein identification,[9] protein function site predictions,[38] protein functional property prediction,[39] etc.

3.3 Discussion

In this section, we will make a theoretical discussion of amino acid-encoding methods. First of all, we investigate the classification criteria of amino acid-encoding methods; second, we discuss the theoretical basis of these methods, and then analyze their advantages and limitations. Finally, we review and discuss the criteria for measuring an amino acid encoding method.

As introduced above, amino acid encoding methods have been divided into five categories according to their information sources and methodologies. However, it should be noted that the methods in one category are not completely different from those in others, and that there are some similarities between the encoding methods belonging to different categories. For example, the 6-bit one-hot encoding method proposed by Wang *et al.*[12] is a dimension-reduced representation of the common one-hot encoding, but it is based on the six amino acid exchange groups which are derived from PAM matrices.[13] There is another classification criterion based on position relevance. In an earlier section, evolution-based encoding methods were discussed, and it was mentioned that they are divided into two categories: position-independent methods and position-dependent methods. We can also group all of the amino acid encoding methods into these position-independent and position-dependent categories. Except for the position-specific scoring matrix (PSSM) and other similar encoding techniques that extract evolution features from multiple sequence alignments which are position-dependent methods, all the other amino acid encoding methods are position-independent methods. The position-dependent methods can capture homologous information, while position-independent ones can reflect the basic properties of amino acids. To some extent, these two types of methods can be complementary to each other. In practice, the combination of position-independent encoding and position-dependent encoding is often used, such as combining one-hot and PSSM,[41] combining physicochemical properties encoding and PSSM,[42] etc.

Theoretically, the functions of a protein are closely related to its tertiary structure, and its tertiary structure is mostly determined by the physicochemical properties of its amino acid sequence.[43] From this perspective, all of the evolution-based encoding, structure-based encoding and machine-learning encoding methods extract information based on the physicochemical properties of the amino acid by using difference strategies. Specifically, different amino acids may have different mutation tendencies in the evolutionary process due to their hydrophobicity, polarity, volume and other properties. These mutation tendencies will be reflected in the sequence alignments and are detected by the evolution-based encoding methods. Similarly, the physicochemical properties of amino acids could affect the inter-residue contact potentials in tertiary protein structures, which form the basis of the structure-based encoding methods. And the machine-learning encoding methods also learn amino acid encoding from its physicochemical representation or evolution information (such as homologous protein structure alignments), which can be seen as another variant of physicochemical properties. Despite the fact that these encoding methods share a similar theoretical basis, their performance is different due to the restrictions in their implementation. As regards the one-hot encoding method, there is no artificial correlation between amino acids, but it is highly sparse and redundant, which leads to a complex machine learning model. The physicochemical properties of amino acids play fundamental roles in the protein folding process; theoretically, the physicochemical property encoding methods should be effective. However, as the protein folding-related physicochemical properties and their digital metrics are unknown, developing an effective physicochemical property encoding method is still an unresolved problem. The evolution-based encoding methods extract evolution information using just protein sequences, which could thus benefit from the dividends of large-scale protein sequence data. In particular, PSSM has shown significant performance in many studies.[44] However, for those proteins without homologous sequences performances of evolution-based methods are limited. The structure-based encoding methods encode amino acids based on the potential of inter-residue contact, which denotes a low-dimensional representation of protein structure. Because of the limited number of known protein structures, their performance scope is limited. Early machine-learning encoding methods also face the problem of insufficient data samples, but several methods developed recently have overcome this problem by taking advantage of unlabeled sequence data.[9, 38, 39]

As discussed, different amino acid encoding methods have specific advantages and limitations; so, what is the most effective encoding method? According to Wang *et al.*,[12] the best encoding method should significantly reduce the uncertainty of the output of the prediction model, or the encoding could capture both the global similarity and the local similarity of protein sequences; here, the global similarity refers to the overall similarity among multiple sequences while the local similarity refers to motifs in the sequences. Riis and Krogh[35] proposed that redundancy encodings will lead the prediction model to be overfitting, and thus it needs to be simplified. Meiler *et al.*[37] also tried to use reduced representations of amino acids' physicochemical and statistical properties for protein secondary structure prediction. Zamani and Kremer[4] stated that an effective encoding must store information associated with the problem at hand while diminishing superfluous data. In summary, an effective amino acid encoding method should be information-rich and non-redundant. "Information-rich" means the encoding contains enough information that is highly relevant to the protein structure and function, such as the physicochemical properties, evolution information, contact potential, and so on. "Non-redundant" means the encoding is compact and does not contain noise or other unrelated information. For example, in neural network-based protein structure and function prediction, redundancy encoding will lead to complicated networks with a very large number of weights, which leads to overfitting and restricts the generalization ability of the model. Therefore, under the premise of containing sufficient information, a more compact encoding will be more useful and generate more results.

Over the past two decades, several studies have been proposed to investigate effective amino acid encoding methods.[5] David[45] examined the effectiveness of various hydrophobicity scales by using a parallel cascade identification algorithm to assess the structure or functional classification of protein sequences. Zhong *et al.*[46] compared orthogonal encoding, hydrophobicity encoding, BLOSUM62 encoding and PSSM encoding utilizing the Denoeux belief neural network for protein secondary structure prediction. Hu *et al.*[6] combined orthogonal encoding, hydrophobicity encoding and BLOSUM62 encoding to find the most optimal encoding scheme by using the SVM with a sliding window training scheme for protein secondary structure prediction. From their test results, it can be seen that the combination of orthogonal and BLOSUM62 matrices showed the highest accuracy compared with all other encoding schemes. Zamani and Kremer[4] investigated the efficiency of 15 amino acid encoding schemes, including orthogonal encoding, physicochemical encoding, and secondary structures- and BLOSUM62-related encoding, by training artificial neural networks to approximate the substitution matrices. Their experimental results indicate that the number (dimension) and the types (properties) of amino acid encoding methods are the two key factors playing a role in the efficiency of the encoding performance. Dongardive and Abraham[47] compared the orthogonal, hydrophobicity, BLOSUM62, PAM250 and hybrid encoding schemes of amino acids for protein secondary structure prediction and found that the best performance was achieved using the BLOSUM62 matrix. These studies thus explored amino acid encoding methods from different perspectives, but they all just evaluated one part of the encoding methods on small datasets. To present a comprehensive and systematic comparison, in this chapter, we performed a large-scale comparative assessment of various amino acid encoding methods based on two tasks — protein secondary structure prediction and protein fold recognition — proposed in the following sections. It should be noted that our aim is assessing how much effective information is contained in different encoding methods, rather than exploring the optimal combination of encoding methods.

3.4 The Assessment of Encoding Methods for Protein Secondary Structure Prediction

In computational biology, protein sequence labeling tasks, such as protein secondary structure prediction, solvent accessibility prediction, disorder region prediction and torsion angle prediction, have gained a great deal of attention from researchers. Among those sequence labeling tasks, protein secondary structure prediction is the most representative task,[48] and several previous amino acid encoding studies have also paid attention to this topic.[6, 35, 46, 47] Therefore, we first assess the various amino acid encoding methods based on the protein secondary structure prediction task.

3.4.1 Encoding methods selection and generation

To perform a comprehensive assessment of different amino acid encoding methods, we select 16 representative encoding methods from each category for evaluation. A brief introduction of the 16 selected encoding methods is shown in Table 3-2. Except for PSSM and HMM encodings, most of these encodings are position-independent encodings and can be used directly to encode amino

Table 3-2 A brief introduction of the 16 selected amino acid encoding methods.

Category	Encoding method	Dimension	Description
Binary	One-hot	20	The general one-hot method with one bit to encode one amino acid type.
	One-hot (6-bit)	6	The dimension-reduced one-hot method by using six bits.[13]
	Binary 5-bit	5	The binary encoding method by using five binary bits.[15]
Physicochemical properties	Hydrophobicity matrix	20	The hydrophobicity matrix based on the hydrophobicity index.[20]
	Meiler parameters	7	Seven parameters of physicochemical-related properties provided by Meiler *et al.*[36]
	Acthely factors	5	Five numerical values reflecting various physicochemical properties provided by Atchley *et al.*[7]
Evolution-based	PAM250	20	The 250 PAM matrix proposed by Dayhoff.[14]
	BLOSUM62	20	The BLOSUM 62 matrix proposed by Henikoff and Henikoff.[22]
	PSSM	20	The position weight matrix generated by using the PSI-BLAST.[26]
	HMM	20	The position weight matrix generated by using the HHblits.[27]
Structure-based	Miyazawa energies	20	The inter-residue contact energies estimated by Miyazawa and Jernigan.[7]
	Micheletti potentials	20	The residue interaction potentials extracted from coarse-grained descriptions of proteins.[34]

(*Continued*)

Table 3-2   (*Continued*)

Category	Encoding method	Dimension	Description
Machine-learning	AESNN3	3	An amino acid encoding learned from protein structure alignments.[8]
	ANN4D	4	A reduced representation of amino acids learned from physicochemical and statistical properties.[37]
	ProtVec	100	A distributed representation of 3-grams amino acids learned from Swiss-Prot sequences.[9]
	ProtVec-3mer	163	ProtVec concatenated with 3-mer.[9]

acids. It should be noted that some protein sequences may contain unknown amino acid types; these amino acids will be expressed by the average value of the corresponding column if the original encodings do not deal with this situation. For the ProtVec,[9] which is a 3-gram encoding, we encode each amino acid by adding its left and right adjacent amino acid to form the corresponding 3-gram word. Since the start and end amino acids do not have enough adjacent amino acids to form 3-grams, they are represented by the "<unk>" encoding in ProtVec. Recently, further work on ProtVec (ProtVecX[49]) has demonstrated that the concatenation of ProtVec and k-mers could achieve better performance; here, we also evaluate the performance of ProtVec concatenated with 3-mers (named as ProtVec-3mer). For position-dependent encoding methods PSSM and HMM, we follow the common practice of generating them. Specifically, for the PSSM encoding of each protein sequence, we ran the PSI-BLAST[26] tool with an e-value threshold of 0.001 and three iterations against the UniRef9[50] sequence database which is filtered at 90% sequence identity. HMM encoding is extracted from the HMM profile by running HHblits[27] against the UniProt20[50] protein database with parameters "-n 3 -diff inf -cov 60". According to the HHsuite user guide, we use the first 20 columns of the HMM profile and convert the integers in the HMM profile to amino acid emission frequencies by using the formula: $h^{\text{fre}} = 2^{-0.001*h}$, where h is the initial integer in the HMM profile and h^{fre} is the corresponding amino acid emission frequency. h is set to 0 if it is an asterisk.

3.4.2 Benchmark datasets for protein secondary structure prediction

Following several representative protein secondary structure prediction works[11,42,51] published in recent years, we use the CullPDB dataset[52] as training data and use four widely used test datasets — the CB513 dataset,[53] the CASP10 dataset,[54] the CASP11 dataset[55] and the CASP12 dataset[56] — as test data to evaluate the performance of different features. The CullPDB dataset is a large non-homologous sequence set produced by using the PISCES server,[52] which culls subsets of protein sequences from the Protein Data Bank based on sequence identity and structural quality criteria. Here, we retrieved a subset of sequences that have structures with better than 1.8 Å resolution and share less than 25% sequence identity with each other. We also remove those sequences sharing more than 25% identity with sequences from the test dataset to ensure there is no homology between the training and the test datasets, and finally the CullPDB dataset contained 5748 protein sequences with lengths ranging from 18 to 1455. The CB513 dataset contains 513 proteins with less than 25% sequence similarity. The Critical Assessment of techniques for protein Structure Prediction (CASP) is a highly recognized community experiment to determine state-of-the-art methods in protein structure prediction from amino acids[56]; the recently released CASP10, CASP11 and CASP12 datasets are adopted as test datasets. It should be noted that the protein targets from CASP used here are based on the protein domain. Specifically, the CASP10 dataset contains 123 protein domains whose sequence lengths range from 24 to 498, the CASP11 dataset contains 105 protein domains whose sequence lengths range from 34 to 520, and the CASP12 dataset contains 55 protein domains whose sequence lengths range from 55 to 463.

Protein secondary structure labels are inferred by using the DSSP program[57] from corresponding experimentally determined structures. The DSSP specifies 8 secondary structure states to each residue; here, we adopt 3-state secondary structure prediction as a benchmark task by converting 8 assigned states to 3 states: G, H, and I to H; B and E to E; and S, T, and C to C.

3.4.3 Performance comparison by using the Random Forests method

In order to use the information of neighboring residues, many previous protein secondary structure prediction methods apply the sliding window scheme and have demonstrated considerably good results.[48] Referring to those methods, we also used the sliding window scheme to evaluate different amino acid encoding methods, and the diagram for this is shown in Fig. 3-3. The evaluation is based on the Random Forests method from the Scikit-learn toolboxes,[58] the

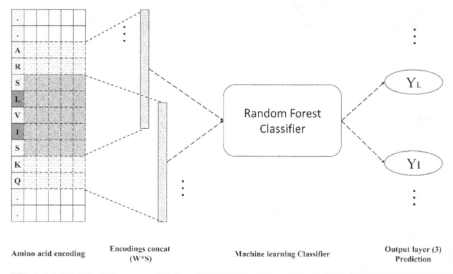

Figure 3-3 The diagram of the sliding window scheme by using the Random Forests classifier for protein secondary structure prediction. The two target residues are Leu (L) and Ile (I) separately, the input for each target residue is independent.

window size is 13 and the number of trees in the forest is 100. The comparison results are shown in Table 3-3.

First, we analyze and discuss the performance of different methods in the same category. For the binary encoding methods, one-hot encoding is the most widely used encoding method. The one-hot (6-bit) encoding and the binary 5-bit encoding are two dimension-reduced representations of the one-hot encoding. As can be seen from Table 3-3, the best performance is achieved by the one-hot encoding method, which demonstrates that some effective information could be lost after the artificial dimension reduction for one-hot (6-bit) encoding and binary 5-bit encoding. For the physicochemical properties encodings, the hydrophobicity matrix just contains hydrophobicity-related information and performs poorly, while the Meiler parameters and the Acthely factors are constructed from multiple physicochemical information sources and perform better. This shows that the integration of multiple physicochemical information sources and parameters is valuable. For evolution-based encodings, it is obvious that the position-dependent encodings (PSSM and HMM) are much more powerful than position-independent encodings (PAM250 and BLOSUM62), which shows that the homologous information is strongly associated with the protein structures. For the two structure-based encodings, they have comparative performances. For the three machine-learning encodings, the ANN4D performs better than the AESNN3 and the ProtVec, while the ProtVec-3mer encoding achieves similar performance compared with the ProtVec encoding. Second, on the whole, the position-dependent evolution-based encoding methods (PSSM and HMM) achieved the best performance. This result suggests that the evaluation information extracted from the MSAs is more conserved than the global information extracted from other sources. Third, the performances of different encoding methods show a certain degree of correlation with encoding dimensions, and the low-dimensional encodings, i.e. the one-hot (6-bit), binary 5-bit and two machine-learning encodings, have poorer performances than the high-dimensional encodings. This correlation could be due to the sliding window scheme and Random Forests algorithm; larger feature

Table 3-3 Protein secondary structure prediction accuracy of 16 amino acid encoding methods by using the Random Forests method.

Category	Encoding method	Dimension	CB513	CASP10	CASP11	CASP12	Mean
Binary	One-hot	20	60.21	56.72	59.31	59.70	58.98
	One-hot (6-bit)	6	50.00	47.97	48.86	48.78	48.90
	Binary 5-bit	5	48.09	44.76	45.78	47.59	46.55
Physicochemical properties	Hydrophobicity matrix	20	56.46	54.08	55.48	54.33	55.09
	Meiler parameters	7	62.29	59.67	61.19	60.63	60.94
	Acthely factors	5	61.42	59.04	60.44	60.49	60.35
Evolution-based	PAM250	20	61.65	59.62	60.85	60.54	60.67
	BLOSUM62	20	62.30	59.84	61.53	60.89	61.14
	PSSM	20	72.80	71.58	71.79	71.75	71.98
	HMM	20	72.20	72.27	69.04	68.51	70.50
Structure-based	Miyazawa energies	20	61.83	59.68	61.20	60.86	60.89
	Micheletti potentials	20	59.61	56.60	58.19	58.85	58.31
Machine-learning	AESNN3	3	54.80	51.71	52.60	53.77	53.22
	ANN4D	4	58.01	55.26	56.41	57.97	56.91
	ProtVec	100	50.00	49.00	50.29	51.63	50.23
	ProtVec-3mer	163	51.87	47.94	49.41	51.51	50.18

dimension is more conducive to recognizing the secondary structure states, but too large of a dimension will lead to poor performance (ProtVec and ProtVec-3mer).

3.4.4 Performance comparison by using the BRNN method

In recent years, deep learning-based methods for protein secondary structure prediction have achieved significant improvements.[48] One of the most important advantages of deep learning methods is that they can capture both neighboring and long-range interactions, which could avoid the shortcomings of sliding window methods with handcrafted window size. For example, Heffernan *et al.*[42] have achieved state-of-the-art performances by using the long short-term memory (LSTM) bidirectional recurrent neural networks. Therefore, to exclude the potential influence of the handcrafted window size, we also perform an assessment by using the bidirectional recurrent neural networks (BRNN) with long short-term memory cells. The model used here is similar to the model used in Heffernan's work,[42] as shown in Fig. 3-4, which contains two BRNN layers with 256 LSTM cells and two fully connected (dense) layers with 1024 and 512 nodes, and it is implemented based on the open-sourced deep learning library TensorFlow.[59]

The corresponding comparison results of the 16 selected encoding methods are shown in Table 3-4. From the overall view,

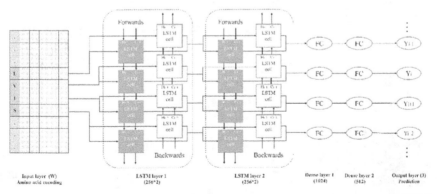

Figure 3-4 The architecture of the long short-term memory (LSTM) bidirectional recurrent neural networks for protein secondary structure prediction.

Table 3-4 Protein secondary structure prediction accuracy of 16 amino acid encoding methods by using the BRNN method.

Category	Encoding method	Dimension	CB513	CASP10	CASP11	CASP12	Mean
Binary	One-hot	20	66.32	66.54	68.75	67.87	67.37
	One-hot(6-bit)	6	58.42	59.84	59.81	59.14	59.3
	Binary5-bit	5	55.04	52.39	52.43	52.31	53.04
Physicochemical properties	Hydrophobicity matrix	20	55.69	56.27	57.24	58.57	56.94
	Meiler parameters	7	52.88	47.98	49.69	49.97	50.13
	Acthely factors	5	63.79	61.54	63.7	64.07	63.28
Evolution-based	PAM250	20	66.67	68.02	70.22	68.74	68.41
	BLOSUM62	20	66.18	64.85	67.58	66.36	66.24
	PSSM	20	80.46	82.25	81.45	79.44	80.9
	HMM	20	70.51	68.55	67.32	66.3	68.17
Structure-based	Miyazawa energies	20	65.44	61.19	61.42	61.46	61.46
	Micheletti potentials	20	70.85	70.65	72.76	70.01	71.07
Machine-learning	AESNN3	3	49.8	51.19	51.74	51.72	51.72
	ANN4D	4	57.18	53.09	54.53	54.67	54.87
	ProtVec	100	67.48	66.39	68.62	67.13	67.41
	ProtVec-3mer	163	70.69	69.43	72.43	72.43	71.24

the BRNN-based method was found to have better performance compared with the Random Forests-based method, but there are also some specific similarities and differences between them. For binary encoding methods, one-hot encoding still shows the best performance, which once again confirms the information loss of the one-hot (6-bit) and the binary 5-bit encoding methods. For the physicochemical property encodings, the Meiler parameters do not perform as well as the Acthely factors, suggesting that the Acthely factors are more efficient for deep learning methods. For the evolution-based encodings, the PSSM encoding achieves the best accuracy, while the HMM encoding just achieves as much accuracy as those position-independent encodings (PAM250 and BLOSUM62). The difference could be due to the different levels of homologous sequence identity. The HMM encoding is extracted from the UniProt20 database with 20% sequence identity, while the PSSM encoding is extracted from the UniRef90 database with 90% sequence identity. Therefore, for a certain protein sequence, its MSA from the UniProt20 database mainly contains remote homologous sequences, while its MSA from the UniRef90 database usually contains more homologous sequences. From the results in Table 3-4, the evaluation information of homologous sequences is more powerful for distinguishing different protein secondary structures than that of remote homologous sequences. For the structure-based encodings, the Micheletti potentials have much better performance when the BRNN method is used than when the Random Forests method is used. For machine-learning encodings, the ProtVec and ProtVec-3mer achieve significantly better performance compared with the values given in Table 3-4, which demonstrates the potential of machine-learning encoding. It is worth noting that ProtVec-3mer has better performance than ProtVec on the BRNN algorithm, corresponding to the authors' recent work.[49] Overall, for the deep learning algorithm BRNN, the position-dependent PSSM encoding still performs best among all encoding methods. For the position-independent encoding methods, the Micheletti potentials achieve the best performance, which demonstrates that the structure-related information has application potential in protein structure and function studies.

3.5 Assessments of Encoding Methods for Protein Fold Recognition

In addition to the protein sequence labeling tasks, protein sequence classification tasks have also received a lot of attention, such as protein remote homology detection[60] and protein fold recognition.[61,62] Here, we perform another assessment of the selected 16 amino acid encoding methods based on the protein fold recognition task. Many machine learning methods have been developed to classify protein sequences into different fold categories for protein fold recognition.[60] The deep learning methods can automatically extract discriminative patterns from variable-length protein sequences and achieve significant success.[61] Referring to Hou's work,[61] we used the one-dimensional deep convolution neural network (DCNN) to assess the usefulness of 16 selected encoding methods for protein fold recognition. As shown in Fig. 3-5, the deep convolution neural network used here has 10 hidden layers of convolution, 10 filters of each convolution layer with two window sizes (6 and 10), 20 maximum values at the max pooling layer and a flatter layer which is fully connected with the output layer to output the corresponding probability of each fold type.

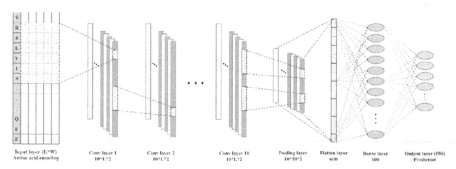

Figure 3-5   The architecture of the one-dimensional deep convolution neural network for protein fold recognition.

3.5.1 Benchmark datasets for protein fold recognition

The most commonly used dataset to evaluate protein fold recognition methods is the SCOP database[63] and its extended version, the SCOPe database.[64] The SCOP is a manual structural classification of proteins whose three-dimensional structures have been determined. All of the proteins in SCOP are classified into four hierarchy levels: class, fold, superfamily and family. Folds represent the main characteristics of protein structures, and the protein fold could reveal the evolutionary process between the protein sequence and its corresponding tertiary structure.[65] Here we use the F184 dataset which was constructed by Xia *et al.*[66] based on the SCOPe database. The F184 dataset contains 6451 sequences with less than 25% sequence identity from 184 folds. Each fold contains at least 10 sequences, which could ensure that there are enough sequences for training and test purposes. Then we randomly selected 20% of the sequences as test data from each fold, leaving 80% of the sequences as training data. Finally, we got 5230 sequences for training and 1221 sequence for testing.

3.5.2 Performances of different encodings on protein fold recognition task

The comparison results of 16 selected encoding methods for protein fold recognition are listed in Table 3-5. It should be noted that the training process for each encoding method is repeated 10 times to eliminate stochastic effects. Different from the performances of protein secondary structure prediction, the performances of most position-independent encoding methods are similar. All of the binary, physicochemical and machine-learning-based encoding methods (except the ProtVec) achieve about 30% mean accuracies, demonstrating that the position-independent encodings could just offer limited information for protein fold classification. The two structure-based encodings have better accuracies — near 33% — demonstrating that the structure potential is more related with the protein fold type. The two evolution-based methods PAM250 and BLOSUM62 perform best among the 12 position-independent

Table 3-5   The performance differences between the various kinds of encodings.

Category	Encoding method	Dimension	Top1	Top5	Top10	Mean
Binary encoding	One-hot	20	13.5	35.5	48.09	32.37
	One-hot(6-bit)	6	13.39	35.01	47.87	32.09
	Binary5-bit	5	12.57	33.05	46.26	30.63
Physicochemical properties	Hydrophobicity matrix	20	12.68	33.56	46.53	30.92
	Meiler parameters	7	12.62	33.05	45.82	30.5
	Acthely factors	5	14.97	36.93	50.7	34.2
Evolution-based	PAM250	20	18.7	43.69	56.66	39.68
	BLOSUM62	20	16.86	41.8	55.25	37.97
	PSSM	20	47.04	74.38	84.57	68.66
	HMM	20	20.02	43.51	56.4	39.98
Structure-based	Miyazawa energies	20	13.95	36.32	49.62	33.3
	Micheletti potentials	20	14.86	37.61	50.3	34.26
Machine-learning	AESNN3	3	11.85	32.58	45.63	30.02
	ANN4D	4	11.77	31.91	45	29.58
	ProtVec	100	6.18	22.91	33.42	20.84
	ProtVec-3mer	163	12.01	33.41	45.12	30.18

Notes: Top 1: the accuracy calculated in the case that the first predicted folding type is the actual folding type. Top 5: the accuracy calculated in the case that the top 5 predicted fold types contain the actual fold type. Top 5: the accuracy calculated in the case that the top 10 predicted fold types contain the actual fold type. Mean: the mean value of accuracies on Top 1, Top 5, and Top 10.

encoding methods, which means the evaluation information is more coupled with the protein structure. The position-dependent encoding methods PSSM and HMM achieve better performances, especially PSSM. It again indicates that the protein evaluation information is tightly coupled with the protein structure, and the homologous information is more useful than remote homologous information. The machine-learning-based AESNN3 and ANN4D encodings achieve comparable performances with other position-independent encoding methods but have much lower dimensions (3 for the AESNN3 and 4 for the ANN4D), showing its potential for further application.

The performance of the ProtVec encoding is poor, and this could be caused by the overlapping strategy that has also been mentioned by the author.[9] The ProtVec-3mer encoding has better performance, demonstrating the effectiveness of the combination of ProtVec and 3-mer.

It should be noted that the benchmark presented here is based on the DCNN method, and these encodings may achieve different performances by using other machine learning methods. The DCNN method could handle variable-length sequences and achieve significant success on fold recognition tasks, which are the main reasons for its selection here.

3.6 Conclusions

Amino acid encoding is the first step of protein structure and function prediction, and it is one of the foundations to achieve final success in those studies. In this chapter, we proposed the systematic classification of various amino acid encoding methods and reviewed the methods of each category. According to information sources and information extraction methodologies, these methods are grouped into five categories: binary encoding, physicochemical properties encoding, evolution-based encoding, structure-based encoding and machine-learning encoding. To benchmark and compare different amino acid encoding methods, we first selected 16 representative methods from those five categories. And then, based on the two representative protein-related studies, protein secondary structure prediction and protein fold recognition, we construct three machine learning models referring to the state-of-the-art studies. Finally, we encoded the protein sequence and implemented the same training and test phase on the benchmark datasets for each encoding method. The performance of each encoding method is regarded as the indicator of its potential in protein structure and function studies.

The assessment results show that the evolution-based position-dependent encoding method PSSM consistently achieves the best performance both on protein secondary structure prediction and protein fold recognition tasks, suggesting its important role in protein structure and function prediction. However, another evolution-based position-dependent encoding method — HMM — does not perform well, and the main reason for this could be that the remote homologous sequences only provide limited evaluation information for the target residue. For the one-hot encoding method, it is highly sparse and leads to complex machine learning models, while its two compressed representations, one-hot (6-bit) encoding and binary 5-bit encoding, lose more or less valuable information and cannot be widely used in related researches. More reasonable strategies to reduce the dimension of one-hot encoding need to be developed. For the physicochemical property encodings, the variety of properties and the extraction methodologies are two important factors needed to construct a valuable encoding. Structure-based encodings and machine-learning encodings achieve comparable or even better performances when compared with other widely used encodings, suggesting more attention needs to be paid to these two categories.

In a time when the dividends of data and algorithms have been highly released, exploring more effective encoding schemes for amino acids should be a key factor to further improve the performance of protein structure and function prediction. In the following, we provide some perspectives for future related studies. First, updated position-independent encodings should be constructed based on new protein datasets. Except for one-hot encoding, all other position-independent encoding methods construct their encodings based on the information extracted from the native protein sequences or structures. There is no doubt that random errors are unavoidable for those encodings and larger datasets will help to reduce those errors. As the development of sequencing and structure detection techniques has progressed and continues to progress, the number of protein sequences and structures has grown rapidly in the past years. Considering that most of the position-independent encoding methods were proposed one decade ago, it would be valuable to reconstruct them by using new datasets. Second, structure-based or function-based encoding methods require more attention. It has been demonstrated that structure-based encoding methods have ability in protein secondary structure prediction and protein fold recognition. These encodings reflect the structural potential of amino acids, which should be highly correlated with the protein structure and function. With the growing of number of proteins with known structure, the future prospect of structure-based encodings is considerable. Furthermore, the encodings reflecting function potentials may be more useful than others for protein function prediction; thus, exploring function-based encoding methods is a worthwhile topic. Third, the machine-learning encoding methods can be promising topics for future studies. As the amino acid encoding is an open problem, most encoding methods are based on an artificially defined basis, i.e. the physicochemical property encodings are constructed from protein fold-related properties observed by researchers, which will inevitably bring some unknown deviations. However, the machine-learning methods can avoid those artificial deviations by learning the amino acid encoding from biological data automatically. The protein sequences and natural languages share some similarities to a certain extent; for instance, the protein sequences can be comparable to sentences, and the amino acid or polypeptide chains can be comparable to words in languages. Considering that the word distributed representation has achieved comprehensive improved performances in natural language processing tasks, the protein sequences should also gain improvements by using the distributed representations of amino acids or n-gram amino acids. Some recent studies have demonstrated the potential of amino acid-distributed representations in protein family classification, disordered protein identification and protein functional property prediction, but most of these methods are concerned with the n-gram amino acid-distributed representations that cannot be directly used to predict the residue-level properties. Thus, residue-level distributed representations of amino acid is a topic that needs more attention.

References

[1] Liu B., Wang X., Lin L., Dong Q., Wang X. A discriminative method for protein remote homology detection and fold recognition combining Top-n-grams and latent semantic analysis. *BMC Bioinfo*, 2008, 9(1): 510.

[2] Liu B., Liu F., Wang X., Chen J., Fang L., Chou K.-C. Pse-in-One: A web server for generating various modes of pseudo components of DNA, RNA, and protein sequences. *Nucleic Acids Res*, 2015, 43(W1): W65–W71.

[3] Liu B. BioSeq-Analysis: a platform for DNA, RNA and protein sequence analysis based on machine learning approaches. *Briefings in Bioinformatics*, 2019, 20(4): 1280–1294.

[4] Zamani M., Kremer S.C. Amino acid encoding schemes for machine learning methods. In the *2011 IEEE International Conference on Bioinformatics and Biomedicine Workshops (BIBMW)*, 2011, pp. 327–333.

[5] Yoo P.D., Zhou B.B., Zomaya A.Y. Machine learning techniques for protein secondary structure prediction: An overview and evaluation. *Curr Bioinfo*, 2008, 3(2): 74–86.

[6] Hu H.-J., Pan Y., Harrison R., Tai P.C. Improved protein secondary structure prediction using support vector machine with a new encoding scheme and an advanced tertiary classifier. *IEEE Trans NanoBiosci*, 2004, 3(4): 265–271.

[7] Miyazawa S., Jernigan R.L. Self-consistent estimation of inter-residue protein contact energies based on an equilibrium mixture approximation of residues. *Proteins*, 1999, 34(1): 49–68.

[8] Lin K., May A.C.W., Taylor W.R. Amino acid encoding schemes from protein structure alignments: Multi-dimensional vectors to describe residue types. *J Theor Biol*, 2002, 216(3): 361–365.

[9] Asgari E., Mofrad M.R.K. Continuous distributed representation of biological sequences for deep proteomics and genomics. *Plos One*, 2015, 10(11): e0141287.

[10] Kawashima S., Pokarowski P., Pokarowska M., Kolinski A., Katayama T., Kanehisa M. AAindex: Amino acid index database, progress report 2008. *Nucleic Acids Res*, 2008, 36(suppl_1): D202–D205.

[11] Wang S., Peng J., Ma J., Xu J. Protein secondary structure prediction using deep convolutional neural fields. *Sci Rep*, 2016, 6.

[12] Wang J.T.L., Ma Q., Shasha D., Wu C.H. New techniques for extracting features from protein sequences. *IBM Syst J*, 2001, 40(2): 426–441.

[13] Dayhoff M.O. A model of evolutionary change in proteins. *Atlas Prot Seq Struct*, 1978, 5: 89–99.

[14] White G., Seffens W. Using a neural network to backtranslate amino acid sequences. *Electronic J Biotechnol*, 1998, 1(3): 17–18.

[15] Atchley W.R., Zhao J., Fernandes A.D., Drüke T. Solving the protein sequence metric problem. *Proc Natl Acad Sci USA*, 2005, 102(18): 6395–6400.

[16] Rose G., Geselowitz A., Lesser G., Lee R., Zehfus M. Hydrophobicity of amino acid residues in globular proteins. *Science*, 1985, 229(4716): 834–838.

[17] Betts M.J., Russell R.B. Amino acid properties and consequences of substitutions. *Bioinfo Genet*, 2003, 317: 289.

[18] Fauchère J.-L., Charton M., Kier L.B., Verloop A., Pliska V. Amino acid side chain parameters for correlation studies in biology and pharmacology. *Chem Biol Drug Design*, 1988, 32(4): 269–278.

[19] Radzicka A., Wolfenden R. Comparing the polarities of the amino acids: side-chain distribution coefficients between the vapor phase, cyclohexane, 1-octanol, and neutral aqueous solution. *Biochemistry*, 1988, 27(5): 1664–1670.

[20] Reinhard L., Gisbert S., Dirk B., Paul W. A neural network model for the prediction of membrane spanning amino acid sequences. *Prot Sci*, 1994, 3(9): 1597–1601.

[21] Elofsson A. A study on protein sequence alignment quality. *Proteins*, 2002, 46(3): 330–339.

[22] Oren E.E., Tamerler C., Sahin D., Hnilova M., Seker U.O.S., Sarikaya M., Samudrala R. A novel knowledge-based approach to design inorganic-binding peptides. *Bioinformatics*, 2007, 23(21): 2816–2822.

[23] Henikoff S., Henikoff J.G. Amino acid substitution matrices from protein blocks. *Proc Natl Acad Sci USA*, 1992, 89(22): 10915–10919.

[24] Henikoff S., Henikoff J.G. Automated assembly of protein blocks for database searching. *Nucleic Acids Res*, 1991, 19(23): 6565–6572.

[25] Stormo G.D., Schneider T.D., Gold L., Ehrenfeucht A. Use of the 'Perceptron' algorithm to distinguish translational initiation sites in E. coli. *Nucleic Acids Res*, 1982, 10(9): 2997–3011.

[26] Altschul S.F., Koonin E.V. Iterated profile searches with PSI-BLAST — A tool for discovery in protein databases. *Trends Biochem Sci*, 1998, 23(11): 444–447.

[27] Remmert M., Biegert A., Hauser A., Söding J. HHblits: lightning-fast iterative protein sequence searching by HMM-HMM alignment. *Nat Meth*, 2012, 9(2): 173.

[28] Tanaka S., Scheraga H.A. Medium- and long-range interaction parameters between amino acids for predicting three-dimensional structures of proteins. *Macromolecules*, 1976, 9(6): 945–950.

[29] Miyazawa S., Jernigan R.L. Estimation of effective interresidue contact energies from protein crystal structures: Quasi-chemical approximation. *Macromolecules*, 1985, 18(3): 534–552.

[30] Miyazawa S., Jernigan R.L. Residue–residue potentials with a favorable contact pair term and an unfavorable high packing density term, for simulation and threading. *J Mol Biol*, 1996, 256(3): 623–644.

[31] Skolnick J., Godzik A., Jaroszewski L., Kolinski A. Derivation and testing of pair potentials for protein folding. When is the quasichemical approximation correct? *Prot Sci*, 1997, 6(3): 676–688.

[32] Simmons, K.T., Ingo R., Charles K., A. F.B., Chris B., David B. Improved recognition of nativelike protein structures using a combination of sequence-dependent and sequence-independent features of proteins. *Proteins: Structure, Function, and Bioinformatics*, 1999, 34(1): 82–95.

[33] Zhang C., Kim S.-H. Environment-dependent residue contact energies for proteins. *Proc Natl Acad Sci USA*, 2000, 97(6): 2550–2555.

[34] Cristian M., Flavio S., R. B.J., Amos M. Learning effective amino acid interactions through iterative stochastic techniques. *Proteins*, 2001, 42(3): 422–431.

[35] Riis S.K., Krogh A. Improving prediction of protein secondary structure using structured neural networks and multiple sequence alignments. *J Comput Biol*, 1996, 3(1): 163–183.

[36] Jagla B., Schuchhardt J. Adaptive encoding neural networks for the recognition of human signal peptide cleavage sites. *Bioinformatics*, 2000, 16(3): 245–250.

[37] Meiler J., Müller M., Zeidler A., Schmäschke F. Generation and evaluation of dimension-reduced amino acid parameter representations by artificial neural networks. *Mol Model Annu*, 2001, 7(9): 360–369.

[38] Xu Y., Song J., Wilson C., Whisstock J.C. PhosContext2vec: A distributed representation of residue-level sequence contexts and its application to general and kinase-specific phosphorylation site prediction. *Sci Rep*, 2018, 8.

[39] Yang K.K., Wu Z., Bedbrook C.N., Arnold F.H. Learned protein embeddings for machine learning. *Bioinformatics*, 2018, 34(15): 2642–2648.

[40] Mikolov T., Sutskever I., Chen K., Corrado G.S., Dean J. Distributed representations of words and phrases and their compositionality. *Proceedings of the 26th International Conference on Neural Information Processing Systems*, Curran Associates inc., New York, USA, 2013, 3111–3119.

[41] Hou J., Adhikari B., Cheng J. DeepSF: Deep convolutional neural network for mapping protein sequences to folds. *Bioinformatics*, 2017, 34(8): 1295–1303.

[42] Heffernan R., Yang Y., Paliwal K., Zhou Y. Capturing non-local interactions by long short term memory bidirectional recurrent neural networks for improving prediction of protein secondary structure, backbone angles, contact numbers, and solvent accessibility. *Bioinformatics*, 2017: btx218.

[43] Anfinsen C.B. Principles that govern the folding of protein chains. *Science*, 1973, 181(4096): 223–230.

[44] Chen J., Guo M., Wang X., Liu B. A comprehensive review and comparison of different computational methods for protein remote homology detection. *Brief Bioinfo*, 2018, 19(2): 231–244.

[45] David R. Applications of nonlinear system identification to protein structural prediction. Thesis (S.M.) — Massachusetts Institute of Technology, Dept. of Mechanical Engineering, 2000.

[46] Zhong W., Altun G., Tian X., Harrison R., Tai P.C., Pan Y. Parallel protein secondary structure prediction based on neural networks. *IEEE*, 2004: 2968–2971.

[47] Dongardive J., Abraham S. Reaching optimized parameter set: Protein secondary structure prediction using neural network. *Neural Comput Appl*, 2017, 28(8): 1947–1974.

[48] Yang Y., Gao J., Wang J., Heffernan R., Hanson J., Paliwal K., Zhou Y. Sixty-five years of the long march in protein secondary structure prediction: The final stretch? *Brief Bioinfo*, 2016: bbw129.

[49] Asgari E., McHardy A.C., Mofrad M.R. Probabilistic variable-length segmentation of protein sequences for discriminative motif discovery (DiMotif) and sequence embedding (ProtVecX). *Sci Rep*, 2019, 9(1): 3577.

[50] Consortium U. UniProt: A hub for protein information. *Nucleic Acids Res*, 2014, 43(D1): D204–D212.

[51] Li Z., Yu Y. Protein secondary structure prediction using cascaded convolutional and recurrent neural networks. *arXiv preprint* arXiv:1604.07176, 2016.

[52] Wang G., Dunbrack R.L. PISCES: A protein sequence culling server. *Bioinformatics*, 2003, 19(12): 1589–1591.

[53] Cuff J.A. and Barton G.J. Evaluation and improvement of multiple sequence methods for protein secondary structure prediction. *Proteins*, 1999, 34(4): 508–519.

[54] John M., Krzysztof F., Andriy K., Torsten S., Anna T. Critical assessment of methods of protein structure prediction (CASP) — Round x. *Proteins*, 2013, 82(S2): 1–6.

[55] Kinch L.N., Li W., Schaeffer R.D., Dunbrack R.L., Monastyrskyy B., Kryshtafovych A., Grishin N.V. CASP 11 target classification. *Proteins*, 2016, 84(S1): 20–33.

[56] Moult J., Fidelis K., Kryshtafovych A., Schwede T., Tramontano A. Critical assessment of methods of protein structure prediction (CASP) — Round XII. *Proteins*, 2018, 86: 7–15.

[57] Wolfgang K., Christian S. Dictionary of protein secondary structure: Pattern recognition of hydrogen-bonded and geometrical features. *Biopolymers*, 2004, 22(12): 2577–2637.

[58] Pedregosa F., Varoquaux G., Gramfort A., Michel V., Thirion B., Grisel O., Blondel M., Prettenhofer P., Weiss R., Dubourg V. Scikit-learn: Machine learning in Python. *J Machine Learning Res*, 2011, 12(Oct): 2825–2830.

[59] Abadi M.N., Barham P., Chen J., Chen Z., Davis A., Dean J., Devin M., Ghemawat S., Irving G., Isard M. Tensorflow: A system for large-scale machine learning. In *12th {USENIX} Symposium on Operating Systems Design and Implementation ({OSDI} 16)*, 2016, pp. 265–283.

[60] Chen J., Guo M., Wang X., Liu B. A comprehensive review and comparison of different computational methods for protein remote homology detection. *Brief Bioinfo*, 2016, 19(2): 231–244.

[61] Hou J., Adhikari B., Cheng J. DeepSF: Deep convolutional neural network for mapping protein sequences to folds. *Bioinformatics*, 2017, 34(8): 1295–1303.

[62] Xia J., Peng Z., Qi D., Mu H., Yang J. An ensemble approach to protein fold classification by integration of template-based assignment and support vector machine classifier. *Bioinformatics*, 2016, 33(6): 863–870.

[63] Murzin A.G., Brenner S.E., Hubbard T., Chothia C. SCOP: A structural classification of proteins database for the investigation of sequences and structures. *J Mol Biol*, 1995, 247(4): 536–540.

[64] Fox N.K., Brenner S.E., Chandonia J.-M. SCOPe: Structural Classification of Proteins — Extended, integrating SCOP and ASTRAL data and classification of new structures. *Nucleic Acids Res*, 2014, 42(D1): D304–D309.

[65] Damoulas T., Girolami M.A. Probabilistic multi-class multi-kernel learning: On protein fold recognition and remote homology detection. *Bioinformatics*, 2008, 24(10): 1264–1270.

[66] Xia J., Peng Z., Qi D., Mu H., Yang J. An ensemble approach to protein fold classification by integration of template-based assignment and support vector machine classifier. *Bioinformatics*, 2017, 33(6): 863–870.

Chapter 4

Remote Homology Detection

4.1 Motivation and Basic Idea

Predicting the structure or function of a protein from its amino acid sequence is one of the most important tasks in computational biology. Protein structures and functions are more conserved than their sequences in the evolution process, and proteins sharing similar structures or functions may have low sequence identities. For protein structure prediction, template-based prediction methods have been proven to be more effective, and many methods have been presented during the last decades.[1] A protein structure can be accurately modeled when the homologous templates are identified. For protein function prediction, the easiest way to annotate newly sequenced proteins is to transfer function annotations from well-characterized homologous proteins[2]; so detecting homologous proteins for a target protein sequence is a central problem in computational biology.[3] Most methods can detect homologous proteins with a high level of similarity, while remote homology is difficult to differentiate from pairs of proteins that share similarities due to chance. Therefore, the development of efficient algorithms for protein homology detection is of great importance. The detection of homologous relationships with low sequence identities, also known as remote homology detection, remains an especially challenging problem in computational biology.[4]

4.2 Related Work

The major methods for homology detection can be split into three basic groups[5]: pair-wise sequence comparison algorithms, generative models for protein families and discriminative classifiers. Early methods looked for pair-wise similarities between proteins. Among those algorithms, the Smith–Waterman dynamic programming algorithm[6] is one of the most accurate methods, whereas heuristic algorithms such as BLAST[7] and FASTA[8] trade reduced accuracy for improved efficiency. The methods have since obtained higher rates of accuracy by collecting statistical information from a set of similar sequences. PSI-BLAST[9] used BLAST to iteratively build a probabilistic profile of a query sequence and obtained a more sensitive sequence comparison score. Generative models such as profile hidden Markov models (HMM)[10] used positive examples of a protein family, which can be trained iteratively using both positively labeled and unlabeled examples by pulling in close homologues and adding them to the positive set.[11] Finally, the discriminative algorithms such as Support Vector Machine (SVM)[12] used both positive and negative examples and provided state-of-the-art performance with an appropriate kernel. Many SVM-based methods have been proposed, such as SVM-fisher,[13] SVM-k-spectrum,[14] Mismatch-SVM,[15] SVM-pairwise,[15] SVM-I-sites,[16] SVM-LA and SVM-SW.[17] A comparison of SVM-based methods can be seen in the paper by Saigo *et al.*[18]

4.3 Latent Semantic Analysis

The success of an SVM classification method for homology detection depends on the choice of the feature set to describe each protein. Most of these research efforts focus on finding useful representations of protein sequence data for SVM training by using either explicit feature vector representations or kernel functions. The features are usually very large, and noise data may be introduced. Focusing on feature extraction for SVM protein classification, a Latent Semantic Analysis (LSA) model from natural language processing[19] is introduced to condense the original protein vectors. The length of the resulting vector is much shorter than that of the original vector, leading to the noise removal and efficient description of the protein sequence.

As a proven method in the case of natural language processing LSA has been used to generate summaries, compare documents and help further information retrieval.[19] LSA was also introduced in computational biology and used to predict the secondary structure of proteins.[20] Furthermore, the similarity between biological sequences and natural language has attracted much attention. Many methods of natural language processing have been applied to biological sequences. The n-grams of whole genome protein sequences have been analyzed and some statistical features have been extracted.[21] The probabilistic models from speech recognition have been employed to enhance protein domain discovery.[22] Protein classification based on text document classification techniques has provided state-of-the-art performance in GPCR classification.[23] The protein sequence language has been discussed extensively by Ganapathiraju *et al.*[24]

4.3.1 Latent semantic analysis for protein remote homology detection

Latent semantic analysis is a theory and method for extracting and representing the contextual-usage meaning of words by applying statistical computations to a large corpus of text.[25] Here, we briefly describe the basic process of LSA.

The starting point of LSA is the construction of a word-document matrix W of co-occurrences between words and documents. The elements of W can be taken as the number of times each word appears in each document; thus, the dimension of W is $M \times N$, where M is the total number of words and N is the number of given documents. To compensate for the differences in document lengths and overall counts of different words in the document collection, each word count can be normalized.[25]

In the word-document matrix W, each document is expressed as a column vector. However, this representation does not recognize synonyms or related words and the dimensions are too large. In the specific application, singular value decomposition is performed on the word-document matrix. Let K be the total ranks of W, so W can be decomposed into three matrices

$$W = USW^T \qquad (4\text{-}1)$$

where U is the left singular matrix with dimensions $(M \times K)$, V is the right singular matrix with dimensions $(N \times K)$, and S is the $(K \times K)$ diagonal matrix of singular values $s_1 \geq s_2 \geq \ldots s_K > 0$. One can reduce the dimensions of the solution simply by deleting the smaller singular values in the diagonal matrix. The corresponding columns of matrix U (rows of matrix V) are also ignored. In practice, only the top $R(R \ll \text{Min}(M, N))$ dimensions for which the elements in S are greater than a threshold are considered for further processing. Thus, the dimensions of matrices U, S and V are reduced to $M \times R$, $R \times R$ and $N \times R$, leading to data compression and noise removal. Values of R in the range [200, 300] are typically used for information retrieval. In the present context, the best results are achieved when R takes a value around 300.

By SVD, the column vectors of the word-document matrix W are projected onto the orthonormal basis formed by the row column vectors of the left singular matrix U. The coordinates of the vectors are given by the columns of SV^T. This in turn means that the column vectors Sv_j^T or, equivalently the row vectors $v_j S$, characterize the position of document d_j in the R dimensions space. Each of the vectors $v_j S$ is referred to as a document vector, uniquely associated with the document in the training set.

For a new document that is not in the training set, it is necessary to add the unseen document to the original training set, and the latent semantic analysis model then needs to be recomputed. However, SVD is a computationally expensive process; performing SVD every time for a new test document is not suitable. From the mathematical properties of the matrices U, S and V, the new vector t can be approximated as:

$$t = dU \qquad (4\text{-}2)$$

where d is the raw vector of the new document, which is similar to the columns of the matrix W.

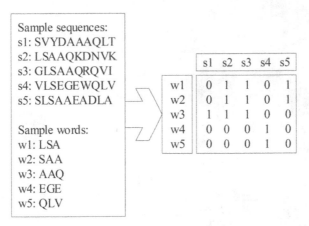

Figure 4-1   Sample construction of the word-document matrix with n-grams as the words. The cell entries are the number of times of occurrence of a word (rows) in a document (columns).

In order to apply LSA to protein remote homology detection, each protein sequence that belongs to a particular class is treated as a "document" that is composed of bags-of-X, where X can be any of the basic building blocks of protein sequences. The word-document matrix needs to be constructed by collecting the weight of each word in the documents. Figure 4-1 presents an example of such matrices. Singular Value Decomposition (SVD) is performed on the word-document matrix to remove the noise from the data and to decrease the dimensions of the protein vectors. The latent semantic representation vectors are evaluated by support vector machines to train classifiers, which are then used to classify the test protein sequences.

In this section, the Gist SVM package implemented by Jaakkola et al.[26] is applied for protein remote homology detection. The parameters of SVM which are used by default are those of the Gist package, except for the kernel function which is the Radius Basis Function (RBF) kernel. Figure 4-2 illustrates the implementation of the method.

4.3.2 Dataset and performance metrics

The evaluation data is the same as the one used by Li et al.,[5] which is taken from the Structural Classification of Proteins (SCOP)

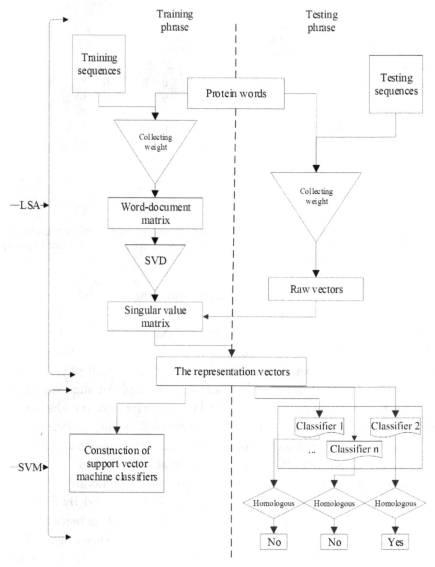

Figure 4-2   Overview of LSA-based SVM for protein classification. The word-document matrix is constructed by the context of protein sequences. The latent semantic analysis is then performed on the matrix to produce the latent semantic representation vectors of protein sequences. The support vector machine is used to evaluate the protein vectors. Such systems can use any building blocks of proteins as the protein words.

database[27] version 1.53. Sequences are selected from the ASTRAL database.[28] The dataset contains 54 families and 4352 distinct sequences. Remote homology is simulated by holding out all members of a target 1.53 family from a given superfamily. Positive training examples are chosen from the remaining families in the same superfamily, and negative test and training examples are chosen from outside the fold of the target family. The held-out family members serve as positive test examples. The above process is iterated until each family has been tested. Details of the datasets are available at http://www1.cs.columbia.edu/compbio/svm-pairwise/.

Two methods are used to evaluate the experimental results: the Receiver Operating Characteristic (ROC) scores[29] and the Median Rate of False Positives (M-RFP) scores.[26] A ROC score is the normalized area under a curve that is plotted with true positives as a function of false positives for varying classification thresholds. A score of 1 indicates the perfect separation of positive samples from negative samples, whereas a score of 0 denotes that none of the sequences selected by the algorithm are positive. The median RFP score is the fraction of negative test sequences that score as high as or better than the median score of the positive sequences. Obviously, the smaller the M-RFP is, the better the results are.

4.3.3 Setup of competing method

Through the experiments reported here, the performances of the following methods are compared: PSI-BLAST, SVM-pairwise, SVM-LA, three SVM-based methods (namely SVM-Ngram, SVM-Pattern and SVM-Motif) and three SVM-based methods after latent semantic analysis (namely SVM-Ngram-LSA, SVM-Pattern-LSA, SVM-Motif-LSA). The setup procedures of these methods are briefly described in the following.

The PSI-BLAST is the most widely applied protein homology detection algorithm that only requires a single sequence as input. But for better performance, multiple sequences are input to PSI-BLAST. First, a random positive training sequence is selected as the initial query. The complete positive training set is then aligned by the

CLUSTALW method.[30] Using the query sequence and the alignment as inputs, PSI-BLAST is run with the test set as a database. The resulting E-values are used to rank the test set.

For the SVM-based method, the key step is to express a protein sequence as a vector or by the calculation of kernels. In the SVM-pairwise method,[31] the feature vector is a list of pairwise sequence similarity scores, computed with respect to all of the sequences in the training set. In the SVM-LA method,[32] the kernel is calculated by summing up scores obtained from the local alignments with the gaps of the sequences. Such a kernel may not be a positive definite kernel, and the authors have provided two solutions for this problem. Due to its performance and simplicity, we have implemented one of the methods, namely, the LA-ekm kernel. The parameters of the LA-ekm kernel take the optimal values provided by the authors ($\beta = 0.5, d = -11, e = -1$). For the SVM method based on three basic words, the length of the feature vector is equal to the number of each type of word. A protein sequence is mapped to a high-dimensional vector by the frequency of occurrence of each word. The protein vectors are then input into SVM to train the classifiers and classify the test protein sequences. Such a representation is also used in related work.[33–35] For the LSA-based method, the word-document matrix is built by collecting the weight of each word in the documents. LSA is then performed on this matrix to produce the latent semantic representative vectors of protein sequences.

4.3.4 Results and discussion

Table 4-1 summarizes the performance of the various methods in terms of average ROC and M-RFP scores over all 54 families tested. As seen in the table, the PSI-BLAST method achieves the lowest performance. The accuracies of the SVM methods based on the basic words are lower than those of SVM-pairwise methods except for the pattern-based SVM method. When the LSA model is used, all the SVM methods based on the three basic words get higher accuracies. The performance of the LAS model is comparable with that of the SVM-LA method and better than that of the SVM-pairwise method. The SVM-pairwise is one of the state-of-the-art methods

Table 4-1   Average ROC and M-RFP scores over 54 families for different methods.

Methods	Mean ROC	Mean M-RFP
PSI-BLAST	0.675393	0.325322
SVM-pairwise	0.825928	0.1173329
SVM-LA	0.887124	0.0653927
SVM-Ngram	0.791415	0.144053
SVM-Pattern	0.835387	0.134893
SVM-motif	0.81356	0.124572
SVM-Ngram-LSA	0.859484	0.101688
SVM-Pattern-LSA	0.878926	0.070287
SVM-Motif-LSA	0.859193	0.0995269

and outperforms many other methods such as FPS,[36] SAM[37] and SVM-Fisher[26]; so, the LSA model is an efficient method for remote homology detection.

When the three basic words are considered, one can find that the method based on patterns performs best whether the LSA model is used or not. The reason for this may be that there are wildcards in patterns. So, patterns can match the protein sequences easily and describe the components of protein sequences effectively.

The homology between the training samples and the test samples is an important factor that influences the performance of various methods. The contribution of homology to various methods is evaluated at the family, the superfamily and the fold level, respectively. At the family level, the members of the target family are divided into two parts, one for positive training and the other for positive test. At the superfamily level, the positive training samples are taken from the same superfamily of the target family, but the members from the family itself are excluded. At the fold level, the positive training samples are taken from the same fold of the target family, but the members from the superfamily of the target family are excluded. The negative training and test samples are the same as those of previous experiments. Since many of the families contain unsuitable positive samples, only one of the families (SCOP ID: 2.1.1.4) is selected as the target family. The number of samples is listed in Table 4-2, and the results of various methods are listed in

Table 4-2   Number of samples at different homology levels.

	Positive train	Positive test	Negative train	Negative test
Family	20	13	3033	1137
Superfamily	88	33	3033	1137
Fold	61	33	3033	1137

Notes: The number of samples of the target family (2.1.1.4) at different homology levels is listed. The selection of the samples for training and test is described in the main text.

Table 4-3   Comparative results of various methods at the family, the superfamily and the fold level.

	Family		Superfamily		Fold	
	ROC	M-RFP	ROC	M-RFP	ROC	M-RFP
PSI-BLAST	0.9874	0.00082	0.8424	0.0219	0.6568	0.6525
SVM-LA	0.9986	0.00084	0.9857	0.0042	0.8942	0.0937
SVM-Ngram	0.8829	0.03078	0.8712	0.0386	0.7875	0.1143
SVM-Pattern	0.9983	0.00096	0.9759	0.0007	0.8639	0.0836
SVM-motif	0.9998	0.00073	0.9885	0.0008	0.8503	0.0993
SVM-Ngram-LSA	0.8929	0.05628	0.8992	0.0659	0.8455	0.1116
SVM-Pattern-LSA	0.9964	0.00098	0.9925	0.0017	0.9127	0.0674
SVM-Motif-LSA	0.9995	0.00087	0.9867	0.0035	0.9084	0.0721

Note: Family (2.1.1.4) is the target family.

Table 4-3. At the family level, all the SVM-based methods perform equally well as PSI-BLAST, while at the superfamily level and the fold level the improvement of SVM-based methods in comparison with PSI-BLAST is significant. So, it can be seen that discriminative methods are more powerful than PSI-BLAST for the detection of remote homology.

Computational efficiency is an important factor for any homology detection algorithm. In this regard, the LSA approaches are better than SVM-pairwise and SVM-LA but a little worse than the methods without LSA and PSI-BLAST. Any SVM-based method includes a vectorization step and an optimization step. The vectorization step of SVM-pairwise takes a running time of $O(n2/2)$, where n is the number of training examples and l is the length of the longest training sequence. The time complexity of the calculation of an LA-ekm kernel matrix is same as that of SVM-pairwise.[32] The time complexity of the vectorization step of the method without LSA is $O(nml)$, where m is the total number of words. The main bottleneck of the LSA method is the additional SVD process, which roughly takes $O(nmt)$, where t is the minimum of n and m. The optimization step of the SVM-based method takes $O(n^2 p)$ time, where p is the length of the latent semantic representation vector. In SVM-pairwise, p is equal to n, yielding a total time of $O(n^3)$. In the method without LSA, p is equal to m, while in the LSA method, p is equal to R. Since $R \ll \text{Min}(n, m)$, the SVM optimization step of the LSA method is much faster than those of the other two methods. The time complexity of running PSI-BLAST is $O(nN)$, where N is the size of the database. In the current situation, N is approximately equal to nl.

The analysis presented here is based on sequences alone without using any evolutionary or structural information. Three basic building blocks of protein sequences are investigated: the n-grams, the patterns and the motifs. All of them show improved performance when the LSA model is used. Obviously, the availability of structural or evolutionary information can further improve the performance of remote homology detection. Han *et al.*[38] used profile–profile alignment and SVM for fold recognition. Hou *et al.*[39] used local sequence–structure correlations for remote homology detection. Multiple profiles have been used for effective detection of remote homologues.[40] Such evolutionary or structural information can also be used in the LSA model, so long as the structural or functional building blocks of proteins are extracted. However, the identification of functional equivalents of "words" in protein sequences is the major hurdle in the use of natural language techniques for a variety of computational biology problems.[24] In essence, the method presented here provides a fertile ground for further experimentation with dictionaries that can be constructed using the different properties of amino acids and proteins.

4.4　Auto-cross Covariance Transformation

Artificial intelligence-based techniques such as SVM and neural networks require fixed-length vectors for training. However, protein sequences often have different lengths. Here the Auto-Cross Covariance (ACC) transformation is introduced to transform protein sequences into fixed-length vectors. As a statistical tool for analyzing the sequences of vectors developed by Wold *et al.*,[41] ACC has been successfully used for protein family classification,[42, 43] protein interaction prediction[44] and protein fold recognition.[45] Since each residue has many physicochemical properties, such as hydrophobicity, hydrophilicity, normalized van der Waals volume, polarity, polarizability, profile, etc., a sequence can be represented as a numeric matrix. ACC can measure the correlation of two different properties (or the same property) along the signal polypeptide and transform the matrix into a fixed-length vector.

In this section, a novel method that combines SVM with ACC is presented for protein remote homology detection. Previous successful applications of the PSI-BLAST profile illustrate that evolutionary information is more informative than the query sequence itself, so the position-specific scoring matrix (PSSM) is transformed into a fixed-length vector by ACC transformation. The resulting vector is then input to a SVM classifier to predict the homology. Experiments are performed on well-established datasets based on the Structural Classification of Proteins (SCOP) database.[27] The proposed method (called ACCRe) outperforms most of the state-of-the-art methods for protein remote homology detection.

4.4.1　Datasets and performance metrics

Two well-constructed datasets are used to access the performance of the proposed method. Both of them are derived from the SCOP database.[27] Remote homology detection is simulated both at the superfamily and the fold level.

SCOP 1.53 superfamily dataset: The dataset was developed by Li and Noble[5] and has been widely used to evaluate the performance of various homology detection methods. The dataset is derived from the SCOP database with version 1.53. Sequences are extracted from the ASTRAL database,[28] and the similarity between any two sequences is less than an E-value of 10^{-25}. The resulting dataset contains 54 families and 4352 distinct sequences. Remote homology is simulated at the superfamily level by holding out all the members of a target family from a given superfamily. Positive training examples are chosen from the remaining families in the same superfamily, and negative test as well as training examples are chosen from outside the fold of the target family. The held-out family members serve as positive test examples. This process is repeated until each family has been tested.

SCOP 1.67 superfamily and fold dataset: The dataset was developed by Haandstad *et al.*,[46] is derived from the SCOP database version 1.67 and contains two subsets that simulate remote homology detection at the superfamily and the fold level, respectively. Redundant sequences that share more than 95% similarity are removed. The data are further filtered according to the principle that each classifier should have at least 10 sequences for test and training, that is, every classifier should have at least 10 sequences in its positive training and test set. The superfamily benchmark contains 102 families and 4019 sequences. The fold benchmark contains 86 superfamilies and 3840 sequences. The goal of the superfamily benchmark is to classify a new protein sequence into an SCOP superfamily, in which the sample partition is the same as that used by the SCOP 1.53 superfamily dataset. The objective of the fold benchmark is to classify an unknown sequence into an SCOP fold. One superfamily is used as the positive test set, while the others in the same fold constitute the positive training set. The negative test set consists of one random superfamily from each of the other folds, and the negative training set consists of the remaining sequences. This benchmark is considerably harder than the superfamily benchmark, as most of the sequences within a fold have a very low degree of similarity.

Performance metrics: Two methods are used to evaluate the experimental results: the receiver operating characteristic (ROC) scores[47] and the median rate of false positives (M-RFP) scores.[13] The ROC score is the normalized area under a curve that is plotted with true positives as a function of false positives for varying classification thresholds. A score of 1 indicates a perfect separation of positive samples from negative samples, whereas a score of 0 denotes that none of the sequences selected by the algorithm is positive. An ROC_{50} score is the area under the ROC curve up to the first 50 false-positives. The median RFP (M-RFP) score is the fraction of negative test sequences that score as high as or better than the median score of the positive sequences. Obviously, the smaller the M-RFP, the better the results.

4.4.2 Auto-cross covariance transformation

Each residue has many physicochemical properties as mentioned earlier, so a protein sequence can be viewed as a time sequence of the corresponding properties. In this study, only the evolutionary information represented in the form of the PSSM is selected as a feature, since it can give promising results according to the experiments. The profile of each sequence is generated by running PSI-BLAST[9] against the NCBI's NR dataset with parameters ($-j$ 3, $-e$ 0.01). The element S_{ij} in the matrix reflects the probability of amino acid i occurring at position j.

Here, each amino acid is taken as one property and the PSSMs are considered as the time sequences of all properties. ACC can transform PSSMs of different lengths into a fixed-length vector by measuring the correlation between any two properties. The first step of ACC transformation is to build two signal sequences, and then calculate the correlation between them. ACC results in two kinds of variables: autocovariance (AC) between the same property, and cross-covariance (CC) between two different properties. The AC variable measures the correlation of the same property between two residues separated by a distance of lg along the sequence and can be calculated using the formula

$$AC(i, lg) = \sum_{j=1}^{L-lg} (S_{i,j} - \bar{S}_i)(S_{i,j+lg} - \bar{S}_i)/(L - lg) \qquad (4\text{-}3)$$

where i is one of the residues, L is the length of the protein sequence, $S_{i,j}$ is the PSSM score of amino acid i at position j, and $\bar{S}_\iota$ is the average score for amino acid i along the whole sequence

$$\bar{S}_\iota = \sum_{j=1}^{L} S_{i,j} \tag{4-4}$$

In such a way, the number of AC variables can be calculated as 20^*LG, where LG is the maximum of $lg(lg = 1, 2, \ldots, LG)$. Note that lg is the same as the lag order in many auto-regression models.

The CC variable measures the correlation of two different properties between two residues separated by lg along the sequence and can be calculated by

$$\mathrm{CC}(i1, i2, lg) = \sum_{j=1}^{L-lg} (S_{i1,j} - \overline{S_{\iota1}})(S_{i2,j+lg} - \overline{S_{\iota2}})/(L - lg) \tag{4-5}$$

where $i1, i2$ are two different amino acids and $\overline{S_{\iota1}}$ $(\overline{S_{\iota2}})$ is the average score for amino acid $i1$ $(i2)$ along the sequence. Since the CC variables are not symmetric, the total number of CC variables is 380^*LG.

In this study, each protein sequence is represented as a vector X with elements of either the AC variables or the ACC variables that are a combination of AC and CC.

4.4.3 Results and discussions

The proposed method can use AC variables or ACC variables, and the corresponding methods are referred to as ACCRe_AC and ACCRe_ACC, respectively. The abilities of homology detection at the superfamily and the fold level are accessed and compared with other excellent methods.

Comparative studies on the SCOP 1.53 superfamily dataset

The value of LG may impact the performance of the ACCRe method. The maximum value of LG is the length of the shortest sequence minus one. The average ROC scores for different values of LG are shown in Fig. 4-3. As can be seen, the value of LG has a minor influence on the ROC scores. The optimal values of LG for

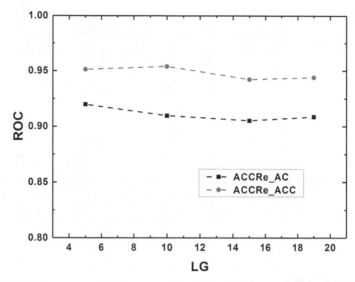

Figure 4-3   The average ROC scores with different values of *lg* on the SCOP 1.53 superfamily dataset.

ACCRe_AC and ACCRe_ACC are 5 and 10, respectively. Since *LG* is the maximum of *lg*, the increase of lag order in the calculation of ACC has a minor influence on the overall performance.

The performance of the ACCRe method on the SCOP 1.53 superfamily dataset is listed in Table 4-4. To give an unbiased comparison, the results of other excellent methods tested on this dataset are also tabulated, including PSI-BLAST,[9] SVM-pairwise,[5] oligomer-distance,[48] SW-PSSM,[49] profile[50] and five building-block-based methods (*n*-gram, pattern, motif,[51] binary profiles[52] and Top-*n*-grams[53]) as well as the recently developed SVM-RQA[54] and SVM-WCM methods.[55] The distributions of ROC and ROC_{50} scores are plotted in Fig. 4-4. In each graph, a higher curve corresponds to a more accurate homology detection performance. As can be seen, the ACCRe method with AC variable achieves an average ROC score of 0.92, an average ROC_{50} score of 0.83 and an average M-RFP score of 0.049. When the ACC variable is used, the ACCRe method shows improved performance with an average ROC score of 0.954, an average ROC_{50} score of 0.894 and an average M-RFP score of 0.026. Such a result is only slightly lower than that of the SW-PSSM

Table 4-4 Comparative performance of different methods on the SCOP 1.53 superfamily dataset.

Method	ROC	ROC50	M-RFP	Source
ACCRe_ACC	0.954	0.894	0.026	This study
ACCRe_AC	0.92	0.83	0.049	This study
SVM-RQA	0.912	0.441	0.057	54
SVM-WCM	0.904	0.4454	0.079	55
SVM-Top-n-gram-combine-LSA	0.939	0.767	0.037	56
SVM-Ngram-LSA	0.859	0.628	0.102	51
SVM-Pattern-LSA	0.879	0.626	0.07	51
SVM-Motif-LSA	0.859	0.628	0.099	51
SVM-Bprofile-LSA	0.921	0.698	0.046	57
SVM-LA(β =0.5)	0.925	0.649	0.054	17
Oligomer-distance (Monomer)	0.919	0.508	0.066	48
SW-PSSM(3.0, 0.75, 1.5)	0.982	0.904	0.015	49
Profile(6, 9.0)	0.967	0.784	—	50
SVM-Pairwise	0.896	0.464	0.084	17
PSI-BLAST	0.675	0.33	0.325	51

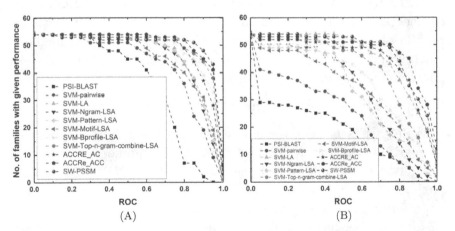

Figure 4-4 Relative performance of homology detection methods on the SCOP 1.53 superfamily dataset. The graph plots the total number of families for which the method exceeds a given (A) ROC and (B) ROC$_{50}$ score.

and profile method, but it is better than those of all the other methods. The SW-PSSM method uses a local alignment-based kernel to calculate the similarity between sequences, which may provide a more accurate measure of homology for proteins.

Both the ACCRe and oligomer-distance methods[48] take the position information between residues of protein sequences into consideration, differently from other methods. However, the ACCRe method uses evolutionary information instead of the basic sequences, and hence better results are obtained in comparison with the oligomer-distance method. In addition, the feature space of the oligomer-distance method is extremely large, and so there exists a data-sparse problem when a multi-oligomer is used. The ACCRe method needs an additional step to produce evolutionary information, which is required by all the profile-based methods.

The ROC score of the ACCRe_ACC method is slightly lower than that of the profile method,[50] but the ROC_{50} score of the ACCRe_ACC method is significantly better than that of the profile method. Both methods utilize evolutionary information for remote homology detection but in different formats. The profile method extends the k-mer-based string kernel by using the profile generated by PSI-BLAST, which omits the order of residues (or profiles) in sequences. The ACCRe method calculates the correlation between profiles along the sequences, as it is a position-dependent method. Another advantage of the ACCRe method is that there are less parameters to be tuned for features (only LG).

Comparative studies on the SCOP 1.67 dataset

This dataset is based on a new version of the SCOP database in comparison with the SCOP 1.53 dataset. The number of classes in this dataset is significantly larger than in the SCOP 1.53 dataset (102 vs. 54 at the superfamily level). The detection of homology is performed at the superfamily level as well as the fold level. So, this dataset can give an extensive evaluation of remote homology detection methods.

The influence of LG on the ACCRe method is illustrated in Fig. 4-5. A very small fluctuation is also observed with ROC scores varying about 1%. The best values of LG for AC and ACC variables are taken as 5 and 10, respectively.

Table 4-5 summarizes the performance of various homology detection methods on the SCOP 1.67 dataset. The corresponding

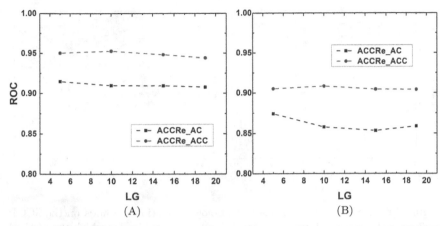

Figure 4-5 The average ROC scores with different values of LG on the SCOP 1.67 dataset. (A) and (B) plot the performance at the superfamily and the fold level, respectively.

Table 4-5 Comparative performance of different methods on the SCOP 1.67 dataset.

Method	Superfamily level		Fold level	
	ROC	ROC_{50}	ROC	ROC_{50}
ACCRe_ACC	0.953	0.892	0.908	0.851
ACCRe_AC	0.915	0.846	0.874	0.823
Gpkernel	0.902	0.591	0.844	0.514
Mismatch	0.878	0.543	0.814	0.467
eMOTIF	0.857	0.551	0.698	0.308
SVM-LA	0.919	0.686	0.834	0.504
SW-PSSM(3.0,0.75,1.5)	0.976	0.915	0.923	0.809
SVM-Pairwise	0.849	0.555	0.724	0.359
PSI-BLAST	0.575	0.175	0.501	0.01

ROC plot is shown in Fig. 4-6. The results of ACCRe and SW-PSSM methods are based on an in-house implementation, while the results of the other methods are taken from the literature.[46] At the superfamily level, the ACCRe method with AC variables gets an average ROC score of 0.915 and a ROC_{50} score of 0.846. The incorporation of CC variables can further improve the performance, with an average ROC score of 0.953 and a ROC_{50} score of 0.908.

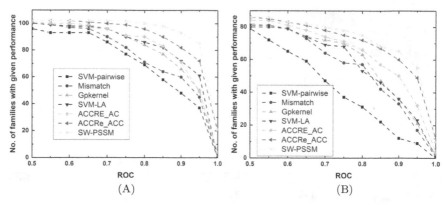

Figure 4-6   Relative performance of homology detection methods on the SCOP 1.67 dataset. The graph plots the total number of families for which the method exceeds a given ROC score. (A) and (B) plot the performance at the superfamily and the fold benchmark, respectively.

In terms of detection performance, the ACCRe_ACC method is comparable with the profile-based kernel method (SW-PSSM), and even outperforms all the other methods. The detection of homology at the fold level is more difficult than that at the superfamily level, since the similarities among sequences in each fold are extremely low. The classic alignment-based method (PSI-BLAST) fails to detect homology on the SCOP 1.67 fold benchmark, which has an average ROC score of 0.5. The other discriminative methods significantly improve the performance. The proposed method with ACC variables achieves an average ROC score of 0.908, which is slightly lower than that of the SW-PSSM method (0.923), but the ROC_{50} score is larger than that of the SW-PSSM method (0.851 vs 0.809). Overall, the proposed ACCRe method is comparable with the SW-PSSM method and superior to all the other methods for protein remote homology detection at both the superfamily and the fold level. To determine whether the two methods have statistically different ROC scores, the Wilcoxon signed-rank test is used. The p-values between the ACCRe_ACC method and SW-PSSM method are 1.215e–05 and 0.08299 on the SCOP 1.67 superfamily and fold datasets, respectively, which indicates that there exists a difference between the results. The two methods provide a different framework for the use of sequence profiles, and the results complement each other.

Correlations between AC/ACC features and protein families

After SVM training, the learned sequence-specific weights can be used to calculate the discriminant weight of each feature for better interpretation of the features. Following a research study,[55] let $\alpha = [\alpha_1, \ldots, \alpha_N]^T$ be the weight vector of a set of N sequences after kernel-based training and let M be the matrix of sequence representatives. Then, the discriminant weight vector ω in feature space can be computed using the formula

$$\omega = M * \alpha \tag{4-6}$$

The magnitude of an entry in ω reflects the discriminative power of the corresponding feature.

Four families are selected from the SCOP 1.67 superfamily dataset, and the ten most discriminative features for the ACCRe_AC and ACCRe_ACC methods are listed in Table 4-6. It is obvious that all families show a preference for the feature with an LG value of 2, which indicates that the signal peptides with lag order of 2 may have an important influence on the remote homology of proteins. Also, some families have a propensity for particular features. For example, when the ACCRe_ACC method is used, the family a.138.1.3 shows

Table 4-6   Ordered list of discriminative features.

	Family a.22.1.3		Family a.138.1.3		Family b.29.1.1		Family b.47.1.3	
	ac	Acc	ac	acc	ac	acc	ac	acc
1	d,2	ia,2	C,3	CH,4	P,5	VP,2	a,3	VT,2
2	e,2	qA,8	h,4	CH,1	T,4	AT,2	G,4	aa,3
3	v,2	va,2	m,5	nh,4	f,1	ra,1	g,2	mp,5
4	q,2	af,9	t,2	CC,3	p,1	RN,6	p,1	pa,2
5	i,2	IA,4	P,3	eh,4	T,3	QT,2	n,4	gg,2
6	E,4	la,2	h,5	qh,4	A,2	RS,6	T,1	DV,4
7	k,2	VM,7	I,5	dh,4	I,2	PT,1	h,3	ph,1
8	m,5	QA,2	A,2	ah,4	Q,2	fa,2	a,5	TY,3
9	Q,4	AE,9	F,2	kh,4	I,5	PN,3	e,4	IT,2
10	V,3	kl,8	K,3	mh,1	N,3	TD,1	d,4	gp,3

a strong preference for the feature with 'H' as the second property and an LG value of 4. For family a.22.1.3, the amino acid 'A' is also overrepresented in its features. Such phenomena indicate that there are family-specific features when auto-cross transformation is used on protein sequences. These family-specific features may contain important structure or function information, which will be explored in a future study.

Evolutionary information can improve the performance of remote homology detection

Protein remote homology detection refers to the detection of a homologous relationship with low sequence similarities. Generally, the homology detection methods are assessed by their abilities to judge whether two sequences belong to the same SCOP hierarchy or not. The traditional alignment-based methods often fail to detect remote homologies while the discriminative methods can provide state-of-the-art performance. A variant of the SVM-based methods has been developed over the last few years. These methods use either the sequence or the profile as features. The sequence composite information has been extensively explored including such techniques as n-gram,[51] Pattern,[58] Motif,[46,59] I-sites,[16] k-spectrum,[60] Mismatch,[15] etc. Among the sequence-based methods, the LA-kernel[17] can provide the best performance, which calculates the similarity between two sequences by local alignments. The profiles of protein sequences contain evolutionary information and are generally represented in the form of the PSSM or its variants. Since the profiles contain more information than the sequence alone, the profile-based methods are more powerful than the sequence-based methods. Some of the profile-based methods focus on the development of more sensitive profiles. The HHSearch method[61] introduces a novel profile based on Hidden Markov Models. SVM-HUSTLE[62] builds profiles using an SVM classifier trained on a collection of representative high-confidence training sets. Other profile-based methods explore the usage of profiles in different manners. The composite information of protein sequences at the profile level[56,57] has been shown to be superior to that at the residue level. Anand *et al.*[40] demonstrated that the use of multiple profiles enables the effective detection of remote homology. The SW-PSSM method calculates the similarities between any two samples by profile–profile alignments. The present study also uses profiles for protein remote homology detection and introduces a novel algorithm to transform the profiles into fixed-length vectors with which the artificial intelligence-based techniques can be subsequently performed. Experimental results show that the proposed method gets comparable results with other superior profile-based methods and is much better than the sequence-based methods. ACC takes the profiles as time sequences of the frequencies of residues and transforms them into fixed-length vectors by measuring the correlation between any two frequencies. The main contribution of this study is to introduce a simple, fast and interpretable algorithm for the usage of profiles, which can also be used for other related studies.

4.5 Conclusions

Remote homology detection between protein sequences is a central problem in computational biology. This chapter proposed the LSA model and a general framework for the conversion of protein sequences to fixed-length vectors by ACC transformation (ACCRe) for protein remote homology detection. Based on LSA, each document is represented as a linear combination of hidden abstract concepts, which arise automatically from the SVD mechanism. LSA defines a transformation between high-dimensional discrete entities (the vocabulary) and a low-dimensional continuous vector space S, the R-dimensional space spanned by the U's, leading to noise removal and efficient representation of the protein sequence. As a result, the LSA model achieves better performance than the methods without LSA. For ACCRe, first the ACC transformation is used to convert the PSSMs into fixed-length vectors, and then these vectors are input to SVM for remote homology detection. Testing on the SCOP 1.53 and SCOP 1.67 datasets has shown that the results of the ACCRe method are comparable or even better than other existing methods.

There are many problems in the biology domain similar to protein remote homology detection, such as fold prediction, tertiary structure and functional properties of proteins, which are considered to be challenging problems. Thus, these tasks are potential areas for applications of the LSA model and ACC transformation.

References

[1] Moult J., Fidelis K., Kryshtafovych A., Schwede T., Tramontano A. Critical assessment of methods of protein structure prediction (CASP) — Round XII. *Proteins*, 2018, 86: 7–15.

[2] Kouranov A., Xie L., de la Cruz J., Chen L., Westbrook J., Bourne P.E., Berman H.M. The RCSB PDB information portal for structural genomics. *Nucleic Acids Rese*, 2006, 34(suppl_1): D302–D305.

[3] Weston J., Zhou D., Elisseeff A., Noble W.S., Leslie C.S. Semi-supervised protein classification using cluster kernels. In *Advances in Neural Information Processing Systems*, Vancouver, Canada, 2004, pp. 595–602.

[4] Webb-Robertson B.-J.M., Oehmen C.S., Shah A.R. A feature vector integration approach for a generalized support vector machine pairwise homology algorithm. *Comput Biol Chem*, 2008, 32(6): 458–461.

[5] Liao L., Noble W.S. Combining pairwise sequence similarity and support vector machines for detecting remote protein evolutionary and structural relationships. *J Comput Biol*, 2003, 10(6): 857–868.

[6] Smith T.F., Waterman M.S. Identification of common molecular subsequences. *J Mol Biol*, 1981, 147(1): 195–197.

[7] Altschul S.F., Gish W., Miller W., Myers E.W., Lipman D.J. Basic local alignment search tool. *J Mol Biol*, 1990, 215(3): 403–410.

[8] Pearson W.R. Rapid and sensitive sequence comparison with FASTP and FASTA. *Methods Enzymol*, 1990, 183(1): 63–98.

[9] Altschul S.F., Madden T.L., Schäffer A.A., Zhang J., Zhang Z., Miller W., Lipman D.J. Gapped BLAST and PSI-BLAST: A new generation of protein database search programs. *Nucleic Acids Res*, 1997, 25(17): 3389–3402.

[10] Karplus K., Barrett C., Hughey R. Hidden Markov models for detecting remote protein homologies. *Bioinformatics* (Oxford, England), 1998, 14(10): 846–856.

[11] Qian B., Goldstein R.A. Performance of an iterated T-HMM for homology detection. *Bioinformatics*, 2004, 20(14): 2175–2180.

[12] Vapnik V., Vapnik V. *Statistical Learning Theory*. 1998. New York: Wiley, pp. 156–160.

[13] Jaakkola T., Diekhans M., Haussler D. A discriminative framework for detecting remote protein homologies. *J Comput Biol*, 2000, 7(1–2): 95–114.

[14] Leslie C., Eskin E., Noble W.S. The spectrum kernel: A string kernel for SVM protein classification, in *Biocomputing 2002*. 2001. Singapore: World Scientific, pp. 564–575.

[15] Leslie C.S., Eskin E., Cohen A., Weston J., Noble W.S. Mismatch string kernels for discriminative protein classification. *Bioinformatics*, 2004, 20(4): 467–476.

[16] Hou Y., Hsu W., Lee M.L., Bystroff C. Efficient remote homology detection using local structure. *Bioinformatics*, 2003, 19(17): 2294–2301.

[17] Saigo H., Vert J.-P., Ueda N., Akutsu T. Protein homology detection using string alignment kernels. *Bioinformatics*, 2004, 20(11): 1682–1689.

[18] Saigo H., Vert J.-P., Akutsu T., Ueda N. Comparison of SVM-based methods for remote homology detection. *Genome Inform*, 2002, 13: 396–397.

[19] Bellegarda J. Exploiting latent semantic information in statistical language modeling. *Proc IEEE*, 2000, 88(8): 1279–1296.

[20] Ganapathiraju M., Klein-Seetharaman J., Balakrishnan N., Reddy R. Characterization of protein secondary structure: Application of latent semantic analysis using different vocabularies. *IEEE Signal Process*, 2004, 21(3): 78–87.

[21] Ganapathiraju M., Weisser D., Rosenfeld R., Carbonell J., Reddy R., Klein-Seetharaman J. Comparative n-gram analysis of whole-genome protein sequences. In *Proceedings of the Human Language Technologies Conference*, San Diego 2002, pp. 1367–1375.

[22] Coin L., Bateman A., Durbin R. Enhanced protein domain discovery by using language modeling techniques from speech recognition. *Proc Natl Acad Sci USA*, 2003, 100(8): 4516–4520.

[23] Cheng B.Y., Carbonell J.G., Klein-Seetharaman J. Protein classification based on text document classification techniques. *Proteins*, 2005, 58(4): 955–970.

[24] Ganapathiraju M., Balakrishnan N., Reddy R., Klein-Seetharaman J. Computational Biology and Language. Ambient Intelligence for Scientific Discovery, *LNAI*, 2005, 3345: 25–47.

[25] Landauer T.K., Foltz P.W., Laham D. Introduction to Latent Semantic Analysis. *Discourse Process*, 1998, 25(2&3): 259–284.

[26] Jaakkola T., Diekhans M., Haussler D. A discriminative framework for detecting remote protein homologies. *J Comput Biol*, 2000, 7(1–2): 95–114.

[27] Andreeva A., Howorth D., Brenner S.E., Hubbard T.J.P., Chothia C., Murzin A.G. SCOP database in 2004: Refinements integrate structure and sequence family data. *Nucleic Acids Res*, 2004, 32(database issue): D226–D229.

[28] Chandonia J.M., Hon G., Walker N.S., Conte L.L., Koehl P., Levitt M., Brenner S.E. The ASTRAL Compendium in 2004. *Nucleic Acids Res*, 2004, 32(database issue): 189–192.

[29] Gribskov M., Robinson N.L. Use of receiver operating characteristic (ROC) analysis to evaluate sequence matching. *Comput Chem*, 1996, 20(1): 25–33.

[30] Thompson J.D., Higgins D.G., Gibson T.J. CLUSTAL W: Improving the sensitivity of progressive multiple sequence alignment through sequence weighting, position-specific gap penalties and weight matrix choice. *Nucleic Acids Res*, 1994, 22(22): 4673–4680.

[31] Li L., Noble W.S. Combining pairwise sequence similarity and support vector machines for detecting remote protein evolutionary and structural relationships. *J Comput Biol*, 2003, 10(6): 857–868.

[32] Saigo H., Vert J.P., Ueda N., Akutsu T. Protein homology detection using string alignment kernels. *Bioinformatics*, 2004, 20(11): 1682–1689.

[33] Leslie C., Eskin E., Noble W.S. The spectrum kernel: A string kernel for SVM protein classification. In *Proceedings of the Pacific Symposium on Biocomputing*, Singapore, 2002, pp. 564–575.

[34] Ben-Hur A., Brutlag D. Remote homology detection: A motif based approach. *Bioinformatics*, 2003, 19 (Suppl 1): i26–i33.

[35] Dong Q.W., Lin L., Wang X.L., Li M.H. A pattern-based SVM for protein remote homology detection. In *The Fourth International Conference on Machine Learning and Cybernetics*, GuangZhou, China. 2005, pp. 3363–3368.

[36] Bailey T.L., Grundy W.N. Classifying proteins by family using the product of correlated p-values. In *Proceedings of the Third International Conference on Computational Molecular Biology (RECOMB99)*, Tokyo, Japan, 1999, pp. 10–14.

[37] Krogh A., Brown M., Mian I.S., Sjolander K., Haussler D. Hidden Markov models in computational biology: Applications to protein modeling. *J Mol Biol*, 1994, 235(5): 1501–1531.

[38] Han S., Lee B.C., Yu S.T., Jeong C.S., Lee S., Kim D. Fold recognition by combining profile-profile alignment and support vector machine. *Bioinformatics*, 2005, 21(11): 2667–2673.

[39] Hou Y., Hsu W., Lee M.L., Bystroff C. Remote homolog detection using local sequence-structure correlations. *Proteins*, 2004, 57(3): 518–530.

[40] Anand B., Gowri V.S., Srinivasan N. Use of multiple profiles corresponding to a sequence alignment enables effective detection of remote homologues. *Bioinformatics*, 2005, 21(12): 2821–2826.

[41] Wold S., Jonsson J., Sjostrom M., Sandberg M., Rannar S. DNA and peptide sequences and chemical processes multivariately modelled by principal component analysis and partial least-squares projections to latent structures. *Anal Chim Acta*, 1993, 277(2): 239–253.

[42] Lapinsh M., Gutcaits A., Prusis P., Post C., Lundstedt T., Wikberg J.E. Classification of G-protein coupled receptors by alignment-independent extraction of principal chemical properties of primary amino acid sequences. *Protein Sci*, 2002, 11(4): 795–805.

[43] Guo Y., Li M., Lu M., Wen Z., Huang Z. Predicting G-protein coupled receptors-G-protein coupling specificity based on autocross-covariance transform. *Proteins*, 2006, 65(1): 55–60.

[44] Guo Y., Yu L., Wen Z., Li M. Using support vector machine combined with auto covariance to predict protein-protein interactions from protein sequences. *Nucleic Acids Res*, 2008, 36(9): 3025–3030.

[45] Dong Q.W., Zhou S.G., Guan J.H. A new taxonomy-based protein fold recognition approach based on autocross-covariance transformation. *Bioinformatics*, 2009, 25(20): 2655–2662.

[46] Haandstad T., Hestnes A.J., Saetrom P. Motif kernel generated by genetic programming improves remote homology and fold detection. *BMC Bioinform*, 2007, 8(1): 23.

[47] Fawcett T. An introduction to roc analysis. *Pattern Recog Lett*, 2006, 27(8): 861–874.

[48] Lingner T., Meinicke P. Remote homology detection based on oligomer distances. *Bioinformatics*, 2006, 22(18): 2224–2231.

[49] Rangwala H., Karypis G. Profile-based direct kernels for remote homology detection and fold recognition. *Bioinformatics*, 2005, 21(23): 4239–4247.

[50] Kuang R., Ie E., Wang K., Wang K., Siddiqi M., Freund Y., Leslie C. Profile-based string kernels for remote homology detection and motif extraction. *J Bioinform Comput Biol*, 2005, 3(3): 527–550.

[51] Dong Q.-W., Wang X.-L., Lin L. Application of latent semantic analysis to protein remote homology detection. *Bioinformatics*, 2006, 22(3): 285–290.

[52] Dong Q.W., Wang X.L., Lin L. Protein remote homology detection based on binary profiles. *Lecture Notes in Computer Science* (1st International Conference on Bioinformatics Research and Development, BIRD 2007), Berlin, Germany, 2007, 4414: 212–223.

[53] Liu B., Chen J., Wang X. Protein remote homology detection by combining Chou's distance-pair pseudo amino acid composition and

principal component analysis. *Mol Genet Genomics*, 2015, 290(5): 1919–1931.

[54] Yang Y., Tantoso E., Li K.B. Remote protein homology detection using recurrence quantification analysis and amino acid physicochemical properties. *J Theor Biol*, 2008, 252(1): 145–154.

[55] Lingner T., Meinicke P. Word correlation matrices for protein sequence analysis and remote homology detection. *BMC Bioinform*, 2008, 9: 259.

[56] Liu B., Wang X., Lin L., Dong Q., Wang X. A discriminative method for protein remote homology detection and fold recognition combining Top-n-grams and latent semantic analysis. *BMC Bioinform*, 2008, 9(1): 510.

[57] Qiwen Dong L.L., Xiaolong Wang. Protein Remote Homology Detection Based on Binary Profiles. *First International Conference, BIRD* 2007, Berlin, Germany, 2007, pp. 212–223.

[58] Floratos A., Rigoutsos I., Parida L., Gao Y. DELPHI: A pattern-based method for detecting sequence similarity. *IBM J Res Dev*, 2001, 45(3/4): 455–473.

[59] Kuang R., Weston J., Noble W.S., Leslie C. Motif-based protein ranking by network propagation. *Bioinformatics*, 2005, 21(19): 3711–3718.

[60] Leslie C., Eskin E., Noble W.S. The spectrum kernel: A string kernel for SVM protein classification. In *Proceedings of the Pacific Symposium on Biocomputing*, Singapore, 2002, pp. 564–575.

[61] Soding J. Protein homology detection by HMM-HMM comparison. *Bioinformatics*, 2005, 21(7): 951–960.

[62] Shah A.R., Oehmen C.S., Webb-Robertson B.J. SVM-HUSTLE — An iterative semi-supervised machine learning approach for pairwise protein remote homology detection. *Bioinformatics*, 2008, 24(6): 783–790.

Chapter 5

Structure Prediction

5.1 Motivation and Basic Idea

Due to the rapid development of protein sequencing technology and the relative lag of structural determination technology, the sequence data in the current molecular database far exceeds the amount of structural data, while the acquisition of structural information is very important to reveal the biological function of proteins. In view of this, it is imperative and necessary to predict the spatial structure of proteins with known sequences. The coding relationship from the amino acid sequence to the three-dimensional structure of the protein, called the second genetic code, has become the primary task of biology in the 21st century. Studying protein structure prediction has great theoretical and practical value. In theory, to understand the basic problem of how the primary structure of the protein determines its high-level structure, it is beneficial for people to systematically and completely understand the whole process of transferring biological information from DNA to biologically active proteins, and to clarify the central law more completely. It also enables people to have a deeper understanding of the various phenomena in the life process, and ultimately promotes the rapid development of life sciences. In terms of application, it is beneficial for people to analyze disease pathogenesis and find treatment methods as well as design proteins with novel biological functions, thereby promoting the rapid development of medicine, agriculture and animal husbandry.

This chapter uses techniques related to biological language to study several problems in protein structure prediction, including protein domain boundaries, protein local structure assessment, protein flexibility prediction and knowledge-based potential energy functions.

5.2 Related Work

5.2.1 Domain boundary prediction

Domains are generally regarded as compact, semi-independent units[1] that can fold autonomously. The identification of structural domain boundaries is not only of theoretical interest but also of great practical importance. Successful domain boundary determination in proteins[2] is useful in structure analysis, function annotation,[3] database searching,[4] protein modeling,[5] etc.

A number of methods for predicting domain boundaries from the amino acid sequences have been developed. Early approaches to domain boundary prediction were based on information theory,[6] statistical potentials[7] or similarity searches.[8] Subsequent methods relied on expert knowledge of protein families to construct models like hidden Markov models[9] and artificial neural networks[10] to identify other members of the family. However, the most useful and straightforward way to predict domains was by sequence homology or multiple sequence alignment. The ProDom[11] method generated a comprehensive set of protein domain families automatically from the SWISS-PROT and TrEMBL sequence databases.[12] DOMAINA-TION[13] delineated domains through analyzing position-specific iterative database search[14] alignments. Similarly, CHOP[15] identified potential domain boundaries through hierarchical searches against databases of more or less well-defined domains. PPRODO[16] used the neural network with the position-specific scoring matrix (PSSM) generated by PSI-BLAST[14] to predict the domain boundary of two-domain proteins. Although all these methods provide valuable information about putative domains for proteins with similar sequences, they fail for small families or in the absence of homologous domain assignments. Some novel methods have been developed to predict domain boundaries directly from sequences. The "Domain Guess by Size" (DGS) algorithm[17] "guessed" domain boundaries solely based on observed domain size distributions. SnapDragon[18] predicted the domain by statistical analysis of the structure model generated by the *ab initio* protein structure prediction method Dragon.[19] A hybrid learning system has also been presented for domain boundaries prediction.[20] In general, most approaches predict the number of domains and only a few predict domain boundaries with reported sensitivity of between 50% and 70% for proteins with single domains and considerably less (<30%) for multi-domain proteins.[21]

Domain boundaries can be extended to form domain linkers that separate the domains of multi-domain proteins.[22] The amino acid compositions in domain regions are different from those in domain linker regions and many methods used these differences to predict the domain. DomCut[23] used the preference of amino acids in linker regions for domain linker prediction. The Domain Linker propensity Index (DLI) is obtained from the observed distribution of amino acids in domain linkers as compared to those in compact protein domains.[21] The residue entropy index (REI) is based on the number of degrees of freedom on the angles φ, ψ and χ, for each amino acid residue.[24] The residue index GHL is derived from the amino acid propensity of all linkers examined in that study.[22] The KDH index refers to the amino acid propensity of residues in the protein hydrophobic core.[25] There are many other domain boundary prediction methods that also work by analyzing the domain linkers.[26–28]

5.2.2 Building block of protein local structure

Proteins have recurrent local sequence patterns that reflect evolutionary selective pressures to fold into stable three-dimensional structures.[29] Local structure prediction, that is, the prediction of tertiary structures of short protein segments based solely on the sequence information contained in the segments, has been paid increasing attention of late. Success in resolving local structure prediction can improve the performance of *ab initio* structure prediction,[30, 31] protein threading and remote homology detection.[32, 33] The accurate prediction of the local protein will be a major milestone in understanding the folding process of proteins.[34] The secondary structure provides a three-state description of the backbone structure, comprised of α-helices, β-strands and coils. This description of protein structures is very crude. Although secondary structure can be predicted with more than 70% average accuracy,[35, 36] it lacks sufficient detail for geometrical modeling of the local structure. Hence, many research groups have clustered fragments into Structure Alphabets (SA) or Building Blocks (BB) to try and describe the local structural features of known protein structures more accurately.

One of the most interesting structural alphabets is the I-Sites library,[29, 31] which, together with a sophisticated procedure for three-dimensional reconstruction, has been used with great efficiency to improve *ab initio* prediction methods.[37] Camproux *et al.* first derived a 12-letter alphabet of fragments by using the Hidden Markov Model[38] and then extended it to 27 letters by using the Bayesian information criterion.[39] This approach simultaneously learns the geometry and connections of the alphabets and has been used for protein structure mining.[40] De Brevern *et al.*[41] proposed a 16-letter alphabet generated by a self-organizing map based on a dihedral angle similarity measure. The prediction accuracy of local three-dimensional structures has been steadily increased by taking sequence information and secondary structure information into consideration.[42] The prediction performance on this alphabet was improved by Benros *et al.*[43] A comprehensive evaluation of these and other structural alphabets was done by Karchin *et al.*[44] Besides being used for the local structure prediction, such structure alphabets have also been used for constructing a substitution matrix,[45] structure similarity searching,[40, 46] developing a structure analysis web-server,[47] etc. Many researchers adopt different features and methods for the local structure prediction of proteins. Hunter and Subramaniam[48] developed a probability model to predict centroids from the amino acid sequence. Pei and Grishin devised evolutionary and structural profiles for the local structure prediction of proteins.[49] The discriminative model has been employed to get better performance.[50,51] The correlation between the local sequence and the local structure has been discovered and the dual-layer model was introduced for local structure prediction with great success.[52]

5.2.3 Characterization of protein flexibility based on structural alphabets

Proteins are dynamic molecules that are in constant motion. Their conformations depend on environmental factors like temperature, pH and interactions.[53] Some regions are more susceptible to change than others. This constant motion of proteins plays a critical role in many biological processes, such as protein–ligand binding,[54] virtual screening,[55] antigen–antibody interactions,[56] protein–DNA binding,[57] structure-based drug discovery,[58] fold recognition,[59,60] etc.

Many studies try to predict protein flexibilities using either sequence or structure information of proteins.[61] Sonavane *et al.*[62] analyzed the local sequence features and the distribution of the B-factor in different regions of protein three-dimensional structures. Yuan *et al.*[63] adopted the support vector regression (SVR) approach with multiple sequence alignment as input to predict the B-factor distribution of a protein from its sequence. Schlessinger and Rost[64] found that flexible residues differ from regular and rigid residues in local features such as secondary structure, solvent accessibility and amino acid preferences. They combined these local features and global evolution information for protein flexibility prediction. Several sequence-based B-factor prediction methods were compared by Radivojac *et al.*[65] Different models have been proposed to predict B-factor distribution based on protein atomic coordinates. Normal mode analysis can identify the most mobile parts of the protein as well as their directions by focusing on a few C_α atoms that move the most.[66,67] The translation liberation screw model[68] simplified the protein as a rigid body with movement along translation, liberation and screw axes. The Gaussian network model (GNM)[69] transformed the protein as an elastic network of C_α atoms that fluctuate around their mean positions. Recently, Yang *et al.*[70] predicted the B-factor by combining local structure assembly variations with sequence-based and structure-based profiling. There are also many other methods for protein flexibility prediction.[71–73]

All the above methods use the B-factor or temperature factors as a result of X-ray crystallography to elucidate the flexibilities of proteins. The B-factor reflects the degree of thermal motion and static disorder of an atom in a protein crystal structure.[74] However, there is noise while experimentally determining the B-factor. Many factors can affect the value of the B-factor such as the overall resolution of the structure, crystal contacts and importantly, the particular refinement procedures.[75] B-values from different structures can therefore not be reasonably compared.[64] Some researchers consider that the upper limit of accuracy for the prediction of B-factors is no more than 80%.[63]

Protein structures are not static and rigid. The polypeptide backbones, and especially the side chains, are constantly moving due to thermal motion and the kinetic energy of the atoms (Brownian motion).[76] A recent study[53] used the continuum prediction of secondary structures to identify the region undergoing conformational change. Other researchers have pointed out that continuous secondary structure assignment can capture protein flexibility.[77] Furthermore, the MolMovDB database[78] consists of structures that are experimentally determinate to exhibit conformational flexibility thus enabling detection of a variety of protein motions. The Morph Server[79] in particular has been used by many scientists to analyze pairs of conformations and produce realistic animations.

5.2.4 Novel nonlinear knowledge-based mean force potentials

Proteins are the most structurally advanced known molecules. The prediction of the three-dimensional structures of the native states of proteins from the sequences of their amino acids is one of the most challenging problems in molecular biology.[80] The basic energetic model most commonly used to solve this problem is based on Anfinsen's hypothesis,[81] which states that for a given set of physiological conditions the native structure of a protein corresponds to the global minimum of Gibbs free energy. The development and evaluation of new energy functions is critical for accurately modeling the properties of biological macromolecules.[82]

A good energy function should be able to distinguish between the native and nonnative conformers of a protein based on its energy estimation.[83] To this end, two different classes of potential functions are currently in usage.[84] One class is the physical-based potentials, which are based on the fundamental analysis of forces between atoms including van der Waals interactions, hydrogen bonding, electrostatic interactions, etc.[85,86] The other class is the knowledge-based mean force potentials, which extract parameters from experimentally solved protein structures.[87,88] In principle, the physical-based potentials can be derived based on the basic laws of physics, but the calculation of free energy is very difficult since the atomic description of a protein and the surrounding solvent have to be taken into account. Some of the well-established force fields in this category include CHARMM,[89] AMBER,[90] and GROMOS.[91] Currently, this type of computation is generally too expensive for protein folding.[92] But, with today's computing resources, knowledge-based potentials can be quite successful in fold recognition[93] and *ab initio* structure prediction.[94,95]

Knowledge-based mean force potentials, as the name suggests, are derived from the statistical analysis of proteins of known structures. Regardless of their vague physical basis, knowledge-based potentials have the advantage of being fast and easy to construct, so these potentials are widely used in fold recognition or threading,[96,97] the selection of native structures of proteins,[98,99] the estimation of protein stability,[100] *ab initio* protein structure prediction,[50,101,102] etc. A comprehensive, recent review on such potentials can be found in Floudas *et al.*[103] Knowledge-based potentials can be classified based on different criteria. For example, when taking protein representation into consideration, they can be divided into residue-level potentials[104] and atom-level potentials;[105] when taking the number of interactions into consideration, they can be grouped into single-body potentials,[96] two-body potentials[106] and multi-body potentials.[107] Here, knowledge-based potentials are classified into three generations in terms of the methods to derive the potentials.

The first generation of knowledge-based potentials is derived by the statistical analysis of solely the native structures, which are referred to as Boltzmann-based potentials here. The theoretical foundation is the inverse Boltzmann equation that converts the occurrence frequency of a structural interaction into the estimate of its free energy.[108] The resulting energy is often equal to the difference between the energy of a structure and that of the reference state. Generally, these potentials use a simple one- or two-point-per-residue representation, which results in potentials being obtained at the residue level. Each residue in a protein sequence is represented by one or two points in three-dimensional space. These points are usually located at the coordinates of each residue's C_α atoms, C_β atoms or at the coordinates of the center of each side chain. The discrimination of native structures from decoys is based on each residue's preference to be buried or exposed,[109] its preference for a particular secondary structure conformation,[110] its preference for the contact number with other residues[96] and its preference to be in contact at a particular distance or sequence separation.[108-111] Other knowledge-based mean force potentials at the atom level or binary profile level have also been developed.[112-114] These potentials can provide better discriminatory power than those at the residue level. The reference state has great effect on potentials. The commonly used reference states include the conditional probability function,[115] the quasi-chemical approximation[116] and the finite ideal-gas reference state.[117] However, there are several conceptual difficulties with this approach, such as the ignoring of chain connectivity in the reference state, the problematic implicit assumption of Boltzmann distribution, etc.[118] Some researchers criticized the usage of Boltzmann law for protein structures since the Boltzmann formalism assumes an equilibrium distribution of atom–atom preference, the physical nature of the reference state is not clear and the probability of observing a system at a given state must be changed with respect to the temperature.

The second generation of knowledge-based potentials is obtained by optimization techniques using both native structures and decoy structures. The potentials are still in the form of the weighted linear sum of interaction pairs, but the parameters of potentials are obtained by using optimization methods. These potentials are referred to as linear potentials here. The advantage of these potentials is that they include information contained in the decoys, which is absent in native structures. The potential parameters are derived from a set of training proteins and decoys by optimizing a certain scoring function (e.g. maximizing the score difference between native conformation and a set of decoy conformations). Many researchers have contributed to this field. Vendruscolo *et al.*[119] presented a new method in which energy parameters are optimized by the condition of the stability of the native state. Wang *et al.*[120] presented the density scores calculated from the decoys and improved the performance of the original RAPDF potential[115] by statistical analysis on weighted decoys. The linear programming method has been widely used to derive the parameters of the pairwise contact potentials, including the HRSC potential,[106] the LKF potential[121] and the TE-13 potential.[122] Because the potential parameters are derived by optimization techniques, the linear potentials can perform better in discriminating native structures from a set of decoys than the Boltzmann-based potentials.

The third generation of knowledge-based potentials is further improved by nonlinear classifiers, which are thus referred to as nonlinear potentials here. The previous two generations of knowledge-based potentials are all in the form of weighted linear sums of the interacting pairs, from which it can get difficult to discriminate a large number of native protein structures against a large number of decoy conformations.[119] Hu *et al.*[123] developed an optimal nonlinear design scoring function that perfectly discriminates a set of 440 native proteins from 14 million sequence decoys. They found that no linear scoring function could succeed in this task. Zhang *et al.*[124]

developed an empirical potential function for simplified protein models by combining descriptors derived from residue–residue contact and local sequence–structure relationships. Tan and Jones[125] used neural networks with evolutionary information, pairwise distance and relative solvent accessibility as input to perform decoy discrimination. The SVMod program[126] used a support vector machine with several scoring functions as inputs to evaluate model quality. Because of the intrinsic superiority of the nonlinear classifiers in comparison with the linear classifiers, they will be widely used to derive powerful knowledge-based potentials for protein structure prediction.

5.3   Domain Boundary Prediction

5.3.1   Materials and method

5.3.1.1   *The protein dataset*

Standard evaluation data are taken from the Structural Classification of Proteins (SCOP) database version 1.67. Sequences are selected using the ASTRAL database[127] with sequence identity less than 40%. The proteins are then filtered with the following rules:

1. Remove the proteins that contain unknown amino acids.
2. Remove the proteins with only one chain domain.
3. Remove the proteins with domain length less than 50 residues.

The resulting dataset contains 774 proteins and is divided into two subsets for usage. First, we randomly selected about one-third of the two-domain proteins as the SCOP-2 dataset, and then the remaining two-domain proteins and the other multidomain proteins are grouped into the SCOP-1 dataset. The SCOP-1 subset contains 610 proteins with two or more SCOP domains and at least one linker, of which 487 proteins have continuous domains and 123 proteins have discontinuous domains. The SCOP-2 subset contains 164 proteins with only two continuous domains and only one linker. The SCOP-2 dataset is treated as a separate test set. There are two reasons for doing so. The first one is because the separate dataset can test the generality of the method since the optimal parameters on the SCOP-1 dataset may not be suitable for other situations. The second reason is that two-domain proteins are easier to predict than the multiple-domain proteins, and most methods can only predict two-domain proteins to a certain degree, such as the PPRODO method.[16] The results thus obtained from this dataset can be compared with those of other methods.

5.3.1.2 *Identifying domain linkers*

There are many methods of domain assignment for protein structures: SCOP,[123] CATH,[128] VAST,[129] etc. The distribution of domain segments among them can have different levels of variations. There are no consistent assignments of structural domains in proteins.[130] Since SCOP[123] is fully based on expert-driven visual domain assignments, it has been used to identify domain linkers in this study. Domain boundaries were derived from SCOP domain annotation, which typically fell between elements of secondary structures. DSSP[131] was used to assign the secondary structures of proteins. The definition of domain linkers is the same one adopted by earlier studies.[10,21] The linker start residue is defined as the last residue of the secondary structure (DSSP codes H, G, I, B, E) before coil elements (DSSP codes T, S or blank). The linker end residue is defined as the first residue of the next secondary structure element. A total of 952 domain linkers (9199 residues) were extracted from the SCOP-I dataset, with a minimum length of three residues and an average length of 9.7 residues.

5.3.1.3 *Generation of profiles*

PSI-BLAST[14] is used to generate the profiles of amino acid sequences with default parameter values except for the number of iterations set to 10. The search is performed against the nrdb90 database (http://www.ebi.ac.uk/~holm/nrdb90/) from EBI.[132] The frequency profiles are directly obtained from the multiple sequence alignments output by PSI-BLAST. The target frequency reflects the probability of an amino acid occurrence in a given position of the sequences. The method of target frequency calculation is similar to that implemented in PSI-BLAST. We use a subset of the multiple sequence alignments with a sequence identity of less than 98% to calculate the frequency profiles. The sequence weight is assigned by the position-based sequence weight method.[133] Given the observed frequency of amino acid i (f_i) and the background frequency of amino acid i (p_i), the pseudo-count for amino acid i is computed as follows:

$$g_i = \sum_{j=1}^{20} f_i(q_{ij}/p_j) \qquad (5\text{-}1)$$

where q_{ij} is the score of amino acid i being aligned to amino acid j in the BLOSUM62 substitution matrix.

The target frequency is then calculated as

$$Q_i = \frac{\alpha f_i + \beta g_i}{\alpha} + \beta \qquad (5\text{-}2)$$

where α is the number of different amino acids in a given column minus one and β is a free parameter set to a constant value of 10, the value initially used by PSI-BLAST.

Because the frequency profile is a matrix of frequencies for all amino acids, it cannot be used directly and needs to be converted into a binary profile by a probability threshold P_h. When the frequency of an amino acid is larger than p, it is converted into an integral value of 1, which means that the specific amino acid can occur at a given position of the protein sequence during evolution. Otherwise, it is converted into 0. A substring of amino acid combinations is then obtained by collecting the binary profile with non-zero value for each position of the protein sequences. These substrings have approximately represented the amino acids that possibly occur at a given sequence position during evolution. Each combination of the 20 amino acids corresponds to a binary profile and vice versa.

5.3.1.4 *Profile domain linker propensity index*

The amino acid frequencies between domains and domain linkers are different. This difference has been used to produce the Domain Linker propensity Index (DLI).[21] Compared with that, a novel index based on the binary profile is introduced here, namely, the Profile Domain Linker propensity Index (PDLI), which is defined as the negative log ratio between the profile frequency in linkers and that in domains.

$$\text{PDLI}_f = -\log\left(P_{f,l}/P_{f,d}\right) \tag{5-3}$$

where f is a binary profile and $P_{f,l}$ and $P_{f,d}$ are the frequencies of f in domain linkers and in domains respectively. The profile frequency refers to the ratio of occurrence of a profile to the occurrence of all profiles that is determined from the SCOP-1 database. The PDLI is then normalized to a zero mean and unit standard deviation. PDLIs describe the likelihood of profiles to be found in domain linkers. These discriminative indexes can be used to predict the domain linkers.

The total number of binary profiles is extremely large (2^{20}), and the small dataset cannot provide sufficient statistics for such a huge parameter space. In fact, only a small fraction of binary profiles appears, which is dependent on the choice of probability threshold P_h. Based on the optimal value of 0.17 (see the Results and Discussion section for more details), there are only 104 binary profiles, and their PDLIs are shown in Table 5-1. The PDLIs of the other absent binary profiles are set to zero, which indicates that they have the same frequencies in domains and in domain linkers. Note that we also ignore the profiles with low occurrence times (< 2), since these profiles may introduce much noise. Only 84 dipeptide binary profiles occur. All the 3-, 4- and 5-residue binary profiles are not obtained. There are two reasons for this phenomenon. The first one is that the multi-domain protein sequences are not sufficient. Only 774 non-redundant multi-domain proteins have been obtained from the SCOP database. The second reason is that the threshold of converting the frequency profiles to binary profiles is too large, so many of the multi-residue binary profiles do not occur.

Each combination of amino acids corresponds to a binary profile. The profile domain linker propensity index is derived by analyzing the frequencies of profiles in domain linkers as compared to those in domains. PDLI is normalized to zero mean and unit standard deviation.

Table 5-1   Profile domain linker propensity index.

Binary profile	PDLI	Binary profile	PDLI	Binary profile	PDLI	Binary profile	PDLI
A	0.728927	DL	0.107439	R	0.082775	AV	2.66241
C	0.223109	FL	0.99251	AR	0.742276	DV	−0.79875
AC	0.624896	GL	0.572175	GR	−1.07739	EV	0.175227
D	0.0675	HL	−1.32197	KR	0.724427	FV	0.473246
E	0.679002	IL	0.791371	LR	−0.78742	GV	1.51191
AE	1.27879	KL	−0.30417	S	0.402267	IV	0.601008
DE	0.528386	M	1.69393	AS	−0.13248	KV	−0.79875
F	0.116705	LM	0.804137	DS	−0.57677	LV	0.841925
G	0.300691	N	0.485542	ES	0.762462	ILV	1.25532
AG	0.763598	DN	0.454796	GS	−0.46471	PV	−0.50544
CG	−0.76125	GN	1.2802	KS	0.175227	RV	−1.48022
DG	0.120286	KN	0.99929	LS	−0.63577	SV	−1.08543
EG	−0.16718	LN	−0.82739	NS	0.309558	TV	−0.18375
H	0.379085	P	−1.22291	PS	−0.67782	W	0.941671
AH	−1.42593	AP	−1.44671	RS	−1.36026	FW	1.55396
DH	−1.20459	DP	−1.29034	T	0.19272	Y	0.186486
I	0.689667	EP	−0.33101	AT	0.951073	DY	−1.08543
AI	0.988685	GP	−0.23421	DT	0.344535	FY	−0.00934
DI	−1.27214	IP	−2.67592	ET	0.912666	GY	0.44287
K	0.178344	KP	−1.79536	GT	−0.53917	HY	0.344535
AK	1.71308	LP	−1.7847	IT	−0.60997	IY	−1.17639
DK	0.272394	NP	−0.68849	LT	−0.62713	LY	−0.24933
EK	0.155715	Q	0.487427	NT	−1.04161	PY	−0.58453
GK	−0.66721	DQ	−0.74278	PT	−1.75423	QY	−3.65167
L	0.421129	EQ	1.4862	ST	0.828692	VY	0.82171
AL	1.15848	KQ	0.88285	V	0.557439	WY	1.12195

5.3.1.5 *Prediction of domain linker*

Two kinds of methods for domain linker prediction have been implemented. The first one is a simple method that directly uses the indexes. The second one is the entropy-based method of the Armadillo system.[21] The simple method for domain linker prediction on an amino acid sequence occurs as follows. First, the frequency profiles of a query sequence are calculated with the output of PSI-BLAST and then converted into binary profiles. As a result, the amino acid sequence is represented as a sequence of binary profiles. Second, a numeric profile is generated by assigning each binary profile of the sequence a corresponding index from the PDLIs. The numeric profile is smoothed by an 11-residue moving window that assigns the average value of ±5 residues to the central residue of the window. Finally, the numeric profile distribution is transformed to a standard normalized distribution using the mean μ and standard deviation σ of the smooth profile distribution:

$$Z = (x - \mu)/\sigma \qquad (5\text{-}4)$$

All Z-scores less than the threshold Z_h are proposed as domain linker candidates. Predicted domain linkers are made a minimum of 11 residues long conforming to an average linker size[22] by extending five residues in each direction from the candidate positions.

For the entropy-based method of the Armadillo system, the numeric profile is further smoothed before being transformed to a normalized distribution. A discrete Fourier transform is performed on the numeric profile and then a low-pass filter is added. The smoothening process is completed with an inverse discrete Fourier transform. The other part of this method is the same as the simple method.

5.3.1.6 *Performance metrics*

Domain linker predictions are correct when the predicted domain linker overlapped wholly or in part between the correct linker boundaries with a ±20 residue margin of error added to each boundary, as was done in earlier studies.[21] Occasionally, two predictions will lie within the ±20 residue margin of error for a real linker. In this case, the prediction with the better score is kept, since keeping both as correct predictions will bias the results towards an improved accuracy.[21] Two performance measures are adopted, that is, sensitivity and specificity. Sensitivity is defined as TP/(TP+FN) where TP is the number of true positive boundary predictions and FN is the number of false negatives. Specificity is defined as TP/(TP+FP), where FP is the number of false positives.

5.3.2 Results and discussion

5.3.2.1 *Parameter optimization and cross-validation*

The SCOP-1 dataset is randomly divided into 10 groups. We use eight groups to produce PDLIs, one for validation and the other for testing. The above process is iterated until each group has been tested. There are two parameters for optimizing, namely, the probability threshold P_h of converting a frequency profile into a binary profile and the Z-scores threshold Z_h for domain linker prediction. The validation set is used to optimize the parameters of P_h and Z_h and the testing set is used to give the final results. That is, we select the values of P_h and Z_h that give the best results on the validation set, and then such parameters are used to test on the testing set to give the final results. A comprehensive experiment has been carried out for various combinations of the two parameters. Some results are shown in Fig. 5-1. The best results are obtained when P_h takes the value of 0.17 and Z_h takes the value of -1.5.

The results of cross-validation are then obtained with the optimal parameters as shown in Table 5-2. We compare the results of PDLI with those of other indexes. They are DLI,[21] REI,[24] GHL[22] and KDH.[25] We also compare the results of PDLI with the entropy-based method of the Armadillo system using PDLI and DLI as indexes. The normalized values of those indexes are taken from Dumontier *et al.*[21]

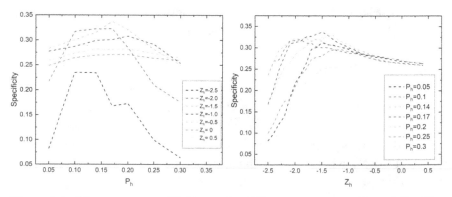

Figure 5-1   The average specificities under different parameters P_h and Z_h. The specificity is obtained as the results of the cross-validation of the validated dataset.

Table 5-2   The results of cross-validation.

Method	Specificity	Sensitivity
PDLI-Armadillo	0.35	0.72
DLI-Armadillo	0.29	0.62
PDLI	0.34	0.71
DLI	0.27	0.59
REI	0.27	0.54
GHL	0.29	0.59
KDH	0.25	0.57

The process of predicting domain linkers based on these indexes is the same as that of PDLI except for the Z-score threshold Z_h, which is set to -1.8, since this threshold gives the best performance and is used in the Armadillo system.

The specificities of various indexes are very low, but the sensitivities are acceptable. The overall low success rate in the SCOP-1 dataset may be caused by the inherent difficulty of the domain prediction of multi-domain proteins. PDLI prediction is more sensitive (12%–17%) and slightly more specific (5%–9%) than other indexes.

5.3.2.2 *Benchmark test on two-domain proteins*

The second evaluation is performed on the SCOP-2 dataset, since most methods can only predict the two-domain proteins with a certain degree.[16] We compare the methods in this study with two other methods, namely, the Biozon method[20] and the Domcut method.[23] The Biozon method implements a complex hybrid learning system for domain boundary prediction. The Domcut method is a simple method that also uses the amino acid indexes. The results are shown in Table 5-3. Detailed results of various methods (Biozon, Domcut and PDLI-Armadillo) on the SCOP-2 dataset are available on our website (http://www.insun.hit.edu.cn/news/view.asp?id=436). The specificities of PDLI are a little lower than those of multi-domain proteins, but the sensitivity is more or less improved. Overall, PDLI still outperforms other indexes and is comparable with the complex method of Biozon.

Table 5-3   The results tested on two-domain proteins.

Method	Specificity	Sensitivity
Biozon	0.40	0.70
PDLI-Armadillo	0.38	0.66
DLI-Armadillo	0.35	0.59
PDLI	0.31	0.72
DLI	0.26	0.62
REI	0.27	0.52
GHL	0.28	0.58
KDH	0.21	0.57
Domcut	0.09	0.23

The PDLI results are obtained by crossvalidating on the SCOP-1 dataset. The average results of other indexes are also given. PDLI-Armadillo and DLI-Armadillo refer to the entropy-based methods of the Armadillo system using PDLI and DLI as the indexes, respectively.

All the various methods were tested on the SCOP-2 dataset. The results of the Biozon and Domcut method were obtained from the corresponding web-server (http://biozon.org/tools/domains/ and http://www.bork.embl-heidelberg.de/~suyama/domcut/).

5.3.2.3 *Testing on the CASP6 target proteins*

We investigated the CASP6 targets for multi-domain proteins and found that only six proteins are available that have only two continuous domains. They are T0199, T0204, T0222, T0228, T0247 and T0260. Because the CASP6 targets are included in the latest SCOP database (version 1.69), none of the targets are present in our training set that is derived from SCOP database version 1.67. The single linker predictions are made at the position with the global minimum score, which is similar to the GBEST measure originally described by Galzitskaya and Melnik.[24] The results are shown in Table 5-4. The performance of PDLI is reasonable.

N_{res} is the length of the protein chains. The true boundary is obtained by the domain annotation of SCOP. The prediction is made

Table 5-4 Domain linker prediction on CASP6 targets with two continuous domains.

		T0199	T0204	T0222	T0228	T0247	T0260
	N_{res}	338	351	373	430	364	224
	True boundary	100	195	296	149	267	88
PDLI-Armadillo	Prediction	105	155	331	146	292	92
	Error	5	40	35	3	25	2
DLI-Armadillo	Prediction	108	130	254	170	273	85
	Error	8	65	42	21	6	3
PDLI	Prediction	110	107	272	144	286	87
	Error	10	88	24	5	19	1
DLI	Prediction	111	62	332	204	304	87
	Error	11	133	36	55	37	1
REI	Prediction	118	190	248	226	250	90
	Error	18	5	48	77	17	2
GHL	Prediction	110	192	336	177	295	86
	Error	10	3	40	28	28	2
KDH	Prediction	183	105	216	157	274	77
	Error	83	90	80	8	7	11

at the position with the global minimum score. The error indicates the distance between the prediction boundary and the true boundary.

5.3.2.4 *A profile usage bias exists in domains and linkers*

The profile frequencies in domains are different from those in linkers. These differences can be used to produce the discriminative profile domain linker propensity index. As can be seen from Table 5-1, an increased propensity of Pro in domain linkers has been observed, which is the same as that from DLI.[21] Small hydrophobic residues like Ala, Gly and Val and some charged residues like Glu and His have been observed as preferred residues in domains, which is in agreement with related studies.[18] Although some amino acids are preferred in domains, such as Ala and Asn for example, the combination of these amino acids with other amino acids may be preferred in domain linkers such as AS, AH. An interesting result is that any combinations of Pro and other amino acids are found to be preferred in domain linkers. None of the other amino acids has such a propensity. For example, the profiles AT, DT, ET, ST are preferred in domains while the profiles GT, IT, LT, NT, DT are preferred in domain linkers. On the basis of the experimental results, we can infer that the propensities at the profile level may be more accurate than those at the amino acid level.

5.3.2.5 *Using evolution information can improve the prediction of domain linkers*

The frequency profile contains the evolution information of protein sequences, that is the probabilities of amino acids occurring in specific positions of the protein sequences. Such profiles are used to produce a more discriminative index — PDLI. PDLI is prior to other indexes at amino acid level according to the experiments, so evolution information can improve the prediction of domain linkers. This conclusion is not surprising, since the evolution information is also used by other methods for domain boundary prediction, either in the form of the position-specific scoring matrix (PSSM)[16] or the homologous sequences[13] generated by PSI-BLAST.

5.4 Building Blocks of Protein Local Structure

5.4.1 Materials and methods

5.4.1.1 *Overview of the method*

The flowchart of our method is schematically shown in Fig. 5-2. During the training phase, the proteins with known structures are split by the "Protein Peeling" algorithm[134] to get the initial partitions. These initial partitions are taken as the old partitions. The model is then constructed from the old partitions including clustering the fragments to produce the building-block library and the statistical calculation of the bi-gram between any two building blocks. The training proteins are then split using the "My-Peeling" algorithm to produce new partitions. The above process is repeated until the partitions of the training proteins remain unchanged.

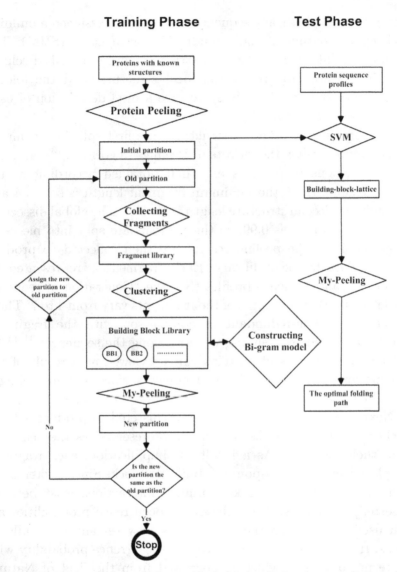

Figure 5-2   The overview of the method for local structure prediction. The native protein structures are split using the "Protein Peeling" algorithm. The fragments in the initial partition are clustered to obtain the building block library. The bi-gram model is then constructed. The original proteins are then resplit by the library. The above process is repeated until the partition remains unchanged. The final building block library is then used to predict the local structures and folding fragments of protein sequences. The building-block lattice is then constructed and the My-Peeling algorithm is used to find the optimal folding fragments.

During the test phase, any sequence segments are assigned a building block by the output of the Support Vector Machine (SVM). The building-block-lattice is then constructed, and the "My-Peeling" algorithm is used to predict the local structures and the folding fragments of the proteins. Here, we give a brief description of each step and some of the results.

The proteins with known structures are first split into compact sub-structures using the "Protein Peeling" algorithm,[134] and the initial partitions of proteins are then obtained according to the peeling results. Here, the minimum fragment length is set as 4 and the minimum second structure length is set as 3. The global dissection criterion R is taken as 0.99, so the proteins are split into pieces as far as possible. The peeling results are then collected to produce the candidate fragment library. Each fragment is represented by its dihedral and sequence profiles (See the "Generation of sequence profile" section). The lengths of the fragments vary from 4 to 7. These fragments are non-redundant in comparison with the fragments that are collected by a sliding window along the sequences.[34, 43, 135] The native structures of proteins can be viewed as a result of the combinational assembling of these fragments, since protein peeling is also a hierarchical process.

Next, the candidate fragments are clustered to produce a finite number of building blocks, which are represented as the centroids of all their members. As a result of simplification, each fragment is replaced by the corresponding building block. Since proteins are assembled by building blocks, complex interactions exist between these building blocks. The adjacent co-occurrence probabilities are then used to represent the connections between any two building blocks. Here, we refer to the adjacent co-occurrence probability with the term "bi-gram", which is borrowed from the field of Natural Language Processing (NLP).[136] Detailed calculations of the bi-grams are explained in the section "Construction of the bi-gram model".

A Building Block Library (BBL) contains two components: one is the building block; the other is the bi-gram between any two building blocks. Once the building-block library has been constructed, it can be used to predict the local structures and the folding fragments of any protein sequence. Here the support vector machine is used to classify a sequence fragment into a specific building block and the building-block lattice is constructed to describe the folding spaces of proteins. A building-block lattice is a directed acyclic graph (DAG) which contains all the possible folding fragments of proteins. The dynamic programming algorithm is used to find the optimal folding fragments (for further details, see the section "My-Peeling algorithm").

One of the problems of constructing the BBL is that the new partitions of the training proteins using the BBL are not the same as the original partitions from which the BBL is derived, so an iterative process is used to construct the BBL. The BBL is first constructed based on the initial partition given by "Protein Peeling".[134] The training proteins are then repeeled by using the "My-peeling" algorithm. In this stage, each node in the word-lattice is assigned the correct building block, that is, the nearest one according to the distance function of Eq. (5-4). A new version of the BBL is then constructed based on the new partitions. The above process is repeated until the partitions of the training proteins remain unchanged.

5.4.1.2 *Generation of sequence profile*

Sequence profiles are generated using PSI-BLAST.[14] Each protein sequence is queried with the default PSI-BLAST parameter values except for the number of iterations being set to 10. The search is performed against the NRDB90 database, which is derived from the NR database of NCBI (ftp://ftp.ncbi.nih.gov/blast/db) by removing the redundancy sequence with sequence identity larger than 90%, using the Perl script from EBI.[132]

Here, the frequency profiles rather than the position-specific score matrix (PSSM) are used for the sake of convenience in the calculation. The frequency profiles are directly obtained from the multiple sequence alignments outputted by PSI-BLAST. The target frequency reflects the probability of an amino acid in a given position of the sequences. The method of target frequency calculation is similar to that implemented in PSI-BLAST. We use a subset of the multiple sequence alignments with sequence identity less than 98% to calculate the frequency profiles. The sequence weight is assigned by the position-based sequence weight method.[133] Given the observed frequency of amino acid $i(f_i)$ and the background frequency of amino acid i (p_i), the pseudo-count for amino acid i is computed as follows:

$$g_i = \sum_{j=1}^{20} f_i * (q_{ij}/P_j) \qquad (5\text{-}5)$$

where q_{ij} is the score of amino acid i being aligned to amino acid j in the BLOSUM62 substitution matrix (the default score matrix of PSI-BLAST).

The target frequency is then calculated as

$$Q_i = (\alpha f_i + \beta g_i)/(\alpha + \beta) \qquad (5\text{-}6)$$

where α is the number of different amino acids in a given column minus one and β is a free parameter set to a constant value of 10, the value initially used by PSI-BLAST.

5.4.1.3 *Protein peeling*

The initial partitions of proteins are obtained by the method that is a reimplementation of the "Protein Peeling" algorithm.[134] The method works from the contact probability matrix, which is a translation of the inter-Cα distances. It uses the principle of conventional hierarchical clustering, leading to a series of nested partitions of the 3D structure. Every step aims at optimally dividing a unit into 2 or 3 sub-units according to a criterion called "partition index" assessing the structural independence of the sub-units newly defined. Moreover, an entropy-derived squared correlation R is used for assessing the protein structure dissection globally.

5.4.1.4 *Clustering of fragments*

There are many clustering methods seen in related studies. Most of them are transmutations of the standard k-means algorithm, such as the simulated annealing k-means algorithm[137] and leader

k-means algorithm.[50] Due to its simplicity and similar performance, the standard k-means clustering is chosen in this study. The initial centers are selected using the maximum–minimum distance criterion. The depth of each initial center is defined as follows:

$$\text{Depth}(C_i) = |\min C_i - \min C_{i-1}| + |\min C_i + \min C_{i-1}| \quad (5\text{-}7)$$

where C_i is the initial center, and $\min(C_i)$ is the minimum distance obtained by the maximum–minimum distance criterion for C_i. The cluster number is then selected as the index of the initial center that has the maximum depth.

The distance between two fragments measures both the sequence distance and the structure distance. For each residue i, its tertiary structure is represented by phi (Φ_i) and psi (Ψ_i) angles in degrees, and its sequence information by frequency profiles comprising f_{ij} for amino acid j. Given fragments a and b of length M, their distance $D(a,b)$ is

$$D(a,b) = D\_Struct(a,b) + w_s * D\_Seq(a,b) \quad (5\text{-}8)$$

$$D\_Struct(a,b) = \sqrt{\frac{\sum_{i=1}^{M}\left(\left(\frac{\Delta\phi_i}{360}\right)^2\right) + \left(\frac{\Delta\varphi_{i+1}}{360}\right)^2}{M}} \quad (5\text{-}9)$$

$$D_{Seq(a,b)} = \left(\prod_{i=1}^{M}\left(\sum_{j=0}^{19}\Delta f_{ij}^2\right)\bigg/2\right)^{1/M} \quad (5\text{-}10)$$

where the symbol Δ denotes the absolute difference in the associated quantity and w_s is the weight of the sequence distance.

5.4.1.5 *Construction of the bi-gram model*

The bi-gram is used to represent the adjacent co-occurrence probability between any two building blocks. The maximum likelihood estimation that is used to calculate the bi-grams is as follows:

$$P(BB_2 \,|\, BB_1) = \frac{Count(BB_1, BB_2)}{Count(BB_1)} \quad (5\text{-}11)$$

where $Count(BB_1, BB_2)$ is the number of occurrences when the building block BB_1 is followed by BB_2 in one protein, and $Count(BB_1)$ is the number of occurrences of BB_1 in the training set.

Then, δ smoothing is done to avoid a zero bi-gram

$$P(BB_2 \mid BB_1) = \frac{Count(BB_1, BB_2) + \delta}{Count(BB_1) + \delta * N} \qquad (5\text{-}12)$$

where N is the total number of building blocks. δ is taken as 0.00001, so that the unseen bi-grams take very small values.

5.4.1.6 *Training of SVM classifiers*

Support Vector Machines (SVMs) are a class of supervised learning algorithms first introduced by Vapnik.[138] SVMs have exhibited excellent performance in practice and have a strong theoretical foundation of statistical learning theory. Here, the support vector machine (SVM) is used to judge whether a sequence segment belongs to a specific building block. The input features are the frequency profiles of the sequence segment. The LIBSVM package[139] is used as the SVM implementation with radial basis function as the kernel. The values of γ and regularization parameter C are set to be 0.5 and 10, respectively.

5.4.1.7 *My-Peeling algorithm*

Given a protein sequence, any of its sequence segments can be assigned a building block. However, not all of the sequence segments fold to form the final tertiary structures. Based on the hierarchical schema, part of the sequence segments fold locally, and these segments are then combinatorially assembled to form the final structures. The aim of the My-Peeling algorithm is to find the optimal folding fragments of proteins. The building-block lattice is used to simulate the folding space of proteins, and the dynamic programming algorithm is adopted to find the folding fragments.

A building-block lattice is a directed acyclic graph (DAG) that contains all the possible folding fragments of a protein. Figure 5-3 gives a schematic example of a building-block-lattice, in which both the sequence and the building blocks are represented by amino acids

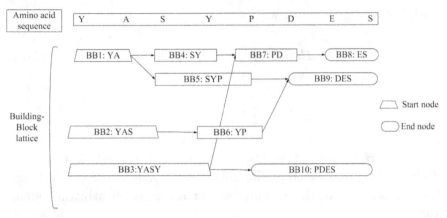

Figure 5-3   A schematic example of a building-block-lattice. Shown in the figure is the building-block lattice of the sequence "YASYP". Both the sequence and the building blocks are represented by amino acids. When a sequence segment matches the sequence of a building block, a node is produced. The edge indicates that two building blocks are adjacent in the sequence. The building blocks that contain the first amino acid of the sequence are defined as the start node. The building blocks that contain the last amino acid of the sequence are defined as the end node. Any pathway from the start node to the end node represents one folding pathway of the protein.

for convenience of understanding. In fact, they are represented by frequency profiles that contain evolutionary information and can help obtain high performance for local structure prediction. During the training phase, each sequence fragment is assigned the correct building block, which is the nearest one according to the distance function of Eq. (5-4). During the test phase, the building block of each sequence segment is assigned by the sequence similarity or the output of the support vector machine.

Any path from the start nodes to the end nodes in the building-block lattice represents one kind of folding fragment of the protein. The optimal folding path is the one that has the maximum path value, which can be the probability, the similarity or a combination of them. Suppose there is a folding path $R = (BB_i, S_i)$, $i = 1, 2, \ldots, K$, where BB_i is the building block of the node and S_i is the sequence similarity between the sequence segment and the building block converted from Eq. (5-6). The probability and the similarity of the path is calculated as follows:

$$P(R) = \prod_{i=1}^{K} P(BB_i \mid BB_{i-1}) \qquad (5\text{-}13)$$

$$S(R) = \prod_{i=1}^{K} S_i \qquad (5\text{-}14)$$

where $P(BB_i \mid BB_{i-1})$ is the bi-gram of BB_i and BB_{i-1}, and $P(BB_1 \mid BB_0)$ is defined as the initial probability of BB_1, which can be estimated from the training set or assigned an arbitrary small value.

The probability and similarity can be combined, which results in the following new equation for calculating the path value:

$$T(R) = \prod_{i=1}^{K} P(BB_i \mid BB_{i-1}) * (S_i)^{w_R} \qquad (5\text{-}15)$$

where w_R is the weight of sequence similarity.

The dynamic programming algorithm is used to find the optimal path in a building-block-lattice. The basic idea is that only the optimal path until each node i is recorded and all other nonoptimal paths are ignored. Two variables are defined for each node i to achieve this goal. One is $\delta(i)$, the path value of the optimal path until i. The other is $\alpha(i)$, the previous node in the corresponding path. For example, when the probability is used as the path value, the two variables are calculated as follows:

$$\delta(i) = \max(\delta(u_j^i) * P(BB_i \mid BB_{u_j^i})) \quad j = 1, \ldots, K_i \qquad (5\text{-}16)$$

$$\alpha(i) = \arg\max(\delta(u_j^i) * P(BB_i \mid BB_{u_j^i})) \qquad (5\text{-}17)$$

where u_j^i is the set of the adjacently previous node of node i and K_i is the size of the set.

In practice, the logarithm forms of Eqs. (5-9)–(5-11) are used to avoid overflow. Finally, each end node is scanned and the one with maximum path value is selected. By tracing, the optimal path can be found.

5.4.1.8 *Dataset*

The dataset of proteins used in this study is a subset of the PDB database[140] obtained from the PISCES web server.[141] There is less than 25% sequence identity between any two proteins, and any protein has a resolution better than 2.5 Å. The structures with missing atoms and chain breaks are also excluded. The resulting dataset contains 1219 chains and is divided into a training set and a test set with a ratio of 9:1.

5.4.1.9 *Performance metrics*

Two criteria for evaluating the local structure prediction are used here: the prediction accuracy and the classification accuracy.

The local structure prediction accuracy was invented by Lesk.[142] It takes two parameters, a window size w and an RMSD threshold t. Given a true structure and its prediction, the scheme computes the percentage of residues found in length-w segments whose predicted structures are within t from the true structure after superposition. Here, the true structures are reconstructed from the dihedral angles of the native structures with standard bond lengths and standard bond angles since the fragments in this study are represented by dihedrals.

The local structure classification accuracy is the percentage of sequence segments that are assigned the correct building blocks, which are the nearest ones according to the distance function.

5.4.2 Results and discussions

5.4.2.1 *Building-block library*

The final building-block library contains 180 building blocks with fragment lengths varying from 4 to 7. Table 5-5 gives the statistics of the building-block library. The average structure distance (calculated using Eq. (5-5)) of all fragments from their centroids is 0.135, with a standard deviation of 0.096. The average sequence distance (calculated using Eq. (5-6)) is 0.11, with a standard deviation of 0.0232. The average sequence + structure distance (calculated using

Table 5-5   The statistics of the building-block library.

Fragment length	Number of fragments	Number of building blocks	Average structure distance[a]	Average sequence distance[b]	Average distance[c]	Average RMSD[d]
4	15,473	43	0.126 (0.093)[e]	0.1081 (0.0233)	0.774 (0.172)	0.334 (0.302)
5	5764	50	0.136 (0.099)	0.1093 (0.0224)	0.792 (0.169)	0.416 (0.330)
6	4958	51	0.135 (0.101)	0.1088 (0.0242)	0.787 (0.178)	0.485 (0.364)
7	10,691	36	0.147 (0.095)	0.1139 (0.0224)	0.830 (0.164)	0.553 (0.371)
All	36,886	180	0.135 (0.096)	0.1100 (0.0232)	0.795 (0.172)	0.430 (0.349)

Notes: [a]The average structure distance of all fragments to their centroid; [b]The average sequence distance of all fragments to their centroid; [c]The average sequence + structure distance of all fragments to their centroid; [d]The average root-mean-squared-deviation of all fragments to their centroid measured in cartesian coordinates space; [e]Shown in the brackets are the standard deviations.

Eq. (5-4)) is 0.795, with a standard deviation of 0.172. Here, the weight of sequence distance w_s is taken as 6, which leads to a very similar performance in classifying each training fragment into the correct building block by the nearest neighbor classifier using sequence distance (41%) and structure distance (63%), respectively. Because the clustering algorithm is based on the sequence + structure distance, the classification accuracy using the distance is 100%.

The average Root-Mean-Squared-Deviation (RMSD) of all fragments to their centroids is 0.430 Å, with a standard deviation of 0.349 Å. Because the fragments are represented in dihedral space, the tertiary structures of the fragments and the centroids are reconstructed with the standard bond length and bond angle, which are taken from the CHARMM force field.[143] The large standard deviation indicates that proteins are dynamic molecules, since the minor inaccuracies in bond angles can cause >6 Å RMSD for the proteins with 150 residues.[144] Some sample building blocks are shown in Fig. 5-4. One representative building block for each length is selected. The features shown in the figure are the secondary structure probability, the dihedral angles, the frequency

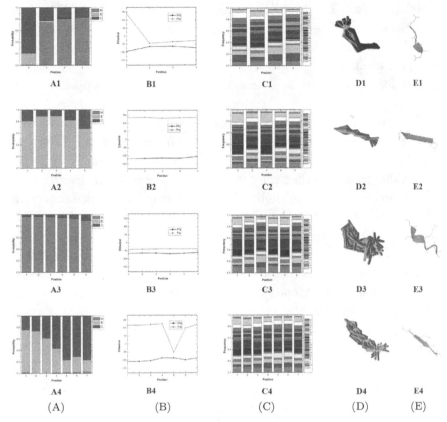

Figure 5-4   Sample building blocks in the building block library. Each row figure corresponds to one building block. The building block indices are 15, 75, 126 and 176, respectively. The lengths of the four building blocks are 4, 5, 6 and 7, respectively. Each column figure represents one feature of the corresponding building block. The sub-figures of column A represent the secondary structure probability matrix, in which the helix, strand and coil are represented as H, E, C, respectively. The sub-figures of column B represent the backbone dihedral angles. The frequency profiles are shown in the sub-figures of column C. A superposition of 30 cluster members is depicted in the sub-figures of column D. Shown in the sub-figures of column E are the cartoon representations of a representative fragment. The representative fragments are 1OTKA 62-65, 1NIJA 278-282, 1QR0A 222-227 and 1GUDA 106-112, respectively.

profiles, the superposition of 30 cluster members and the cartoon representations of a representative fragment. The building block in the first row consists of most helix structures with coil structures at the N-terminal. It may connect helix and coil structures in actual proteins. The building block in the second row is a typical helix structure. The building block in the third row is a typical strand structure. The building block in the last row is composed of strand and coil structures. The complete building-block library in text format and the bi-grams are provided in the supplementary materials.

The correlations between any two building blocks are represented by bi-grams, which are shown in Fig. 5-5. Some of the bi-grams have large values, while others have values close to zero. A large bi-gram value indicates that the two building blocks are often adjacent in one protein. The long helix structures may be divided into two sub-structures, so the corresponding bi-grams are very high. For example, the bi-gram value between the building blocks 121 and 158 is 0.7479, in which both of the building blocks are typical helix structures. Such phenomena also exist for strand structures. Some bi-grams that connect coils and helices are also very high, such as the bi-gram between the building blocks 19 and 136. The former

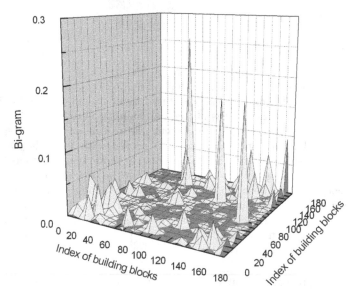

Figure 5-5   The schematic plot of the bi-grams between any two building blocks. Note that the bi-grams have been smoothed to plot the three-dimensional surface. For the actual bi-gram, please refer to the supplementary materials.

building block is composed of coil structures at the N-terminal and helix structures at the C-terminal, while the latter building block is a complete helix structure. Most of the low bi-grams exist in the building blocks in which three secondary structures occur in the two building blocks. These bi-grams describe the connections and propensities of the building blocks when they are organized to form the tertiary structures of proteins. The folding space of proteins is infinite in theory, but only a finite number of folds have been discovered thus far.[145] The basic idea used here is that the proteins fold in the most common way, which can be captured by the bi-gram model.

5.4.2.2 *Prediction results*

The local structures and the folding fragments of protein sequences are predicted using the "My-Peeling" algorithm. Here, three optimal paths are compared. They are the maximum similarity path, the maximum probability path and the maximum combination path, calculated using Eqs. (5-9)–(5-11), respectively. Two criteria are used to evaluate the local structure prediction: the classification accuracy and the prediction accuracy (see the "Performance metrics" section). As regards prediction accuracy, the RMSD thresholds should be dependent on the lengths of the fragments, since long fragments are difficult to be superposed and result in large RMSD. Here, the RMSD thresholds are taken as $\mu + \sigma$, where μ and σ are the means and the standard deviations of all training fragments to their centroids. The final RMSD thresholds are 0.635, 0.746, 0.849 and 0.924 Å for fragment lengths of 4, 5, 6 and 7, respectively. Such thresholds are more rigid than those of other studies. For example, some researchers take the RMSD threshold as 1.4 Å for a fragment length of 8.[29,34]

When only one path with maximum path value is returned, the results are given in Table 5-6. The maximum similarity path achieves the lowest performance with a classification accuracy of 0.4259 and a prediction accuracy of 0.5774. The maximum probability path improves the classification accuracy up to 0.5302 and the prediction accuracy up to 0.6381. The maximum combination path outperforms the other two paths, by obtaining a classification accuracy of 0.6140

Table 5-6   The local structure prediction results of the optimal paths.

Path	The classification accuracy	The prediction accuracy
The maximum similarity path	0.4259	0.5774
The maximum probability path	0.5302	0.6381
The maximum combination path	0.614	0.6486

Table 5-7   The local structure prediction results of multiple paths.

Number of paths[a]	Path	The classification accuracy	The prediction accuracy
10	The maximum similarity path	0.4534	0.5858
	The maximum probability path	0.5927	0.6492
	The maximum combination path	0.6578	0.6578
100	The maximum similarity path	0.4709	0.5803
	The maximum probability path	0.6478	0.6682
	The maximum combination path	0.6973	0.6697
500	The maximum similarity path	0.5711	0.6029
	The maximum probability path	0.6974	0.6697
	The maximum combination path	0.7227	0.6772

Note: [a]The number of paths that have the highest path value.

and a prediction accuracy of 0.6486. The weight of sequence distance w_s is taken as 40, which is based on the observation that the standard deviation of the bi-gram is about 40 times that of the sequence distance (SVM output).

Sometimes the optimal path may not be the correct one, so multiple paths should be returned and the best results are given in Table 5-7. As can be seen, the performance increases as the number of paths increases. When 500 paths with optimal values are returned, the classification accuracy is 0.7227 and the prediction accuracy is 0.6772.

There are false positives in the local structure classification, that is, some of the sequence segments are not assigned the correct building blocks, so the corresponding building-block lattices are not accurate and the correct path cannot be found. To solve this problem, a loose manner is adopted when the building-block lattices are constructed, that is, multiple building blocks can match one node. The results are shown in Table 5-8. As the number of building blocks and the number of paths increase, the performance also increases. But such a schema is not excellent since much noise is introduced to the building-block lattices. More paths should be returned to include the correct one.

Overall, the classification accuracy seems to be lower than the prediction accuracy. Two reasons are provided here. The first one is that the number of building blocks in the library is very large (180). The classifier needs to classify each fragment into one of the 180 classes. Decreasing the number of classes can lead to better results, for example, the secondary structure prediction in three states can lead to an accuracy of nearly 80%.[36] The other reason is the different evaluation methods. For the prediction accuracy, the RMSD threshold is taken as $\mu + \sigma$, which means that if the fragments are correctly classified, their local structures can be correctly predicted with a probability of 0.84. If the fragments are not correctly classified, their local structures may also be correctly predicted, because the classification accuracy needs to take the sequence similarity and structure similarity into consideration while the prediction accuracy only considers structure similarity. That is, the building block incorrectly assigned to a fragment may have high structure similarity with the fragment.

The initial number of building blocks in the library is selected as the depth of the initial clustering center (see the "Clustering of fragments" section). During the iterative training process, the number of building blocks may change according to new partitions of the training proteins. The final library contains 180 building blocks and remains unchanged because the library and the model are

Table 5-8   The local structure prediction results of multiple paths when multiple building blocks can match one node in the building-block lattice.

Number of building blocks[a]	Number of paths	Path	The classification accuracy	The prediction accuracy
2	1	The maximum similarity path	0.4162	0.5749
		The maximum probability path	0.4696	0.6233
		The maximum combination path	0.6126	0.6486
	10	The maximum similarity path	0.4287	0.5779
		The maximum probability path	0.5475	0.6362
		The maximum combination path	0.6598	0.6603
	100	The maximum similarity path	0.4478	0.5816
		The maximum probability path	0.6065	0.6519
		The maximum combination path	0.6989	0.6693
	500	The maximum similarity path	0.4597	0.5872
		The maximum probability path	0.6438	0.6663
		The maximum combination path	0.7244	0.6759
3	1	The maximum similarity path	0.4088	0.5745
		The maximum probability path	0.4523	0.6124
		The maximum combination path	0.6121	0.6488
	10	The maximum similarity path	0.4239	0.5782
		The maximum probability path	0.5301	0.6351
		The maximum combination path	0.6605	0.6595
	100	The maximum similarity path	0.4487	0.5871
		The maximum probability path	0.5964	0.6453
		The maximum combination path	0.7004	0.6698
	500	The maximum similarity path	0.4495	0.5797
		The maximum probability path	0.6275	0.6621
		The maximum combination path	0.7236	0.6779

Note: [a]The number of building blocks that match one node in the building-block lattice.

Table 5-9 The local structure prediction results with different numbers of building blocks.

No. building blocks[a]	Path	The classification accuracy	The prediction accuracy
52	The maximum similarity path	0.4584	0.5024
	The maximum probability path	0.5625	0.5492
	The maximum combination path	0.6325	0.5673
308	The maximum similarity path	0.3428	0.3863
	The maximum probability path	0.3987	0.4024
	The maximum combination path	0.4538	0.4597

Note: [a]The number of building blocks in the library.

convergent. Here, we manually select the initial number of building blocks to get different libraries, which demonstrate their influence on the prediction accuracy. Two other libraries with different numbers of building blocks (52 and 308) are developed and their performances are explained in Table 5-9. Only the classification accuracy of the 52-letter library is improved; all other performances are lower than those of the 180-letter library. According to machine learning theory, samples with a small number of classes are easier to classify than those with a large number of classes, so the classification accuracy of the 52-letter library is better than that of the 180-letter library. The library with a small number of building blocks cannot provide sufficient descriptions of the local structures of proteins, so the prediction accuracy of the 52-letter library is lower than that of the 180-letter library. The 302-letter library contains more classes than the 180-letter library, so its classification accuracy is lower than that of the 180-letter library. The prediction accuracy of the 302-letter library is also lower than that of the 180-letter one, which may be caused by the data sparsity problem, since more bi-grams need to be estimated in the 302-letter library than those in the 180-letter library. The current dataset cannot provide sufficient statistics for

120 Biological Language Model: Theory and Application

the bi-grams in the 302-letter library, and we find that many of the bi-grams are zero.

5.4.2.3 *Sample prediction*

A practical prediction is provided here. The T4 lysozyme, used for this sample prediction, is one of the most frequently used proteins to study protein folding. The native-state hydrogen exchange experiment has identified an intermediate with the N-terminal domain (from residues 14 to 65) unfolded and C-terminal domain (from residues 1 to 13 and 66 to 164) folded.[146, 147]

The sequence of the T4 lysozyme was submitted to our system to predict the local structures and the folding fragments. The result of the maximum combination path is evaluated. When only one path with maximum path value is returned, the classification accuracy is 0.967 and the prediction accuracy is 0.667. Such high classification accuracy may be caused by the homology between the T4 lysozyme and the proteins from the training set. When 500 paths are returned, many paths get improved results. The native protein structure is shown in Fig. 5-6. The path that is most similar to the experimental results is selected. Its rank is 272. Some segments on that path are shown in Fig. 5-7. A clear separation between the three folding intermediates is identified by the fragments 2 and 3 and the fragments 4 and 5. The fragments at the N-terminal and C-terminal are also shown. The method used in this study can predict all the folding fragments that are involved in the folding process. With the development of advanced experimental techniques, more data about the folding process will be available and folding fragments will be observed, and then the supervised machine learning method will be used to build a smart model. The current method cannot predict the folding orders of these fragments, namely the folding pathway. Future works will be carried out to explore it.

5.4.2.4 *Comparison with related studies*

Early work on protein local structure prediction was performed by Bystroff and Baker,[29] who presented a library of short sequence

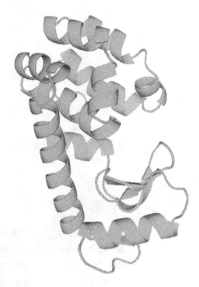

Figure 5-6   The native structure of the protein T4 lysozyme in Carton format.

patterns that correlated strongly with protein three-dimensional structural elements. Matching segments are assigned the tertiary structure of the corresponding sequence pattern. The prediction accuracy of local structures is 0.5, with a fragment length of 8 and an RMSD threshold of 1.4 Å. Subsequently, many other studies tried to predict the local structures of proteins by comparing the sequences or profiles of the sequence segments with those of the fragments.[49] Tang *et al.*[34] designed a dynamic programming approach to optimize an objective function that measured the quality of the sequence match. They reported a prediction accuracy of 58.21% with the same fragment length and RMSD threshold. Our method also uses the sequence profiles as inputted, but we use an advanced machine learning approach to predict the local structures of proteins. A significant improvement has been achieved in comparison with the sequence matching method.

Many studies also used the machine learning approaches for local structure classification of proteins, most of which are based on the structure alphabets, such as the SAH alphabet (10 letters),[31] the PB alphabet (16 letters)[42] and the DW alphabet (28 letters).[148] The performance is strongly dependent on the number of letters in the structure alphabet. Sander *et al.*[50] applied a support vector

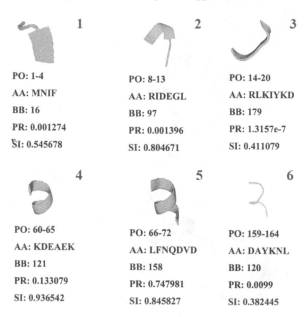

PO: 1-4

AA: MNIF

BB: 16

PR: 0.001274

SI: 0.545678

PO: 8-13

AA: RIDEGL

BB: 97

PR: 0.001396

SI: 0.804671

PO: 14-20

AA: RLKIYKD

BB: 179

PR: 1.3157e-7

SI: 0.411079

PO: 60-65

AA: KDEAEK

BB: 121

PR: 0.133079

SI: 0.936542

PO: 66-72

AA: LFNQDVD

BB: 158

PR: 0.747981

SI: 0.845827

PO: 159-164

AA: DAYKNL

BB: 120

PR: 0.0099

SI: 0.382445

Figure 5-7   Some fragments for the T4 lysozyme protein. PO is the position of the segment on the native structure. AA is the amino acid sequence. BB is the corresponding building block that matches the segment. PR is the bi-gram of the building block with the previous one. The PR of the first segment is the initial probability of the corresponding building block. SI is the similarity of the sequence segment with the corresponding building block (SVM probability out).

machine to local structure prediction and achieved a classification accuracy of only 36.15% on an alphabet with 28 letters. The HYPLOSP method[51] adopted a neural network for local structure prediction and obtained a classification accuracy of 61.53% on the SAH alphabet and 63.24% on the PB alphabet. We previously found that neighboring local structures are strongly correlated and designed a dual-layer model for protein local structure prediction.[52] The classification accuracy obtained was 45.6% on the DW alphabet and 58.5% on the PB alphabet. The study in this paper had a classification accuracy of 61.4% on a 180-letter alphabet. Unlike most previous studies that predict the local structures using only local sequence information and ignore the correlations between these letters, this paper presents a bi-gram model to describe the adjacent co-occurrence probability of any two letters and uses the dynamic programming approach to find the globally optimal fragments.

Our works are also similar to those of Haspel *et al.*[149, 150] and Tsai *et al.*,[151] who presented a hierarchical framework for protein structure prediction. However, they failed to implement a practical method to find the optimal folding fragments of proteins. Here, we use the bi-gram model as implementation and achieve positive results for the local structure prediction of proteins.

The I-sites Library is a set of sequence patterns that strongly correlate with the protein structure at the local level. It has been successfully used to predict local structures,[29] in remote homology detection,[32] for developing complex sequence–structure correlation,[31] etc. This study also derived a 180-letter fragment library. Our library is different from the I-sites library in the following aspects: 1) There is less noise in the fragments used by our library than those used by the I-sites library before clustering; 2) The I-sites library is derived on the sequence space while our library is derived on the sequence + structure space; 3) The correlations between the fragments are ignored in the I-sites library while in our library, such correlations are represented by the bi-gram; 4) The I-sites library is derived by the standard k-means algorithm. Our initial library is derived using the same algorithm, but the final library is derived in an iterative manner such that the final library and the model are convergent on the training data.

The method in this study is compared with the HMMSTR method,[31] which is one of the state-of-the-art methods for protein local structure prediction. The model extends the I-sites library by describing the adjacencies of different sequence–structure motifs as observed in the protein database and by representing overlapping motifs in a much more compact form. The HMMSTR model divides the backbone angles into 11 regions (See Fig. 5-7 of Ref. [31]). Each residue in proteins is assigned one of the 11 labels (E, e, B, b, d, G, H, L, l, x, c). The evaluation criterion used here is the classification accuracy, which is the percent of residues that are correctly classified according to the 11 labels. The results of the HMMSTR method can be obtained from the web server (http://www.bioinfo.rpi.edu/~bystrc/hmmstr/server.php). The 121 testing proteins in this study are submitted to the web server. However, we

Table 5-10   Comparative results with the HMMSTR method.

ID	HMMSTR[a]	BBL_1[b]	BBL_500[c]	ID	HMMSTR[a]	BBL_1[b]	BBL_500[c]
1A34A	0.4275	0.3758	0.4532	1Q8RA	0.6034	0.5431	0.6239
1J27A	0.5312	0.5729	0.6472	1TUWA	0.5288	0.4807	0.5874
1Y0HA	0.6868	0.6869	0.7239	1COZA	0.6613	0.6209	0.6937
1UCRA	0.625	0.5556	0.6458	1YTLA	0.6603	0.5128	0.6428
1VCTA	0.7068	0.5602	0.6649	1SHEA	0.5824	0.5384	0.6987
1SA3A	0.5923	0.4885	0.5736	1WDJA	0.6339	0.5792	0.6745
1T6SA	0.6962	0.6772	0.7394	1V54F	0.4167	0.3729	0.4647
1DZFA	0.6202	0.5673	0.6538	Ave	0.5981	0.5422	0.6325

Notes: [a]Results of HMMSTR are taken from the web-server (http://www. bioinfo.rpi.edu/~bystrc/hmmstr/server.php); [b]The results of our method with only one maximum combination path returned; [c]The results of our method with 500 maximum combination paths returned.

find that the homologue information of many proteins is used by the HMMSTR method. Thus, it is unfair to compare the HMMSTR method with our method, since there is no homologue between the training data and the test data (less than 25% sequence identity) in our method. We selected the test proteins so that the homologue information is not used by the web server. The results are given in Table 5-10. The average classification accuracy of the 15 proteins predicted by the HMMSTR method is 0.5981. When only one path is returned, our method reaches a classification accuracy of 0.5422, which is a little lower than that of the HMMSTR method. When 500 paths are returned, our method outperforms the HMMSTR method and reaches a classification accuracy of 0.6325.

5.4.2.5 *Analysis of the method*

The method in this study outperforms those used most in the previous studies. The advantages of our method are as follows:

1. There is little noise in the fragment library before clustering. The training proteins are first split using the "Protein Peeling" algorithm and the fragments are collected from the initial partitions. While most other related studies adopt fixed-length fragments and collected fragments along the sequence with a sliding window, there can be significant noise using this method.

2. The distance defined in Equation 5-4 takes both sequence similarity and structure similarity into consideration while making the local structure prediction from sequences accurately.
3. The local structures of proteins are predicted by advanced machine learning approaches, not the simple comparison of sequences or profiles.
4. The building-block library is constructed in an iterative manner until convergence. The new partitions of training proteins are the same as the old ones from which the building-block library is derived. The building blocks and their bi-grams can simulate the components and their interactions in protein structures.
5. Our method can predict not only the local structures but also the folding fragments of proteins.

However, there are also several limitations in the current method that may hinder performance, such as the following:

1. The classification accuracies of local structures are not very high, and so the correct folding fragments may not exist in the building-block lattice.
2. The "My-Peeling" algorithm cannot bear much noise. For example, the algorithm cannot find the correct folding fragments when one node in the building-block lattice matches multiple building blocks. The false building blocks in the node may result in a high bi-gram frequency, so the optimal fragment is not the correct one.
3. The current method lacks a rigid theoretical foundation. The basic idea used here is that the proteins fold in the most common way, which is based on the observation that there are only a finite number of folds in the current PDB.[140]

5.5 Characterization of Protein Flexibility Based on Structural Alphabets

5.5.1 Materials and method

5.5.1.1 *Dataset*

Three datasets are used in this study for different experimental validations.

The first dataset is taken from the work of Boden and Bailey[53] and is used for the prediction of protein flexibility. This dataset contains 171 non-redundant protein sequences, with no pair of sequences having larger than 20% sequence identity. All the proteins exhibit conformational flexibility according to the comprehensive database of macromolecular movements (MolMovDB).[78] Each sequence in this dataset has been annotated with a list of residue positions that have more than one local structure according to the structure alphabets.

The second dataset is used to train the support vector machine which is used for the local structure predictions of proteins. This dataset is a subset of the PDB database[140] obtained from the PISCES[141] web server. There is less than 25% sequence identity between any two proteins, and every protein has a resolution better than 2.5 Å. Structures with missing atoms and chain breaks are excluded. The proteins that show homologues with the proteins from the first dataset are also excluded. The resulting dataset thus contains 928 protein chains.

The third dataset is used to test whether the changes of local structures can characterize protein flexibility. To achieve this goal, a variant of conformations for one protein must be provided. We use the Baker decoy sets[152] that were previously used for the evaluation of knowledge-based mean force potentials. This dataset consists of 41 single-domain proteins with varying degrees of secondary structures and lengths from 25 to 87 residues. Each protein is attached with about 1400 decoy structures generated by the *ab initio* protein structure prediction method of Rosetta.[153]

5.5.1.2 *Training and test of local structures*

Many methods have been presented for the prediction of protein local structures. The dual-layer model has been adopted here, which was developed in our previous studies.[154] The method is based on the observation that neighboring local structures are strongly correlated. A dual-layer model is then designed for protein local structure prediction. The position-specific scoring matrix (PSSM), generated by PSI-BLAST,[14] is input to the first-layer classifier, whose output is further enhanced by a second-layer classifier. At each layer, a variant of classifiers can be used, such as Support Vector Machines (SVMs),[50] Neural Networks (NNs)[155] or Hidden Markov Models (HMMs). In this study, the SVM is selected as the classifier, since its performance is better than those of other classifiers. Experimental results show that the dual-layer model provides an efficient method for protein local structure prediction.

5.5.1.3 *Characterization of protein flexibilities by conformational changes*

The conformations of proteins are represented by the local structures in the form of a structure alphabet. All the local structure types can be referred to as structure alphabets. Four different structure alphabets, including the secondary structures in the 3-class and 8-class, the PB structure alphabet[42] and the DW structure alphabet,[148] are investigated here. The three-dimensional protein structures can be represented by one-dimensional structure alphabet sequences according to a specific structure alphabet. Given a protein and its variable conformations, we can convert them into several structure alphabet sequences. The changes of local structures can be used to characterize protein flexibility. For example, consider a protein sequence $a_1 a_2 \cdots a_n$. Its three-dimensional structures and conformations are labeled as structure alphabet sequences; we then obtained a structure alphabet matrix $a_{11}, a_{12}, \ldots, a_{nm}$, where a_{ij} is the probability of the structure alphabet letter of the jth conformation at the amino acid position i, n is the length of the protein sequence and m is the total number of letters in the structure alphabet. Conformational entropy is then used as an indicator of the protein flexibility

$$H(i) = -\sum_{j=1}^{m} a_{ij} \ln a_{ij} \qquad (5\text{-}18)$$

where $H(i)$ is the conformational entropy of the protein at sequence position i.

The correlation between the conformational entropies and the B-factors is calculated as follows:

$$CC = \frac{\sum_{i=1}^{n}(H_i - Ave(H))(B_i - Ave(B))}{\sqrt{\left[\sum_{i=1}^{n}(H_i - Ave(H))^2\right]\left[\sum_{i=1}^{n}(B_i - Ave(B))^2\right]}} \qquad (5\text{-}19)$$

where B_i is the B-factor of the protein at sequence position i, $Ave(H)$ and $Ave(B)$ are the average of the conformational entropy and the average of the B-factor of the protein.

5.5.1.4 *Prediction of protein flexibilities by local structure entropies*

Let the predicted local structure for a given residue be $Y = Y_1, \ldots, Y_m$ where Y_j is the probability that the residue is in the jth local structure class, and m is the number of local structure classes: 3 for a 3-class secondary structure alphabet, 8 for an 8-class secondary structure alphabet, 16 for the PB structure alphabet and 28 for the DW structure alphabet. The conformation entropy of a residue is defined as

$$H = -\sum_{j=1}^{m} Y_j \ln Y_j \qquad (5\text{-}20)$$

High entropy indicates relatively more disorder while lower entropy indicates relatively more order.

5.5.1.5 *Performance metrics*

The following measures are used to evaluate the prediction of protein flexibilities: sensitivity, specificity, precision and the Receiver Operator Characteristic (ROC) curves, which are defined as follows:

$$Sensitivity = \frac{TP}{TP + FN} \qquad (5\text{-}21)$$

$$Specificity = \frac{TN}{TN + FP} \qquad (5\text{-}22)$$

$$\text{Precision} = \frac{TP}{TP + FP} \qquad (5\text{-}23)$$

where TP is the number of true positives (flexible residues correctly classified as flexible residues), FP is the number of false positives (rigid residues incorrectly classified as flexible residues), TN is the number of true negatives (rigid residues correctly classified as rigid residues) and FN is the number of false negatives (flexible residues incorrectly classified as rigid residues).

The ROC curve is plotted with true positives as a function of false positives for varying classification thresholds. A ROC score is the normalized area under the ROC curve. A score of 1 indicates the perfect separation of positive samples from negative samples, whereas a score of 0 denotes that none of the sequences selected by the algorithm are positive.

5.5.2 Results and discussions

5.5.2.1 *Local structure prediction*

Four different structure alphabets are used in this study. They are the secondary structures in the 3-class and 8-class, the PB structure alphabet[42] and the DW structure alphabet.[148] All of them are descriptions of the local structures of proteins.

The 3-class secondary structure provides a three-state description of backbone structures: helices, strands and coils. The 8-class secondary structure provides a more detailed description.[131] However, this description of protein structures is still very crude.[156]

Two other structure alphabets were investigated in this study: the DW structure alphabet and the PB structure alphabet. They are represented in Cartesian coordinate space and in torsion angles space, respectively. The PB alphabet[42] is composed of 16 prototypes, each of which is 5 residues in length and represented by 8 dihedral angles. This structure alphabet remains valid although the size of the databank becomes large.[157] The DW structure alphabet was developed in our previous study,[148] and is represented in Cartesian coordinate space. This structure alphabet contains 28 prototypes that have lengths of 7 residues.

Table 5-11   The average Q-scores of local structure prediction for the four structure alphabets.

	Sec3	Sec8	PB	DW
Number of letters	3	8	16	28
Single-layer model	0.756	0.593	0.564	0.432
Dual-layer model	0.765	0.614	0.585	0.456

The dual-layer model is used to predict the local structures of proteins.[154] The experiment was performed on the second dataset. The Q-score is used to assess the prediction results, that is, the proportion of structure alphabet prototypes correctly predicted. This score is equivalent to the Q_3 value for secondary structure prediction. The results after 5-fold cross-validation are shown in Table 5-11. The accuracy of secondary structure prediction is comparable with the currently state-of-the-art method,[36] while the performances of the other two structure alphabets are significantly better than those of other related works.[34, 42, 43, 50] For detailed results, please refer to Dong *et al.*[154]

The single-layer model uses the position-specific scoring matrix (PSSM) as input and outputs the probability of the structure alphabet letters. The dual-layer model adds an additional classifier, which uses the output of the single-layer model as input and outputs the final prediction. For both models, the support vector machine is used as the classifier.

5.5.2.2   *Results for the characterization of protein flexibilities*

Since proteins are dynamic molecules, we can investigate whether conformational changes can capture protein flexibilities. The protein structures are represented by structure alphabet sequences. The conformational entropy is used as an indicator of protein flexibility. The experiment is performed on the third dataset.

The initial results demonstrate that some of the proteins show high correlations between the conformational entropies and the

Table 5-12   The correlations between the conformational entropies and the *B*-factors.

ID	< 3[a]	3-4	4-5	5-6	> 6	Sec3[b]	Sec8	PB	DW
1res	73	73	73	7	4	0.1105	0.1505	0.2454	0.2605
1am3	571	177	162	161	400	0.1139	0.2993	0.4110	0.5149
1r69	389	119	284	228	300	0.2028	0.4040	0.3909	0.3794
1utg	1	20	401	290	300	0.2003	0.2990	0.2729	0.1653
1a32	364	125	95	142	300	0.2819	0.4818	0.5077	0.4145
1mzm	9	306	317	171	300	0.0118	0.2734	0.3353	0.3144
1hyp	1	0	34	270	300	0.1491	0.3579	0.1893	0.2889
1cei	1	0	4	64	300	0.0821	0.3583	0.4335	0.4932
1pgx	219	342	182	391	300	0.0264	0.2843	0.3339	0.3674
5icb	3	142	481	225	300	0.4255	0.5660	0.5433	0.5635
Ave	163.1	130.4	203.3	194.9	280.4	0.1604	0.3474	0.3663	0.3762

Notes: [a]Shown in the table are the number of decoy structures in this class; [b]Shown in the table are the correlations measured by the specific structure alphabet.

B-factors while the other proteins show low, and even negative, correlations. After detailed analysis, we find that the correlations are influenced by the distribution of the decoy structures. Uniform distribution often leads to high correlation. The decoy structures are first classified by Root-Mean-Squared-Deviation (RMSD) with the native structures. We then select the decoy structures so that they are approximately uniformly distributed between different classes. Some of the proteins and the correlations are listed in Table 5-12 together with the number of decoy structures. As the number of letters increases, the correlations also increase.

According to the law of thermodynamics, the native structure is the one that has the lowest energy. Since proteins are dynamic molecules, their structures often fluctuate upon the native state. The decoy sets used here are generated using the well-known Rosetta algorithm.[153] These sets contain many decoy structures whose energies are close to the native one. The conformational entropies are then derived from the decoy sets. Some of the conformational entropies show high correlation with the protein flexibilities. However, the decoy sets are not the true stories, there still are some proteins that show low correlations between the entropies and the B-factors (data not shown). This experiment only tries to investigate whether the conformational changes can capture protein flexibilities. If the true decoy sets can be obtained, we can then give a definite answer. However, obtaining the true decoy sets is costly and labor-intensive work.

5.5.2.3 *Results for the prediction of protein flexibilities*

The experiment is performed on the first dataset. Each residue is labeled as a rigid or flexible residue. The animations of protein motions provided by the MolMovDB database[78] are converted into structure alphabet letter sequences by the specific structure alphabet. If a residue changes its structure alphabet letter between animations, it is labeled as a flexible residue. Otherwise, it is a rigid residue.

During the prediction process, the protein local structures are first predicted from amino acid sequences by the dual-layer model, and then the entropy function is applied to the predicted class distribution for each residue. Residues with an entropy larger than a given threshold T are predicted to be flexible residues. Otherwise, they are predicted to be rigid residues. Following the work of Boden and Bailey,[53] we use the mean entropy of all residues in our conformation variability dataset as the threshold T.

The results of the four structure alphabets are shown in Table 5-13. The corresponding Receiver Operator Characteristic

Table 5-13 Prediction performance of the protein flexibilities by different structure alphabets.

SA[a]	No.po[b]	No.ne[c]	Sensitivity	Specificity	Precision	Roc
Sec3	6152	54737	0.6291	0.4543	0.1109	0.5457
Sec8	9468	51421	0.5887	0.5677	0.1942	0.5741
PB	10625	50264	0.6209	0.5521	0.2114	0.5901
DW	16012	44877	0.6399	0.5725	0.2586	0.6193

Notes: [a]The structure alphabet types; [b]The number of positive samples (flexible residues); [c]The number of negative samples (rigid residues).

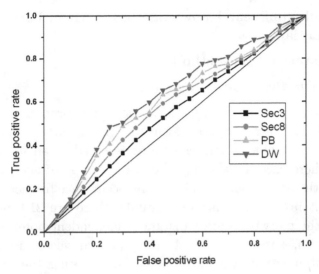

Figure 5-8   The ROC curve of the proposed method by using different structure alphabets on the set of 171 protein sequences.

(ROC) curves are given in Fig. 5-8. The different structure alphabets get different numbers of positive (flexible) and negative (rigid) samples. As the number of letters in the structure alphabet increases, the number of positive samples increases and the prediction performance also increases, which means that more subtle local structures can be captured by a large number of structure alphabet letters. The precision and ROC scores steadily increase. Overall the DW structure alphabet shows the best performance.

The results obtained here are similar to the work of Boden and Bailey.[53] The precision in this study is higher than that of Boden and Bailey (0.05 for Sec3 and 0.12 for Sec8), but the ROC scores are a little lower than those of Boden and Bailey (0.61 for Sec3 and 0.64 for Sec8). The main differences between this study and that of Boden and Bailey are in two aspects. The first one is that two additional structure alphabets (the PB and DW structure alphabet) are investigated here. The second difference is that a decoy set is used to explore whether the conformation change can capture protein flexibility.

5.6   Novel Nonlinear Knowledge-based Mean Force Potentials

5.6.1   Materials and methods

5.6.1.1   *The theoretical framework*

The sequence and structure information of a protein need to be converted into an appropriate form for conveniently computing its energy. Generally, a protein can be represented as an m-dimension vector, where each dimension indicates one type of energy component and the corresponding value is the occurrence frequency of that component in the protein. For example, there are 210 interaction pairs for the pairwise contact distance-independent potential at the residue level, so the length of the potential vector is 210, and the potential vector can be obtained by counting the occurrence frequency of each interaction pair.

Let X be the potential vector of a protein and $E(X)$ be the corresponding energy. It was found that the energy of the native structure is lower than the energy of any decoy,[81] which is formally given as

$$E(X_N) - E(X_D) < 0 \qquad (5\text{-}24)$$

where X_N is the potential vector of the native structure and X_D is the potential vector of the decoy. We can further restrict the difference between $E(X_N)$ and $E(X_D)$ to be greater than a constant $\delta > 0$, that is,

$$E(X_N) - E(X_D) + \delta < 0 \qquad (5\text{-}25)$$

There are various methods for calculating $E(X)$ in the literature, which results in many different potentials. The Boltzmann-based potentials and the linear potentials are all in the form of the linear sum of the elements of a potential vector, that is,

$$E(X) = w'X + b' \qquad (5\text{-}26)$$

Substituting the value in the previous equation, we get

$$w'(X_N - X_D) + \delta < 0 \tag{5-27}$$

The above inequality can be obtained by solving the following two inequalities:

$$\begin{cases} w'X_N + b' < -\delta/2 \\ w'X_D + b' > -\delta/2 \end{cases} \tag{5-28}$$

By defining two variables,

$$w = 2 * w'/\delta, \quad b = 2 * b'/\delta \tag{5-29}$$

The two inequalities can be rewritten as

$$\begin{cases} wX_N + b < -1 \\ wX_D + b > -1 \end{cases} \tag{5-30}$$

which is actually the standard linear classifier formulated by the SVM (Support Vector Machine), in which the native structures have been assigned the value of −1 and the decoys have been assigned the value of +1. The graphical representation of such a classification problem is illustrated in Fig. 5-9. Each structure is represented by a point in the figure. The native structures are depicted as solid points and the decoys are depicted as hollow points. If the distribution of data points is similar to that illustrated in Fig. 5-9(a), then linear classifiers can perfectly discriminate the native structures from the decoys. An SVM constructs the optimal hyperplane by maximizing the gap between the two sets of samples. Other methods such as linear programming have also been used to construct linear classifiers.[158]

If the data points are distributed as illustrated in Fig. 5-9(b), a nonlinear classifier can distinguish the two sets of samples. A major reason for this failure is that the functional form of the linear sum is too simple. For such cases, nonlinear classifiers must be constructed.

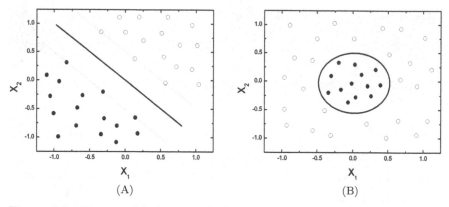

Figure 5-9 The graphical view of the inequality requirement for protein potential. A two-dimensional case has been used here. The solid points denote the native structures and the hollow points denote the decoys. (A) A linear classification function can perfectly discriminate the native structures and the decoys. (B) A nonlinear classification function is needed to distinguish the two sets of samples since the linear classification function cannot succeed in this task.

The nonlinear potentials can be formulated as

$$E(X) = \sum_{i \in D} y_i \alpha_i K(X, X_i) + b \qquad (5\text{-}31)$$

where y_i is -1 for native structures and $+1$ for decoys, D is the vector set containing both native structures and decoys, α_i are parameters to be determined and K is the kernel function that implicitly maps the feature space of the original vectors to another high-dimensional space, in which the optimal hyperplane is expected to be found. The optimal hyperplane should have the largest margin distance separating the native structures and the decoys in the space transformed by the nonlinear kernel. Using statistical learning theory,[138] such a hyperplane can be found by solving the following Lagrange dual form of the quadratic programming problem

$$\min \frac{1}{2} \sum_i \sum_j y_i y_j \alpha_i \alpha_j K(X_i, X_j) - \sum_j \alpha_j \qquad (5\text{-}32)$$

Subject to $\sum_i y_i \alpha_i = 0; 0 \le \alpha_i \le C$

where C is a regularization constant that limits the influence of each misclassified structure. As a result, optimal nonlinear potentials can be obtained such that each native structure has energy close to -1 and each decoy has energy close to $+1$.

Here, the Libsvm package[159] is used as an implementation of the SVM. The Radial Basis Function (RBF) is taken as the kernel function, which is defined as

$$K(X_i, X_j) = \exp(-\gamma \|X_i - X_j\|^2) \qquad (5\text{-}33)$$

The values of γ and the regularization parameter C are optimized on the training set. Additionally, all the potential vectors are normalized by the length of the target proteins.

5.6.1.2 *Datasets*

To evaluate the usefulness of the statistical potentials, large sets of protein structures are needed. Three datasets, including the LKF dataset,[121] the CASP7 dataset[160] and the Decoys 'R' Us set,[161] are used here to train and evaluate the nonlinear potentials. They are briefly described in this section.

The LKF dataset was generated by Loose *et al.*[121] using the program of DYANA,[162] which takes as input the sequence of a protein along with information about its secondary structure that gives bounds for the distances and torsion angles between atoms. Pre-processing on the data is done to ensure the quality of the decoy set. Decoys of 185 proteins were downloaded from the authors' website (http://titan.princeton.edu/Decoys/), and each protein has about 200 decoy structures. Twenty-three of the 185 proteins contain incomplete atoms, so the atom-level potentials cannot be calculated. To give an unbiased comparison with other potentials, these 23 proteins are removed from the decoy set. Totally, there are 161 proteins and 32,047 decoy structures.

The CASP7 dataset was downloaded from the official website http://predictioncenter.org/ and then subjected to a number of stringent filtering processes. The proteins that miss some of the amino acids are removed. The decoy structures that contain incomplete atoms, especially main-chain atoms, are also discarded. The resulting dataset contains 63 proteins and 20,868 decoy structures.

The Decoys 'R' Us dataset[161] contains several well-constructed decoy subsets and has been widely used to evaluate various potentials.[105, 106, 163–165] Six decoy subsets including 4stat_reduced[166] fisa,[94] fisa-casp3,[94] lmds,[167] lattice-ssfit[168, 169] and semfold[170] were selected. These subsets were generated by various researchers using different techniques, and each subset has a different number of decoy conformations. Because there are multiple decoy subsets generated by different methods, this dataset can give a comprehensive evaluation of the potentials.

5.6.1.3 *Knowledge-based mean force potentials*

In addition to the Boltzmann-based potentials and the linear potentials, a class of nonlinear potentials is presented. We introduce five knowledge-based mean force Boltzmann-based or linear potentials and implement the corresponding nonlinear potentials.

The DIH potential: The DIH potential[96] is a single-body residue-level Boltzmann-based potential that is obtained from the propensity of each amino acid for each dihedral Φ/Ψ class. The energy of the amino acid i with respect to a dihedral class Φ_i/Ψ_i can be expressed as

$$\Delta\mathrm{E}(i, \Phi_i, \Psi_i) = -RT \frac{N_{obs}(i, \Phi_i, \Psi_i)}{\ln \sum_{\Phi_i, \Psi_i} N_{obs}(i, \Phi_i, \Psi_i)/N_{bin}^2} \quad (5\text{-}34)$$

where Φ_i and Ψ_i are the dihedral angles at interaction center i, R is the gas const and T is the temperature. The dihedral potential is the logarithm of the number of observed occurrences of the interaction center type i at the dihedral angles of $\Phi/\Psi [N_{obs}(i, \Phi_i, \Psi_i)]$ normalized by the averaged occurrence. Each dihedral angle is divided into 36 bins. That is, N_{bin} is equal to 36. The total potential for any protein or decoy can be obtained by adding up all its amino acids' energies.

There are 20 standard amino acids and 36*36 dihedral bins, so the length of the potential vector is 25,920 (20*36*36) for the corresponding nonlinear potentials. A potential vector is obtained by first simply counting the occurrence of each specific amino acid in the dihedral bin and then normalizing the vector by the length of the protein.

The DFIRE-SCM potential: The DFIRE-SCM potential[104] is a two-body residue-level Boltzmann-based potential. The energy of two interaction amino acids (i, j) at distance r is given by:

$$\Delta E\left(i, j, r\right) = \begin{cases} -\eta RT \ln \dfrac{N_{obs}(i, j, r)}{\left(\frac{r}{r_{cut}}\right)^{\alpha} (\Delta r / \Delta r_{cut}) / N_{obs}(i, j, r_{cut})} & r < r_{cut} \\ \qquad\qquad 0 & r \geq r_{cut} \end{cases}$$

$$(5\text{-}35)$$

where $\eta (= 0.0157)$ is a scaling constant, $N_{obs}(i, j, r)$ is the number of interaction pairs (i, j) within the distance shell r observed in a given structure database, $r_{cut} = 14.5\,\text{Å}$, and $\Delta r(\Delta r_{cut})$ is the bin width at $r(r_{cut})$. ($\Delta r = 2\,\text{Å}$, for $r < 2\,\text{Å}$; $\Delta r = 0.5\,\text{Å}$ for $2\,\text{Å} < r < 8\,\text{Å}$; $\Delta r = 1\,\text{Å}$ for $8\,\text{Å} < r < 15\,\text{Å}$). The exponent α is obtained from the distance dependence of the pair distribution function of uniformly distributed points in finite spheres (finite ideal-gas reference state) and is set to 1.61. The interaction center is taken as the centroid of the side chain for each residue.

The DFIRE-SCM potential is a typical Boltzmann-based potential at the residue level. Its main advantage over other residue-level Boltzmann-based potentials is the reference state, which is a distance-scaled, finite ideal-gas reference state. This potential can reach a similar performance to that of the DFIRE all-atom Boltzmann-based potential[117] and even outperforms other Boltzmann-based potentials at the atom level, such as the RAPDF potential[171] and the KBP potential.[116]

In total, there are 210 (20*20/2) interaction pairs and 20 distance bins, so the length of the vector of the DFIRE-SCM potential is 4200 (210*20).

The FS potential: The FS potential[172] is a two-body atom-level Boltzmann-based potential. The energy of interaction between a pair of atoms (i, j) at distance bin r is given by:

$$\Delta E(i, j, r) = -RT \ln \frac{N_{obs}(i, j, r)}{N(i, j) * \left(0.5 * \left(\frac{N(i, r)}{N(i)} + N(j, r)/N(j)\right)\right)},$$

$$(5\text{-}36)$$

where $N_{obs}(ijr)$ is the observed number of interaction pairs (i, j) within the distance bin r. The reference state in the denominator is calculated by the number of all interaction pairs $N(i, j)$ times the average fraction of atoms of types i and j that interact with any atom within that distance interval.

There are 30 atom types,[172] so the number of interaction pairs is 465 (30*31/2). Two atoms are regarded as being in contact if the surface distance between them is less than 4 Å. The width of the distance bin is set to 0.2, which results in 20 bins. Thus, the length of a potential vector is 9300 (465*20).

The HRSC potential: The HRSC potential is a two-body residue-level linear potential.[106] The energy of each structure is evaluated by the arithmetic sum of pairwise interactions corresponding to each amino acid combination at a particular contact distance. Two amino acids are regarded as in contact if the distance between the centers of the side-chains is less than 9 Å. The energy of each interaction is a function of distance and the identity of the interacting amino acids. The interaction distance between 3 Å and 9 Å is divided into 7 bins. The length of a potential vector is 1470 (210*7). The potential parameters are optimized against a large set of high resolution decoys using a linear programming method. One basic requirement is that the energy of a native structure should be lower than that of its decoys. Additionally, another set of constraints based on physical properties is also introduced such as the hydrophobic–hydrophobic constraints and the charged group constraints. This type of potential is an improvement over the previous HR potential, which takes the C_α atom as the interaction center.[83]

The T32S3 potential: The T32S3 potential is a two-body atom-level linear potential,[114] which is also derived by the linear programming method. The interaction type is at the level of the atom, rather than the residue. Two atoms are regarded as being in contact if the distance between them is less than 6.5 Å and larger than 2 Å. Such a distance range is divided into three bins. The atom types are grouped into 32 classes. The length of a potential vector is 1584 (32*33*3/2). The potential parameters are also optimized against a large set of decoys.

5.6.1.4 *Performance metrics*

The potential functions are evaluated using four criteria, which are as follows:

(1) Accuracy: The fraction of the proteins whose native structures are ranked as 1 on a decoy set.
(2) Rank: The rank of the native structures in the list of decoys sorted by energies.
(3) Z-score: the Z-score of a native structure in a decoy set is defined as

$$Z - \text{Score} = |\langle E^{decoy} \rangle - E^{native}| \Big/ \sqrt{\langle (E^{decoy})^2 \rangle - \langle E^{decoy} \rangle^2}$$

(5-37)

where $\langle \rangle$ denotes the average overall decoy structure, and E^{native} is the energy of the native structure. Z-score is a measure of the bias toward the native structure.

(4) The Pearson correlation coefficient (CC) between energy (x) and RMSD (y), which is defined as:

$$(\text{CC}) = \frac{\sum_{i=1}^{M} (x_i - \bar{x})(y_i - \bar{y})}{\sqrt{\left[\sum_{i=1}^{M} (x_i - \bar{x})^2\right]\left[\sum_{i=1}^{M} (y_i - \bar{y})^2\right]}}$$

(5-38)

where M is the total number of decoys of a specified protein.

5.6.2 Results

5.6.2.1 *Performance on the decoy sets*

Five knowledge-based mean force Boltzmann-based or linear potentials are introduced and the corresponding nonlinear potentials are implemented. These potentials are the DIH potential,[96] the DFIRE-SCM potential,[104] the FS potential,[172] the HRSC potential[106] and the T32S3 potential.[114] They cover various potential types, and also are both residue-level potentials and atom-level potentials, and also single-body potentials and two-body potentials. The potential parameters of the first three Boltzmann-based potentials are calculated from the PDB25 dataset,[173] which is a non-redundant dataset containing proteins that have resolutions better than 2.5 Å and that share no more than 25% sequence identity with each other. The parameters of the other two linear potentials are taken from the supplementary materials of the Refs. [106] and [114]. The interaction centers and the distance partition of the nonlinear potentials are the same as those of the Boltzmann-based or linear potentials, so the potential vectors are just the same. The only difference between the nonlinear potentials and other potentials is that the nonlinear potentials have nonlinear discriminative functions while the Boltzmann-based and linear potentials are all in the form of a weighted linear sum of the components of the potential vectors.

Three datasets including the LKF dataset,[121] the CASP7 dataset[160] and the Decoys 'R' Us dataset[161] are used to evaluate the performance of the nonlinear potentials in comparison with the corresponding Boltzmann-based or linear potentials. These datasets are well constructed and have been widely used to evaluate various potentials. Statistical information regarding these datasets is provided in Table 5-14.

The performance of the potentials on the LKF dataset is listed in Table 5-15. A fourfold cross-validation is employed to test the potential functions. All of the 161 proteins are randomly divided into four groups, in which three groups and their associated decoy structures are used for training and the other group is used for testing. The Boltzmann-based or linear potentials show different results since they differ from each other in the definition of the interaction pairs, the distance partition, the training datasets and the training methods. Surprisingly, the simplest DIH potential, which is a single-body residue-level Boltzmann-based potential, can

Table 5-14   Summary of the decoy sets.

Dataset	Number of proteins	Lengths	Number of decoy structures per protein	RMSD(Å)[a]
LKF	161	32–147	52–200	1.463–43.405 (10.061±2.979)
CASP7	61	42–526	254–465	0.432–225.977 (10.004±5.631)
4state_reduced	7	54–75	629–685	0.805–9.391 (5.209±1.687)
fisa	4	43–76	500–500	2.769–14.130 (7.548±2.2049)
fisa_casp3	5	71–114	971–2411	3.627–20.870 (11.879±1.898)
lattice_ssfit	8	55–98	1994–2000	4.742–15.608 (9.888±1.253)
lmds	10	31–68	214–499	2.446–13.476 (7.747±1.417)
semfold	6	56–95	10000–21080	2.982–15.065 (10.357±1.665)

Notes: [a]RMSD is the C_α Root Mean Square Deviation. Given in brackets are the average and the standard deviation.

Table 5-15   Comparative performance on the LKF dataset.

Potentials[a]	Accuracy	Rank	Z	CC
T32S3_NL	0.988	1.05	32.732	0.236
FS_NL	0.988	1.229	14.787	0.272
HRSC_NL	0.9501	1.317	7.715	0.213
DFIRE-SCM_NL	0.938	2.112	7.502	0.287
DIH_NL	0.932	3.283	8.292	0.169
DFIRE-SCM	0.857	4.981	6.484	0.247
DIH	0.789	9.82	3.754	0.111
T32S3	0.733	7.043	4.824	0.217
HRSC	0.671	8.764	3.798	0.161
FS	0.652	47.348	3.494	0.242

Note: [a]The potentials with the _NL suffix indicate the corresponding nonlinear potentials.

achieve satisfactory results with an accuracy of 0.789. As can be seen, all nonlinear potentials perform better than the corresponding Boltzmann-based or linear potentials. Especially, the two atom-level nonlinear potentials (FS_NL and T32S3_NL) achieve nearly perfect discrimination of the native structures from the decoy structures and obtain large Z-scores (14.787 and 32.732, respectively).

Table 5-16   Comparative performance on the CASP7 dataset.

Potentials	Accuracy	Rank	Z	CC
T32S3_NL	0.772	9.546	3.526	0.332
FS_NL	0.705	26.231	3.066	0.463
T32S3	0.541	17.082	2.17	0.557
DFIRE-SCM	0.525	20.18	1.94	0.546
DFIRE-SCM_NL	0.524	14.734	2.506	0.473
FS	0.508	11.426	1.678	0.234
HRSC_NL	0.438	9.167	2.752	0.386
DIH_NL	0.231	41.654	2.648	0.094
DIH	0.197	29.771	1.269	0.195
HRSC	0.033	74.377	0.981	0.525

CASP7 dataset: Because the CASP7 dataset contains a relatively small number of proteins, a five-fold cross-validation is used to test the potential functions. The results are given in Table 5-16. All the potentials achieve worse results than that obtained using the LKF dataset. This may be caused by the large RMSD range, which varies from 0.432 Å to 225.977 Å in the CASP7 dataset. Besides DFIRE-SCM, the residue-level potentials (DIH and HRSC) get unsatisfactory results with accuracies no higher than 25%. Better performance is observed from the atom-level potentials (FS and T32S3). Again, all the nonlinear potentials outperform the corresponding Boltzmann-based or linear potentials. The HRSC potential gets the worst results, and nearly no native structure has been identified. As pointed out by the authors,[106] this potential is trained on a high-resolution dataset with RMSD less than 8 Å, so it cannot perform well on the datasets that contain far-native decoys.

Decoys 'R' Us dataset: Six subsets are used to evaluate the potential functions. Since there are only a few proteins in each subset, the KLF dataset and CASP7 dataset are merged to produce the training samples, and the trained classifiers are used to test the nonlinear potentials on each subset. The proposed method is also compared with the recently developed contact-count and count-type potentials.[174] The results are given in Table 5-17. Overall, the nonlinear potentials still outperform the corresponding

Table 5-17 Comparative performance on the Decoys 'R' Us dataset.

Potentials	4state_reduced	fisa	fisa_casp3	lattice_ssfit	lmds	semfold
DIH	6/7(2.671)[a]	2/4(1.420)	1/5(1.975)	6/8(3.500)	7/10(1.609)	1/6(0.229)
DIH_NL	5/7(3.556)	2/4(2.205)	2/5(1.377)	7/8(3.899)	7/10(3.367)	1/6(4.813)
DFIRE-SCM	4/7(3.564)	4/4(4.857)	5/5(5.473)	8/8(5.797)	4/10(2.378)	3/6(3.580)
DFIRE-SCM_NL	6/7(3.850)	3/4(3.413)	3/5(3.616)	6/8(4.016)	7/10(1.503)	1/6(2.452)
FS	6/7(2.933)	2/4(2.147)	4/5(5.421)	8/8(4.257)	4/10(2.745)	2/6(2.342)
FS_NL	6/7(3.866)	1/4(3.072)	3/5(3.726)	7/8(4.136)	6/10(1.673)	2/6(2.587)
HRSC	1/7(2.083)	3/4(3.672)	2/5(2.335)	0/8(2.193)	4/10(2.879)	0/6(1.700)
HRSC_NL	5/7(3.549)	3/4(1.927)	3/5(3.727)	5/8(3.845)	5/10(2.572)	1/6(2.210)
T32S3	4/7(3.564)	2/4(2.272)	3/5(3.689)	8/8(6.441)	7/10(3.609)	5/6(4.419)
T32S3_NL	5/7(2.941)	3/4(5.388)	4/5(4.502)	8/8(5.149)	7/10(4.131)	1/6(2.532)
Contact-count[b]	1.94	2.59	1.43	3.36	1.72	—
Contact-type[b]	2.51	1.36	0.03	3.76	0.86	—

Notes: [a]Given are the number of correctly identified proteins in the total number of proteins and the energy Z-scores; [b]Shown in the table are the Z-scores taken from Ref. [174].

Boltzmann-based or linear potentials. Since this is an open test, the amount of performance improvement of the nonlinear potentials on this dataset in comparison with the Boltzmann-based or linear potentials is less than that on the KLF and CASP7 datasets. Even some nonlinear potentials perform worse than the Boltzmann-based or linear potentials. The contact-count potential is a single-body residue-level Boltzmann-based potential, while the contact-type potential is a two-body residue-level Boltzmann-based potential. On average, their performances are comparable with that of the DIH and DFIRE-SCM potentials, but worse than that of the nonlinear potentials.

5.6.2.2 *Analysis of the misclassified proteins*

Another experiment is done to investigate why the native proteins are misclassified. The FS_NL potentials tested on the CASP7 dataset are selected as representatives. There are 18 proteins whose native structures have not been recognized. The Euclidean distances between the vectors of the 18 proteins and the support vector involved in the kernel design scoring function are calculated. There are only a few native support vectors within the top 1000 nearest neighbors of the failed protein, so all misclassifications are due to the fact that the native vectors are too close to the decoys.

5.6.3 Discussion

5.6.3.1 *The performance of nonlinear potentials is better than that of the Boltzmann-based or linear potentials*

One basic requirement for protein structure prediction is an effective potential function, which is used to search and identify native or near-native conformations. The work in this study follows the previous work, including that of Wu *et al.*[164] and Rajgaria *et al.*,[83] with the aim to develop powerful knowledge-based mean-force potentials. There are many ways to improve the potential functions, such as the introduction of multi-body interactions,[175] the usage of local sequence–structure descriptors,[124] the optimization of reference states,[117] the incorporation of information from decoy structures,[120] etc.

Potential functions using a weighted linear combination of interaction pairs have been shown to be inadequate in discriminating native structures from a large number of decoys.[119] In this study, a novel discriminative framework is proposed for developing empirical protein scoring functions, with the goal of simultaneously characterizing the fitness landscapes of many proteins. A kernel function is introduced to map protein vectors to another high-dimensional space, so that the linearly inseparable problem can be transformed into a separable one. The optimization criterion is to maximize the separation distance between the native protein vectors and the decoy vectors in the transformed high-dimensional space. Such an optimal criterion has its foundation in statistical learning theory, where the expected error of classification of new test data is minimized by balancing the minimization of the training error (or empirical risk) and the control of the capacities of specific types of scoring functions.

Because of the intrinsic superiority of the nonlinear classifiers, the nonlinear potentials perform better than the corresponding Boltzmann-based or linear potentials. Such a conclusion is drawn by testing on several datasets and using different potential types, all of which together indicate that nonlinear classifiers are a powerful tool to develop effective knowledge-based mean force potentials. Some other authors have also used a similar idea for developing the empirical functions of proteins. Hu *et al.*[118] adopted an SVM to develop protein design scores. Zhang *et al.*[124] adopted an SVM to develop empirical potentials for simplified protein models. However, these existing studies considered only one type of descriptor for proteins. In this study, we explore several well-established mean force potentials, including both atom-level potentials and residue-level potentials as well as single-body potentials and two-body potentials. Our extensive experiments have demonstrated that, in general, the nonlinear potentials outperform the corresponding Boltzmann-based or linear potentials.

5.6.3.2 *Factors that influence the performance of the mean force potentials*

Five knowledge-based mean force potentials are explored in this study. The performance is different since they adopt different representations of protein structures and different definitions of force fields. A thorough analysis is needed to reveal the essence of knowledge-based mean force potentials.

Overall, the atom-level potentials (FS and T32S3) outperform the residue-level potentials (DIH, DFIRE-SCM and HRSC). This may be attributed to the fact that the whole atoms can give a better description of protein structures than the residues alone can do. For the residue-level potentials, each residue in a protein is represented by one or two points in three-dimensional space. These points are usually located at the coordinates of each residue's C_α atoms or C_β atoms or at the coordinates of the center of each side chain. Such coarse-grained representation may lead to the missing of some important information regarding protein structures. As a result, the atom-level potentials can provide better discriminatory power than the residue-level potentials.[113, 114, 116, 171, 173] Such a conclusion is also valid for the nonlinear potentials. All the experimental results in this study show that the nonlinear potentials at the atom level outperform those at the residue-level.

The reference state has an important impact on the Boltzmann-based potentials. Most researchers adopted the "uniform density" reference state originally proposed by Sippl,[111] where the expected number of occurrences within a certain distance interval is the number of average overall interaction pairs. Some other researchers used the "quasi-chemical approximation",[172] in which the statistical likelihood of forming a chance encounter is estimated by the total number of interactions times the mole fraction of the interaction pairs. The newly developed "finite ideal-gas" reference state can improve the knowledge-based mean force potentials for structure selection and stability prediction.[104, 117] To give an unbiased comparison, the DFIRE-SCM force field is used to derive three types of potentials, namely DFIRE-SCM_UD, DFIRE-SCM_QC and

Table 5-18   Results of the DFIRE-SCM potential using three reference states.

Datasets	DFIRE-SCM_UD[a]	DFIRE-SCM_QC	DFIRE-SCM_FI
LKF	113/161(3.482)[b]	107/161(3.095)	138/161(6.484)
CASP7	36/61(2.395)	31/61(2.383)	32(1.9357)
4state_reduced	6/7(3.489)	5/7(3.434)	7/7(3.952)
Fisa	1/4(2.190)	1/4(2.425)	2/4(4.554)
fisa_casp3	3/5(3.637)	3/5(3.317)	5/5(5.473)
lattice_ssfit	7/8(5.393)	7/8(5.301)	8/8(5.7968)
Lmds	3/10(1.669)	2/10(1.199)	4/10(2.378)
Semfold	3/6(3.234)	2/6(3.107)	3/6(3.580)

Notes: [a]The potentials with _UD, _QC and _FI suffixes refer to the potentials that take the "Uniform Density", "Quasi-Chemical approximation" and "Finite Ideal-gas" as the reference state, respectively; [b]Given are the number of correctly identified proteins in the total number of proteins and the energy Z-scores (in brackets).

DFIRE-SCM_FI, each of which takes "Uniform Density", "Quasi-Chemical approximation" and "Finite Ideal-gas" as the reference state. The potential parameters are computed on the PDB25 dataset. The three potentials are tested on several datasets, and the results are given in the Table 5-18. As can be seen, the DFIRE-SCM_FI potentials have the best performance, which means that the finite ideal-gas reference state is superior to the other two reference states.

The residue-level potentials usually use one-point representation for the residues. The point location is a critical factor to mean-force potentials. The side-chain-based representation is usually better than that based on the C_α atom only. Some other researchers also found a similar phenomenon. Zhang *et al.*[104] have shown that the all-atom knowledge-based potentials (167 atomic types) based on distance-scaled, finite ideal-gas reference states can be substantially simplified to 20 residue types located at the side-chain center of mass without a significant change in their capability of structure discrimination. Rajgaria *et al.*[106] developed a linear potential based on side-chain representation and demonstrated that such a potential outperforms the linear potentials based on C_α representation.

Although minor, other factors also influence knowledge-based mean-force potentials, such as interaction pair, distance interval, distance cutoff, etc. To save space, we do not go into a detailed discussion here.

5.6.3.3 *The correlation between energy and RMSD*

The percentage of correctly detected native proteins provides useful but incomplete information of the energy function. A good potential should assign low scores to the near-native decoy structures and high scores to the far-from-native decoy structures, so that the energy landscape can be fully depicted. The correlation between energy and RMSD is widely used to evaluate this property of the potential.

However, the nonlinear potentials in this study aim to discriminate native proteins from a large number of decoy structures. All the decoy structures are assigned a label of 1 when training. No information about the difference of decoy structures with regard to RMSD is included during the training process, so a high correlation between energy score and RMSD is not expected for the nonlinear potentials. Even so, the correlation between energy score and RMSD of the nonlinear potentials is comparable with or even better than that of the Boltzmann-based or linear potentials. Figure 5-10 shows some cases that have high correlations when using the nonlinear potentials. The test samples are taken from the CASP7 dataset.

5.7 Conclusions

This chapter examines issues related to protein structure prediction, including protein domain boundaries, protein local structures and knowledge-based potential energy functions. For protein domain linker prediction, a novel index at the profile level is presented, namely, the Profile Domain Linker propensity Index (PDLI), which uses the evolutionary information of profiles for domain linker prediction. Frequency profiles are directly calculated from the multiple sequence alignments outputted by PSI-BLAST and converted into binary profiles with a probability threshold. PDLI is then obtained by the frequencies of binary profiles in domain linkers as compared to those in domains. A smooth and normalized

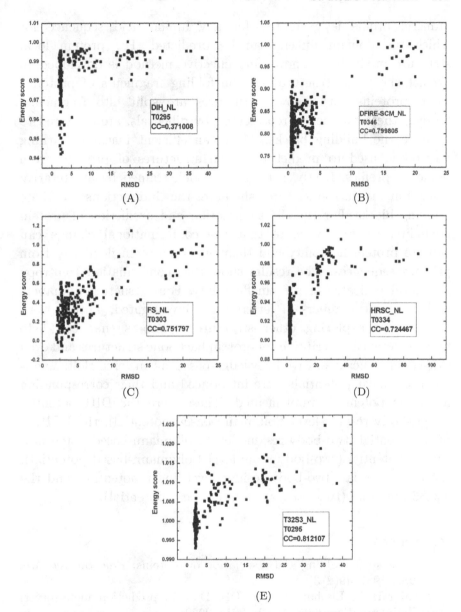

Figure 5-10   Some results of correlation between RMSD and energy score. (A–E) show the RMSD-energy plots for the DIH_NL, DFIRE-SCM_NL, FS_NL, HRSC_NL and T32S3_NL potentials, respectively.

numeric profile is generated for any amino acid sequence for which the domain linkers can be predicted. For protein local structure prediction, a novel and effective method is developed to predict the local structure and the folding fragments of proteins. First, proteins with known structures are split into fragments. Second, these fragments, represented by dihedrals, are clustered to produce the building blocks. Third, an efficient machine learning method is used to predict the local structures of proteins from sequence profiles. Lastly, a bi-gram model, trained by an iterative algorithm, is introduced to simulate the interactions of these building blocks. For the characterization and prediction of protein flexibility, we first validate that the conformational change can capture protein flexibility and then predict protein flexibility from primary sequences. The results show that conformational entropy is a good indicator of protein flexibility. Four structure alphabets with different numbers of letters were investigated. Future work will aim at exploring other structure alphabets that can help provide detailed descriptions of protein backbone structures and even side-chain structures. Five knowledge-based mean force Boltzmann-based or linear potentials were introduced and their corresponding nonlinear potentials implemented. These were the DIH potential (single-body residue-level Boltzmann-based potential), the DFIRE-SCM potential (two-body residue-level Boltzmann-based potential), the FS potential (two-body atom-level Boltzmann-based potential), the HR potential (two-body residue-level linear potential) and the T32S3 potential (two-body atom-level linear potential).

References

[1] Jaenicke R. Folding and association of proteins. *Prog Biophys Mol Biol*, 1987, 49(2–3): 117–237.
[2] Saini H.K., Fischer D. Meta-DP: Domain prediction meta-server. *Bioinformatics*, 2005, 21(12): 2917–2920.
[3] Wen Z.N., Wang K.L., Li M.L., Nie F.S., Yang Y. Analyzing functional similarity of protein sequences with discrete wavelet transform. *Comput Biol Chem*, 2005, 29(3): 220–228.

[4] Nikitin F., Lisacek F. Investigating protein domain combinations in complete proteomes. *Comput Biol Chem*, 2003, 27(4–5): 481–495.

[5] Xiao J.F., Li Z.S., Sun M., Zhang Y., Sun C.C. Homology modeling and molecular dynamics study of GSK3/SHAGGY-like kinase. *Comput Biol Chem*, 2004, 28(3): 179–188.

[6] Busetta B., Barrans Y. The prediction of protein domains. *Biochim Biophys Acta*, 1984, 790(2): 117–124.

[7] Kikuchi T., Nemethy G., Scheraga H.A. Prediction of the location of structural domains in globular proteins. *J Protein Chem*, 1988, 7(4): 427–471.

[8] Gouzy J., Corpet F., Kahn D. Whole genome protein domain analysis using a new method for domain clustering. *Comput Chem*, 1999, 23(3–4): 333–340.

[9] Ponting C.P., Schultz J., Milpetz F., Bork P. SMART: Identification and annotation of domains from signalling and extracellular protein sequences. *Nucleic Acids Res*, 1999, 27(1): 229–232.

[10] Miyazaki S., Kuroda Y., Yokoyama S. Characterization and prediction of linker sequences of multi-domain proteins by a neural network. *J Struct Funct Genomics*, 2002, 2(1): 37–51.

[11] Corpet F., Servant F., Gouzy J., Kahn D. ProDom and ProDom-CG: Tools for protein domain analysis and whole genome comparisons. *Nucleic Acids Res*, 2000, 28(1): 267–269.

[12] Boeckmann B., Bairoch A., Apweiler R., Blatter M.C., Estreicher A., Gasteiger E., Martin M.J., Michoud K., O'Donovan C., Phan I., Pilbout S., Schneider M. The Swiss-Prot protein knowledge base and its supplement TrEMBL in 2003. *Nucleic Acids Res*, 2003, 31(1): 365–370.

[13] George R.A., Heringa J. Protein domain identification and improved sequence similarity searching using PSI-BLAST. *Proteins*, 2002, 48(4): 672–681.

[14] Altschul S.F., Madden T.L., Schaffer A.A., Zhang J.H., Zhang Z., Miller W., Lipman D.J. Gapped Blast and Psi-blast: A new generation of protein database search programs. *Nucleic Acids Res*, 1997, 25(17): 3389–3402.

[15] Liu J.F., Rost B. CHOP proteins into structural domain-like fragments. *Proteins*, 2004, 55(3): 678–688.

[16] Sim J., Kim S.Y., Lee J. PPRODO: prediction of protein domain boundaries using neural networks. *Proteins*, 2005, 59(3): 627–632.

[17] Wheelan S.J., Marchler-Bauer A., Bryant S.H. Domain size distributions can predict domain boundaries. *Bioinformatics*, 2000, 16(7): 613–618.

154   *Biological Language Model: Theory and Application*

[18] George R.A., Heringa J. SnapDRAGON: A method to delineate protein structural domains from sequence data. *J Mol Biol*, 2002, 16(3): 839–851.

[19] Aszodi A., Gradwell M.J., Taylor W.R. Global fold determination from a small number of distance restraints. *J Mol Biol*, 1995, 251(2): 308–326.

[20] Nagarajan N., Yona G. Automatic prediction of protein domains from sequence information using a hybrid learning system. *Bioinformatics*, 2004, 20(9): 1335–1360.

[21] Dumontier M., Yao R., Feldman H.J., Hogue C.W. Armadillo: domain boundary prediction by amino acid composition. *J Mol Biol*, 2005, 350(5): 1061–1073.

[22] George R.A., Heringa J. An analysis of protein domain linkers: their classification and role in protein folding. *Protein Eng*, 2002, 15(11): 871–879.

[23] Suyama M., Ohara O. DomCut: Prediction of inter-domain linker regions in amino acid sequences. *Bioinformatics*, 2003, 19(5): 673–674.

[24] Galzitskaya O.V., Melnik B.S. Prediction of protein domain boundaries from sequence alone. *Protein Sci*, 2003, 12(4): 696–701.

[25] Kyte J., Doolittle R.F. A simple method for displaying the hydropathic character of a protein. *J Mol Biol*, 1982, 157(1): 105–132.

[26] Tanaka T., Kuroda Y., Yokoyama S. Characteristics and prediction of domain linker sequences in multidomain proteins. *J Struct Funct Genomics*, 2003, 4(2–3): 79–85.

[27] Kyounghwa B., Bani K.M., Christine G.E. Prediction of protein inter-domain linker regions by a hidden Markov model. *Bioinformatics*, 2005, 21(10): 2264–2270.

[28] Udwary D.W., Merski M., Townsend C.A. A method for prediction of linker regions within large multifunctional proteins, and its application to a type I polyketide synthase. *J Mol Biol*, 2002, 323(3): 585–598.

[29] Bystroff C., Baker D. Prediction of local structure in proteins using a library of sequence-structure motifs. *J Mol Biol*, 1998, 281(3): 565–577.

[30] Bystroff C., Shao Y. Fully automated *ab initio* protein structure prediction using I-SITES, HMMSTR and ROSETTA. *Bioinformatics*, 2002, 18(Suppl 1): S54–S61.

[31] Bystroff C., Thorsson V., Baker D. HMMSTR: A hidden Markov model for local sequence-structure correlations in proteins. *J Mol Biol*, 2000, 301(1): 173–190.

[32] Hou Y., Hsu W., Lee M.L., Bystroff C. Efficient remote homology detection using local structure. *Bioinformatics*, 2003, 19(17): 2294–2301.

[33] Hou Y., Hsu W., Lee M.L., Bystroff C. Remote homolog detection using local sequence-structure correlations. *Proteins*, 2004, 57(3): 518–530.

[34] Tang T., Xu J., Li M. Discovering sequence-structure motifs from protein segments and two applications. *Pac Symp Biocomput*, 2005: 370–381.

[35] Martin J., Gibrat J.F., Rodolphe F. Analysis of an optimal hidden Markov model for secondary structure prediction. *BMC Struct Biol*, 2006, 6: 25.

[36] Dor O., Zhou Y. Achieving 80% ten-fold cross-validated accuracy for secondary structure prediction by large-scale training. *Proteins*, 2006, 66(4): 838–845.

[37] Simons K.T., Bonneau R., Ruczinski I., Baker D. *Ab initio* protein structure prediction of CASP III targets using ROSETTA. *Proteins*, 1999, Suppl 3: 171–176.

[38] Camproux A.C., Tuffery P., Chevrolat J.P., Boisvieux J.F., Hazout S. Hidden Markov model approach for identifying the modular framework of the protein backbone. *Protein Eng*, 1999, 12(12): 1063–1073.

[39] Camproux A.C., Gautier R., Tuffery P. A hidden Markov model derived structural alphabet for proteins. *J Mol Biol*, 2004, 339(3): 591–605.

[40] Guyon F., Camproux A.C., Hochez J., Tuffery P. SA-Search: A web tool for protein structure mining based on a Structural Alphabet. *Nucleic Acids Res*, 2004, 32(Web Server issue): W545–W548.

[41] de Brevern A.G., Etchebest C., Hazout S. Bayesian probabilistic approach for predicting backbone structures in terms of protein blocks. *Proteins*, 2000, 41(3): 271–287.

[42] Etchebest C., Benros C., Hazout S., de Brevern A.G. A structural alphabet for local protein structures: Improved prediction methods. *Proteins*, 2005, 59(4): 810–827.

[43] Benros C., de Brevern A.G., Etchebest C., Hazout S. Assessing a novel approach for predicting local 3D protein structures from sequence. *Proteins*, 2006, 62(4): 865–880.

[44] Karchin R., Cline M., Karplus K. Evaluation of local structure alphabets based on residue burial. *Proteins*, 2004, 55(3): 508–518.

[45] Tyagi M., Gowri V.S., Srinivasan N., de Brevern A.G., Offmann B. A substitution matrix for structural alphabet based on structural alignment of homologous proteins and its applications. *Proteins*, 2006, 65(1): 32–39.

[46] Yang J.M., Tung C.H. Protein structure database search and evolutionary classification. *Nucleic Acids Res*, 2006, 34(13): 3646–3659.

[47] Tyagi M., Sharma P., Swamy C.S., Cadet F., Srinivasan N., de Brevern A.G., Offmann B. Protein Block Expert (PBE): A web-based protein structure analysis server using a structural alphabet. *Nucleic Acids Res*, 2006, 34(Web Server issue): W119–W123.

[48] Hunter C.G., Subramaniam S. Protein local structure prediction from sequence. *Proteins*, 2003, 50(4): 572–579.

[49] Pei J., Grishin N.V. Combining evolutionary and structural information for local protein structure prediction. *Proteins*, 2004, 56(4): 782–794.

[50] Sander O., Sommer I., Lengauer T. Local protein structure prediction using discriminative models. *BMC Bioinfo*, 2006, 7(1): 14.

[51] Chen C.T., Lin H.N., Sung T.Y., Hsu W.L. HYPLOSP: A knowledge-based approach to protein local structure prediction. *J Bioinform Comput Biol*, 2006, 4(6): 1287–1307.

[52] Dong Q.W., Wang X.L., Lin L. Analysis and prediction of protein local structure based on structure alphabets. *Proteins*, 2008, 72(1): 163–172.

[53] Boden M., Bailey T.L. Identifying sequence regions undergoing conformational change via predicted continuum secondary structure. *Bioinformatics*, 2006, 22(15): 1809–1814.

[54] Li J., Cai J., Su H., Du H., Zhang J., Ding S., Liu G., Tang Y., Li W. Effects of protein flexibility and active site water molecules on the prediction of sites of metabolism for cytochrome P450 2C19 substrates. *Mol Biosyst*, 2016, 12(3): 868–878.

[55] Manoharan P., Chennoju K., Ghoshal N. Target specific proteochemometric model development for BACE1 — Protein flexibility and structural water are critical in virtual screening. *Mol Biosyst*, 2015, 11(7): 1955–1972.

[56] Dunker A.K., Brown C.J., Lawson J.D., Iakoucheva L.M., Obradovic Z. Intrinsic disorder and protein function. *Biochemistry*, 2002, 41(21): 6573–6582.

[57] Dyson H.J., Wright P.E. Coupling of folding and binding for unstructured proteins. *Curr Opin Struct Biol*, 2002, 12(1): 54–60.

[58] Antunes D.A., Devaurs D., Kavraki L.E. Understanding the challenges of protein flexibility in drug design. *Expert Opin Drug Discov*, 2015, 10(12): 1301–1313.

[59] Feng Z., Hu X. Recognition of 27-class protein folds by adding the interaction of segments and motif information. *BioMed Res Int*, 2014, 2014: 9.

[60] Chen J., Liu B., Huang D. Protein remote homology detection based on an ensemble learning approach. *Bio Med Res Int*, 2016, 2016: 11.

[61] Petrovich A., Borne A., Uversky V.N., Xue B. Identifying similar patterns of structural flexibility in proteins by disorder prediction and dynamic programming. *Int J Mol Sci*, 2015, 16(6): 13829–13849.

[62] Sonavane S., Jaybhaye A.A., Jadhav A.G. Prediction of temperature factors from protein sequence. *Bioinformation*, 2013, 9(3): 134–140.

[63] Yuan Z., Bailey T.L., Teasdale R.D. Prediction of protein B-factor profiles. *Proteins*, 2005, 58(4): 905–912.

[64] Schlessinger A., Rost B. Protein flexibility and rigidity predicted from sequence. *Proteins*, 2005, 61(1): 115–126.

[65] Radivojac P., Obradovic Z., Smith D.K., Zhu G., Vucetic S., Brown C.J., Lawson J.D., Dunker A.K. Protein flexibility and intrinsic disorder. *Protein Sci*, 2004, 13(1): 71–80.

[66] Alexandrov V., Lehnert U., Echols N., Milburn D., Engelman D., Gerstein M. Normal modes for predicting protein motions: A comprehensive database assessment and associated Web tool. *Protein Sci*, 2005, 14(3): 633–643.

[67] Krebs W.G., Alexandrov V., Wilson C.A., Echols N., Yu H., Gerstein M. Normal mode analysis of macromolecular motions in a database framework: Developing mode concentration as a useful classifying statistic. *Proteins*, 2002, 48(4): 682–695.

[68] Kuriyan J., Weis W.I. Rigid protein motion as a model for crystallographic temperature factors. *Proc Natl Acad Sci USA*, 1991, 88(7): 2773–2777.

[69] Haliloglu T., Bahar I. Gaussian dynamics of folded proteins. *Phys Rev Lett*, 1997, 79(1616): 3090–3093.

[70] Yang J., Wang Y., Zhang Y. ResQ: An approach to unified estimation of B-factor and residue-specific error in protein structure prediction. *J Mol Biol*, 2016, 428(4): 693–701.

[71] Kovacs J.A., Chacon P., Abagyan R. Predictions of protein flexibility: First-order measures. *Proteins*, 2004, 56(4): 661–668.

[72] Xia K., Wei G.W. Stochastic model for protein flexibility analysis. *Phys Rev E Stat Nonlin Soft Matter Phys*, 2013, 88(6): 062709.

[73] Gu Y., Li D.W., Bruschweiler R. Decoding the mobility and time scales of protein loops. *J Chem Theory Comput*, 2015, 11(3): 1308–1314.

[74] Drenth J. *Principles of Protein Crystallography*. 1994. New York, NY: Springer-Verlag.

[75] Tronrud D.E. Knowledge-based B-factor restraints for the refinement of proteins. *J Appl Crystallogr*, 1996, 29(2): 100–104.

[76] Sharma A., Manolakos E.S. Efficient multicriteria protein structure comparison on modern processor architectures. *Bio Med Res Int*, 2015, 2015: 13.

[77] Andersen C.A., Palmer A.G., Brunak S., Rost B. Continuum secondary structure captures protein flexibility. *Structure*, 2002, 10(2): 175–184.

[78] Flores S., Echols N., Milburn D., Hespenheide B., Keating K., Lu J., Wells S., Yu E.Z., Thorpe M., Gerstein M. The Database of Macromolecular Motions: New features added at the decade mark. *Nucleic Acids Res*, 2006, 34(Database issue): D296–D301.

[79] Krebs W.G., Gerstein M. The morph server: A standardized system for analyzing and visualizing macromolecular motions in a database framework. *Nucleic Acids Res*, 2000, 28(8): 1665–1675.

[80] Cristian M., Flavio S., R. B.J., Amos M. Learning effective amino acid interactions through iterative stochastic techniques. *Proteins*, 2001, 42(3): 422–431.

[81] Anfinsen C.B. Principles that govern the folding of protein chains. *Science*, 1973, 181(4096): 223–230.

[82] Sippl M.J. Knowledge-based potentials for proteins. *Curr Opin Struct Biol*, 1995, 5(2): 229–235.

[83] Rajgaria R., McAllister S., Floudas C. A novel high resolution Cα–Cα distance dependent force field based on a high quality decoy set. *Proteins*, 2006, 65(3): 726–741.

[84] Lazaridis T., Karplus M. Effective energy functions for protein structure prediction. *Curr Opin Struct Biol*, 2000, 10(2): 139–145.

[85] Fujitsuka Y., Takada S., Luthey-Schulten Z.A., Wolynes P.G. Optimizing physical energy functions for protein folding. *Proteins*, 2004, 54(1): 88–103.

[86] Lii J.H., Allinger N.L. Directional hydrogen bonding in the MM3 force field: II. *J Comput Chem*, 1998, 19(9): 1001–1016.

[87] Fang Q., Shortle D. Enhanced sampling near the native conformation using statistical potentials for local side-chain and backbone interactions. *Proteins*, 2005, 60(1): 97–102.

[88] Fang Q., Shortle D. A consistent set of statistical potentials for quantifying local side-chain and backbone interactions. *Proteins*, 2005, 60(1): 90–96.

[89] MacKerell Jr A.D., Bashford D., Bellott M., Dunbrack Jr R.L., Evanseck J.D., Field M.J., Fischer S., Gao J., Guo H., Ha S. All-atom empirical potential for molecular modeling and dynamics studies of proteins. *J Phys Chem B*, 1998, 102(18): 3586–3616.

[90] Cornell W.D., Cieplak P., Bayly C.I., Gould I.R., Merz K.M., Ferguson D.M., Spellmeyer D.C., Fox T., Caldwell J.W., Kollman P.A. A second generation force field for the simulation of proteins, nucleic acids, and organic molecules. *J Am Chem Soc*, 1995, 117(19): 5179–5197.

[91] Christen M., Hünenberger P.H., Bakowies D., Baron R., Bürgi R., Geerke D.P., Heinz T.N., Kastenholz M.A., Kräutler V., Oostenbrink C. The GROMOS software for biomolecular simulation: GROMOS05. *J Comput Chem*, 2005, 26(16): 1719–1751.

[92] Duan Y., Kollman P.A. Pathways to a protein folding intermediate observed in a 1-microsecond simulation in aqueous solution. *Science*, 1998, 282(5389): 740–744.

[93] Bowie J.U., Luthy R., Eisenberg D. A method to identify protein sequences that fold into a known three-dimensional structure. *Science*, 1991, 253(5016): 164–170.

[94] Simons K.T., Kooperberg C., Huang E., Baker D. Assembly of protein tertiary structures from fragments with similar local sequences using simulated annealing and Bayesian scoring functions. *J Mol Biol*, 1997, 268(1): 209–225.

[95] Petrey D., Honig B. Protein structure prediction: inroads to biology. *Mol Cell*, 2005, 20(6): 811–819.

[96] Zhou H., Zhou Y. Single-body residue-level knowledge-based energy score combined with sequence-profile and secondary structure information for fold recognition. *Proteins*, 2004, 55(4): 1005–1013.

[97] Jones D.T. GenTHREADER: an efficient and reliable protein fold recognition method for genomic sequences. *J Mol Biol*, 1999, 287(4): 797–815.

[98] Lüthy R., Bowie J.U., Eisenberg D. Assessment of protein models with three-dimensional profiles. *Nature*, 1992, 356(6364): 83.

[99] Kunin V., Ouzounis C.A. Clustering the annotation space of proteins. *BMC Bioinfo*, 2005, 6(1): 24.

[100] Wiederstein M., Sippl M.J. Protein sequence randomization: Efficient estimation of protein stability using knowledge-based potentials. *J Mol Biol*, 2005, 345(5): 1199–1212.

[101] Chiu T.L., Goldstein R.A. How to generate improved potentials for protein tertiary structure prediction: A lattice model study. *Proteins*, 2000, 41(2): 157–163.

[102] Yang W.Y., Pitera J.W., Swope W.C., Gruebele M. Heterogeneous folding of the trpzip hairpin: Full atom simulation and experiment. *J Mol Biol*, 2004, 336(1): 241–251.

[103] Floudas C., Fung H., McAllister S., Mönnigmann M., Rajgaria R. Advances in protein structure prediction and de novo protein design: A review. *Chem Eng Sci*, 2006, 61(3): 966–988.

[104] Zhang Y., Skolnick J. Scoring function for automated assessment of protein structure template quality. *Proteins*, 2004, 57(4): 702–710.

[105] Lu M., Dousis A.D., Ma J. OPUS-PSP: an orientation-dependent statistical all-atom potential derived from side-chain packing. *J Mol Biol*, 2008, 376(1): 288–301.

[106] Rajgaria R., McAllister S., Floudas C. Distance dependent centroid to centroid force fields using high resolution decoys. *Proteins*, 2008, 70(3): 950–970.

[107] Feng Y., Kloczkowski A., Jernigan R.L. Four-body contact potentials derived from two protein datasets to discriminate native structures from decoys. *Proteins*, 2007, 68(1): 57–66.

[108] Sippl M.J. Boltzmann's principle, knowledge-based mean fields and protein folding. An approach to the computational determination of protein structures. *J Compu Aid Mol Des*, 1993, 7(4): 473–501.

[109] Melo F., Feytmans E. Assessing protein structures with a non-local atomic interaction energy. *J Mol Biol*, 1998, 277(5): 1141–1152.

[110] Gilis D., Rooman M. Identification and *ab initio* simulations of early folding units in proteins. *Proteins*, 2001, 42(2): 164–176.

[111] Sippl M.J. Calculation of conformational ensembles from potentials of mena force: An approach to the knowledge-based prediction of local structures in globular proteins. *J Mol Biol*, 1990, 213(4): 859–883.

[112] Melo F., Feytmans E. Novel knowledge-based mean force potential at atomic level. *J Mol Biol*, 1997, 267(1): 207–222.

[113] Summa C.M., Levitt M., DeGrado W.F. An atomic environment potential for use in protein structure prediction. *J Mol Biol*, 2005, 352(4): 986–1001.

[114] Qiu J., Elber R. Atomically detailed potentials to recognize native and approximate protein structures. *Proteins*, 2005, 61(1): 44–55.

[115] Samudrala R., Moult J. An all-atom distance-dependent conditional probability discriminatory function for protein structure prediction. *J Mol Biol*, 1998, 275(5): 895–916.

[116] Lu H., Skolnick J. A distance-dependent atomic knowledge-based potential for improved protein structure selection. *Proteins*, 2001, 44(3): 223–232.

[117] Zhou H., Zhou Y. Distance-scaled, finite ideal-gas reference state improves structure-derived potentials of mean force for structure selection and stability prediction. *Prot Sci*, 2002, 11(11): 2714–2726.

[118] Hu C., Li X., Liang J. Developing optimal non-linear scoring function for protein design. *Bioinformatics*, 2004, 20(17): 3080–3098.

[119] Vendruscolo M., Najmanovich R., Domany E. Can a pairwise contact potential stabilize native protein folds against decoys obtained by threading? *Proteins*, 2000, 38(2): 134–148.

[120] Wang K., Fain B., Levitt M., Samudrala R. Improved protein structure selection using decoy-dependent discriminatory functions. *BMC Struct Biol*, 2004, 4(1): 8.

[121] Loose C., Klepeis J., Floudas C. A new pairwise folding potential based on improved decoy generation and side-chain packing. *Proteins*, 2004, 54(2): 303–314.

[122] Tobi D., Elber R. Distance-dependent, pair potential for protein folding: Results from linear optimization. *Proteins*, 2000, 41(1): 40–46.

[123] Andreeva A., Howorth D., Brenner S.E., Hubbard T.J.P., Chothia C., Murzin A.G. SCOP database in 2004: Refinements integrate structure and sequence family data. *Nucleic Acids Res*, 2004, 32(database issue): D226–D229.

[124] Zhang J., Chen R., Liang J. Empirical potential function for simplified protein models: Combining contact and local sequence–structure descriptors. *Proteins*, 2006, 63(4): 949–960.

[125] Tan C.-W., Jones D.T. Using neural networks and evolutionary information in decoy discrimination for protein tertiary structure prediction. *BMC Bioinfo*, 2008, 9(1): 94.

[126] Eramian D., Shen M.Y., Devos D., Melo F., Sali A., Marti-renom M.A. A composite score for predicting errors in protein structure models. *Prot Sci*, 2006, 15(7): 1653–1666.

[127] Chandonia J.M., Hon G., Walker N.S., Conte L.L., Koehl P., Levitt M., Brenner S.E. The ASTRAL Compendium in 2004. *Nucleic Acids Res*, 2004, 32(database issue): 189–192.

[128] Pearl F., Todd A., Sillitoe I., Dibley M., Redfern O., Lewis T., Bennett C., Marsden R., Grant A., Lee D., Akpor A., Maibaum M., Harrison A., Dallman T., Reeves G., Diboun I., Addou S., Lise S., Johnston C., Sillero A., Thornton J., Orengo C. The CATH domain structure database and related resources Gene3D and DHS provide comprehensive domain family information for genome analysis. *Nucleic Acids Res*, 2005, 33(Database issue): D247–D251.

[129] Madej T., Gibrat J.F., Bryant S.H. Threading a database of protein cores. *Proteins*, 1995, 23(3): 356–369.

[130] Veretnik S., Bourne P.E., Alexandrov N.N., Shindyalov I.N. Toward consistent assignment of structural domains in proteins. *J Mol Biol*, 2004, 339(3): 647–678.

[131] Kabsch W., Sander C. Dictionary of secondary structure in proteins: Pattern recognition of hydrogenbonded and geometrical features. *Biopolymers*, 1983, 22(12): 2577–2637.

[132] Holm L., Sander C. Removing near-neighbour redundancy from large protein sequence collections. *Bioinformatics*, 1998, 14(5): 423–429.

[133] Henikoff S., Henikoff J.G. Position-based sequence weights. *J Mol Biol*, 1994, 243(4): 574–578.

[134] Gelly J.C., de Brevern A.G., Hazout S. 'Protein Peeling': An approach for splitting a 3D protein structure into compact fragments. *Bioinformatics*, 2006, 22(2): 129–133.

[135] An-Suei Y., Lu-yong W. Local structure prediction with local structure-based sequence profiles. *Bioinformatics*, 2003, 19(10): 1267–1274.

[136] Manning C.D., Schütze H. *Foundation of Statistical Natural Language Processing*. 1999. Cambridge, MA: The MIT Press.

[137] Kolodny R., Koehl P., Guibas L., Levitt M. Small libraries of protein fragments model native protein structures accurately. *J Mol Biol*, 2002, 323(2): 297–307.

[138] Vapnik V.N. *Statistical Learning Theory*. 1998. New York, NY: Wiley.

[139] Chang C.C., Lin C.J. LIBSVM: A library for support vector machines. 2001. Software available at http://www.csie.ntu.edu.tw/~cjlin/libsvm

[140] Kouranov A., Xie L., de la Cruz J., Chen L., Westbrook J., Bourne P.E., Berman H.M. The RCSB PDB information portal for structural genomics. *Nucleic Acids Res*, 2006, 34(Database issue): D302–D305.

[141] Wang G., Dunbrack R.L., Jr. PISCES: A protein sequence culling server. *Bioinformatics*, 2003, 19(12): 1589–1591.

[142] Lesk A.M. CASP2: Report on *ab initio* predictions. *Proteins*, 1997, Suppl 1: 151–166.

[143] MacKerell J., Bashford A.D., Bellott D., Jr. D., Evanseck M.R., Field J., Fischer M., Gao S., Guo J., Ha H., Joseph-McCarthy S., Kuchnir D., Kuczera L., Lau K., Mattos F., Michnick C., Ngo S., Nguyen T., Prodhom D., Reiher B., Roux I., W.B., Schlenkrich M., Smith J., Stote R., Straub J., Watanabe M., Wiorkiewicz-Kuczera J., Yin D., Karplus M. All-atom empirical potential for molecular modeling and dynamics studies of proteins. *J Phys Chem B*, 1998, 102: 3586–3616.

[144] Holmes J.B., Tsai J. Some fundamental aspects of building protein structures from fragment libraries. *Prot Sci*, 2004, 13(6): 1636–1650.

[145] Wolf Y.I., Grishin N.V., Koonin E.V. Estimating the number of protein folds and families from complete genome data. *J Mol Biol*, 2000, 299(4): 897–905.

[146] Llinas M., Gillespie B., Dahlquist F.W., Marqusee S. The energetics of T4 lysozyme reveal a hierarchy of conformations. *Nat Struct Biol*, 1999, 6(11): 1072–1078.

[147] Kato H., Vu N.D., Feng H., Zhou Z., Bai Y. The folding pathway of T4 lysozyme: An on-pathway hidden folding intermediate. *J Mol Biol*, 2007, 365(3): 881–891.

[148] Dong Q., Wang X., Lin L. Methods for optimizing the structure alphabet sequences of proteins. *Comput Biol Med*, 2007, 37(11): 1610–1616.

[149] Haspel N., Tsai C.J., Wolfson H., Nussinov R. Reducing the computational complexity of protein folding via fragment folding and assembly. *Prot Sci*, 2003, 12(6): 1177–1187.

[150] Haspel N., Tsai C.J., Wolfson H., Nussinov R. Hierarchical protein folding pathways: A computational study of protein fragments. *Proteins*, 2003, 51(2): 203–215.

[151] Tsai C.J., Ma B., Sham Y.Y., Kumar S., Wolfson H.J., Nussinov R. A hierarchical building-block-base computational scheme for protein structure prediction. *IBM J Res Dev*, 2001, 45(3/4): 513–523.

[152] Tsai J., Bonneau R., Morozov A.V., Kuhlman B., Rohl C.A., Baker D. An improved protein decoy set for testing energy functions for protein structure prediction. *Proteins*, 2003, 53(1): 76–87.

[153] Simons K.T., Bonneau R., Ruczinski I., Baker D. *Ab initio* protein structure prediction of CASP III targets using ROSETTA. *Proteins*, 1999, 37(Suppl 3): 171–176.

[154] Dong Q., Wang X., Lin L., Wang Y. Analysis and prediction of protein local structure based on structure alphabets. *Proteins*, 2008, 72(1): 163–172.

[155] Hawkins J., Boden M. The applicability of recurrent neural networks for biological sequence analysis. *IEEE/ACM Trans Comput Biol Bioinfo*, 2005, 2(3): 243–253.

[156] Chu W., Ghahramani Z., Podtelezhnikov A., Wild D.L. Bayesian segmental models with multiple sequence alignment profiles for protein secondary structure and contact map prediction. *IEEE/ACM Trans Comput Biol Bioinfo*, 2006, 3(2): 98–113.

[157] de Brevern A.G. New assessment of a structural alphabet. *In Silico Biol*, 2005, 5(3): 283–289.

[158] Tobi D., Shafran G., Linial N., Elber R. On the design and analysis of protein folding potentials. *Proteins*, 2000, 40(1): 71–85.

[159] Chang C.-C., Lin C.-J. LIBSVM: A library for support vector machines. *ACM Trans Intelligent Syst Technol*, 2011, 2(3): 27.

[160] Moult J., Fidelis K., Kryshtafovych A., Rost B., Hubbard T., Tramontano A. Critical assessment of methods of protein structure prediction — Round VII. *Proteins*, 2007, 69(S8): 3–9.

[161] Samudrala R., Levitt M. Decoys 'R'Us: A database of incorrect conformations to improve protein structure prediction. *Prot Sci*, 2000, 9(07): 1399–1401.

[162] Güntert P., Mumenthaler C., Wüthrich K. Torsion angle dynamics for NMR structure calculation with the new program DYANA. *J Mol Biol*, 1997, 273(1): 283–298.

[163] Zhang C., Liu S., Zhou H., Zhou Y. An accurate, residue-level, pair potential of mean force for folding and binding based on the distance-scaled, ideal-gas reference state. *Prot Sci*, 2004, 13(2): 400–411.

[164] Wu Y., Lu M., Chen M., Li J., Ma J. OPUS-Ca: A knowledge-based potential function requiring only Cα positions. *Prot Sci*, 2007, 16(7): 1449–1463.

[165] Benkert P., Tosatto S.C., Schomburg D. QMEAN: A comprehensive scoring function for model quality assessment. *Proteins*, 2008, 71(1): 261–277.

[166] Park B., Levitt M. Energy functions that discriminate X-ray and near-native folds from well-constructed decoys. *J Mol Biol*, 1996, 258(2): 367–392.

[167] Keasar C., Levitt M. A novel approach to decoy set generation: Designing a physical energy function having local minima with native structure characteristics. *J Mol Biol*, 2003, 329(1): 159–174.

[168] Samudrala R., Xia Y., Levitt M., Huang E.S. A combined approach for *ab initio* construction of low resolution protein tertiary structures from sequence. In *Biocomputing '99*. 1999, Singapore: World Scientific, pp. 505–516.

[169] Xia Y., Huang E.S., Levitt M., Samudrala R. *Ab initio* construction of protein tertiary structures using a hierarchical approach. *J Mol Biol*, 2000, 300(1): 171–185.

[170] Samudrala R., Levitt M. A comprehensive analysis of 40 blind protein structure predictions. *BMC Struct Biol*, 2002, 2(1): 3.

[171] Samudrala R., Moult J. An all-atom distance-dependent conditional probability discriminatory function for protein structure prediction. *J Mol Biol*, 1998, 275(5): 895–916.

[172] Fang Q., Shortle D. Protein refolding in silico with atom-based statistical potentials and conformational search using a simple genetic algorithm. *J Mol Biol*, 2006, 359(5): 1456–1467.

[173] Dong Q., Wang X., Lin L. Novel knowledge-based mean force potential at the profile level. *BMC Bioinfo*, 2006, 7(1): 324.

[174] Bolser D.M., Filippis I., Stehr H., Duarte J., Lappe M. Residue contact-count potentials are as effective as residue-residue contact-type potentials for ranking protein decoys. *BMC Struct Biol*, 2008, 8(1): 53.

[175] Deutsch C., Krishnamoorthy B. Four-body scoring function for mutagenesis. *Bioinformatics*, 2007, 23(22): 3009–3015.

Chapter 6

Function Prediction

6.1 Motivation and Basic Idea

The ultimate goal of functional genomics is to determine the functions of genes and proteins as a means to better understand life, health and illness.[1] With the rapid development of a completely sequenced genome, the experimental determination of protein function is no longer sufficient and more automated largescale methods are required. So, it is necessary to use computational methods to predict the function of proteins. In this chapter, the biological language model will be used to solve the problem of protein function including finding information about the binding sites of proteins, protein–protein interaction, gene ontology–based function prediction and identification of the missing proteins.

Protein function is very often encoded in a small number of residues located in the functional active site, and these are dispersed around the primary sequence but packed in a compact spatial region.[2] The recognition of functional sites in proteins is a direct computational approach to the characterization of proteins in terms of biological and biochemical function. The localization of functional sites will allow us to understand how the protein recognizes other molecules, to gain clues about its likely function at the level of the cell and the organism, and to identify important binding sites that may serve as useful targets for pharmaceutical design.[3] Since proteins perform their functions by interacting with one another and with other biomolecules, reconstructing a map of the protein–protein interactions of a cell is the first important step towards understanding protein function and cellular behavior.[4] The Human Genome Sequence Project[5] provides a comprehensive compendium of all the human protein-encoding genes. However, due to the diversity of proteins and the underdevelopment of current proteomics technology, there are many proteins which have not been identified and annotated.

6.2 Profile-level Interface Propensities for Binding Site Prediction

6.2.1 Background

Recently, a series of computational efforts to identify interaction sites or interfaces in proteins has been undertaken. A number of studies on the characteristics of protein interfaces have provided clues for binding site prediction. Several methods have been proposed to predict these sites based on the sequence or structure characteristics of known protein–protein interaction sites.

In terms of physical chemistry, protein interfaces are generally observed to be more hydrophobic than the remainder of the protein surface.[6,7] Moreover, the interfaces of permanent complexes tend to be more hydrophobic when compared to those of transient complexes.[8] Some interfaces have a significant number of polar residues,[9] usually where interactions are less permanent.[10] Charged side-chains are often excluded from protein–protein interfaces with the exception of arginine,[11] which is one of the most abundant interface residues regardless of interaction types.[12]

The evolutionary conservation of residues is another property that may be utilized to predict protein–protein interfaces.[13] The evolutionary trace (ET) method tries to identify functional sites by using the sequence variations and functional divergences found in nature.[14,15] Accurate ET analysis requires functionally relevant sequences and high-quality alignments as input.[16] A structure-independent criterion has been presented to measure the quality of evolutionary trace.[17] Because sequence conservation reflects not only evolutionary selection at binding sites to maintain protein function but also selection throughout the protein to maintain the stability of the folded state,[18] many researchers try to distinguish functional and structural constraints on protein evolution.[19, 20] A comprehensive evaluation of different conservation scores has been performed by Valdar.[21] Other sequence information has also been exploited such as the phylogenetic profile,[22, 23] the sequence motifs,[24] sequence profile,[25, 26] evolution rate,[27, 28] etc.

The features extracted from the three-dimensional structures of protein complexes are critical for a full understanding of the mechanism of interactions because they provide specific interaction details at the atomic level. The accessible surface area (ASA) is one of the most widely used features.[29] Molecular docking seems to be the most principled computational approach for identifying the interaction sites,[30] but it requires the precise design of energy function,[31] either physical energy[32] or empirical scoring functions.[30, 33] 3D-motifs have also been successfully used to identify binding sites of the same type in proteins with different folds.[34-37] Patch analysis using a six-parameter scoring function can distinguish the interface from other surfaces.[6]

Because none of the above-mentioned properties is able to make an unambiguous identification of interface regions or patches, a combination of some of them (via either a linear combination[38] or machine learning[39]) is found to be effective for improving the accuracy of binding-site prediction.[40] The PINUP method predicts interface residues using an empirical score function made of a linear combination of the energy score, interface propensity and residue conservation score.[41] Rossi *et al.* first constructed a scoring function, and then performed a Monte Carlo optimization, to find a good scoring patch on the protein surface.[42]

Machine Learning Methods are well suited to the classification of interface and noninterface surface residues.[43, 44] Neural networks[45] and support vector machines[46, 47] have been applied in this field. These studies take sequential or structural information as input.[9] Other researchers adopted a two-stage model[26] to further improve the performance. Recently, the conditional random field (CRF) model has been introduced, which formalizes the prediction of protein interaction sites as a sequence-labeling task.[48]

In this study, we revisit the difference between amino acid compositions of the interface area and those of other surface areas. Although some researchers have found that there are different amino acid compositions among the interaction sites of different complexes (homo-permanent complexes, homo-transient complexes, hetero-permanent complexes and hetero-transient complexes),[49] such differences have not been integrated into the prediction process. Here, the residue interface propensities of different complexes are collected. These propensities, combined with sequence profiles and accessible surface areas, are given as input to the support vector machine for the prediction of protein binding sites. Such propensities are further improved by taking evolutionary information into consideration. The frequency profiles are directly calculated from the multiple sequence alignment output by PSI-BLAST[50] and converted into binary profiles[51] with a probability threshold. As a result, the protein sequences are represented as sequences of binary profiles rather than sequences of amino acids. Similar to the residue interface propensities, a class of novel propensities at the profile level is introduced. Binary profiles can be viewed as the novel building blocks of proteins. They have been successfully applied in many computational biology tasks, such as domain boundary prediction,[51] knowledge-based mean force potentials,[52] protein remote homology detection,[53] etc. Experimental results show that the binary profile propensities significantly improve the performance of the binding site prediction of proteins.

6.2.2 Profile-level interface propensities

6.2.2.1 *Dataset*

A comprehensive set of complexes is chosen from the Protein Data Bank (PDB)[54] and then subjected to a number of stringent filtering steps. All proteins with multi-chains, non-NMR structures and resolution better than 4 Å are selected. Two chains in a protein are considered as interacting pairs if at least two nonhydrogen atoms in each chain are separated by no more than $5\,\text{Å}$.[45,55] For PDB structures with more than two chains, each chain is selected for at most one time. For protein chains that interact with multiple partners, only one partner with the most interfacial residues is selected as its partner. Protein chains with less than 40 amino acids are removed. The PQS web server[56] is used to eliminate crystal packing complexes rather than biologically functional multimers. The selected chains are further filtered such that no pair of chains has more than 25% sequence identity. Finally, a total of 1139 chains are obtained.

6.2.2.2 *Classification of complexes*

Protein–protein interactions can be divided into different types according to different criteria.[57] In this study, the complexes are classified by the homology of interacting chains (homo versus hetero) and the lifetime of the complexes (transient versus permanent).

Using simple sequence comparisons the complexes can be classified as homo-complexes or hetero-complexes. Two interacting protein chains are defined as homocomplex if over 90% of them are aligned and the sequence identity over the aligned region is more than 95%.[45] All other complexes are classified as hetero-complexes.

A permanent complex is usually very stable and thus only exists in its complexed form. In contrast, a transient complex can exist in the separated state. The method of differentiating the transient complexes and permanent complexes is same as the one used by Ofran and Rost.[49] The guidelines for classifying the hetero-complexes and homo-complexes into permanent and transient states are different. They are briefly described here. If the chains from the hetero-complexes are stored in the same SWISS-PROT files,[58] the complexes are classified as hetero-permanent complexes, otherwise they are classified as hetero-transient complexes. All the homo-complexes that are annotated as monomers in the DIP[59] database are classified as homo-transient complexes; otherwise they are classified as homo-permanent complexes.

Table 6-1   Summary of the four complexes.

	Chains	Res.	Surface res.	Interface res.[a]
Hetero-permanent	123	25157	21737	7136 (32.8%)
Hetero-transient	386	86168	72288	19177 (26.5%)
Homo-permanent	625	174629	142620	38556 (27%)
Homo-transient	5	1555	1267	187 (14.8%)
Total	1139	287509	237912	65056 (27.3%)

Note: [a]Given in the brackets are the fractions of interface residues in the total number of surface residues.

The above dataset is then grouped into four kinds of complexes (hetero-permanent, hetero-transient, homo-permanent, homo-transient). The statistical information of different complexes is tabulated in Table 6-1. An amino acid is defined as a surface amino acid if the ASA of at least one of its atoms is larger than $2 \, \text{Å}^2$.[42] A surface residue is considered as an interface residue if its accessible surface area is decreased by more than $1 \, \text{Å}^2$ upon complexation.[41] The ASA is calculated with the DSSP program.[60] According to this definition, 27.3% of the surface residues are interface residues. Such a ratio is very close to that (28%) in Chung's dataset.[18]

6.2.2.3 *Calculation of propensities*

The amino acid frequencies between the interface and the other surface area are different. Such a difference can be used to produce the residue interface propensity, which is defined as the log ratio between the amino acid frequency in the interface area and that in the surface area, and it is given as

$$P_a = \ln(P_{a,I}/P_{a,S}) \tag{6-1}$$

where P_a is the propensity of amino acid a, $P_{a,I}$ is the frequency of amino acid a in the interface area and $P_{a,S}$ is the frequency of amino acid a in the surface area. The frequencies can be calculated from the training set by maximum likelihood estimation as follows:

$$P_{a,I} = \frac{C_{a,I}}{C_I} \tag{6-2}$$

$$P_{a,S} = \frac{C_{a,S}}{C_S} \qquad (6\text{-}3)$$

where $C_{a,I}$ is the count of amino acid a in the interface area, C_I is the total number of amino acids in the interface area, $C_{a,S}$ is the count of amino acid a in the surface area, C_S is the total number of amino acids in the surface area. The residue interface propensity describes the likelihood of an amino acid to be found in the interface area as compared with the surface area. A propensity of 0 indicates that the amino acid has the same frequency in the interface and surface areas. A positive propensity means that the amino acid is overrepresented in the interface area.

In terms of binary profiles, the protein sequence is represented as a sequence of binary profiles rather than a sequence of amino acids. Each amino acid is replaced by the corresponding binary profiles that are derived from the multiple sequence alignments as described in the following section. The calculation formula for binary profile interface propensities is the same as that for the residue interface propensities except that the subscripts are replaced by binary profiles rather than the amino acid. The formula is

$$P_b = \ln(P_{b,I}/P_{b,S}) \qquad (6\text{-}4)$$

where P_b is the propensity of binary profile b, $P_{b,I}$ is the frequency of binary profile b in the interface area and $P_{b,S}$ is the frequency of binary profile b in the surface area. The frequencies can also be calculated by maximum likelihood estimation in the same manner as that for the amino acid. The binary profile interface propensity contains evolution information and provides a more accurate prediction of binding sites than the amino acid interface propensity as can be seen from the experimental results.

Here, an example for calculating the propensities of binary profiles is provided. Suppose there is a frequency profile:

A: 0.09	C: 0.02	D: 0.07	E: 0.04	F: 0.03	**G: 0.1**	H: 0.07	I: 0.04	K: 0.02	**L: 0.09**
M: 0.02	**N: 0.09**	P: 0.05	Q: 0.04	R: 0.03	S: 0.04	T: 0.05	V: 0.01	W: 0.05	Y: 0.05

When the probability threshold P_h is taken as 0.08, we get the following binary profile:

A: 1	C: 0	D: 0	E: 0	F: 0	**G:** 1	H: 0	I: 0	K: 0	**L:** 1
M: 0	**N:** 1	P: 0	Q: 0	R: 0	S: 0	T: 0	V: 0	W: 0	Y: 0

By collecting the non-zero terms in the binary profile, the amino acid combination AGLN is obtained. Suppose the frequency of AGLN is 0.00042 in the interface area and 0.00021 in the surface area. These frequencies are calculated by the maximum likelihood estimate using Eqs. (6-2) and (6-3). Thus, the propensity of AGLN is 0.693147 (ln (0.00042/0.00021)) as calculated using Eq. (6-4).

6.2.2.4 *Generating binary profiles*

A binary profile can be expressed by a vector with dimensions of 20, in which each element represents one kind of amino acid and can only take a value of 0 or 1. When the element takes a value of 1, it means that the corresponding amino acid can occur during evolution. Otherwise, it means that the corresponding amino acid cannot occur. A binary profile can also be expressed by a substring of amino acid combinations, which is obtained by collecting each element of the vector with non-zero value. Each combination of the 20 amino acids corresponds to a binary profile and vice versa. Below we describe the process of generating the binary profiles.

PSI-BLAST[50] is used to generate the profiles of amino acid sequences with parameters $j = 3$ and $e = 0.001$. The search is performed against the nonredundant (NR) database from NCBI. The frequency profiles are directly obtained from the multiple sequence alignments output by PSI-BLAST. The target frequency reflects the probability of an amino acid occurrence in a given position of the sequences. The method of target frequency calculation is similar to that implemented in PSI-BLAST.

Because the frequency profile is a matrix of frequencies for all amino acids, it cannot be directly used and needs to be converted into a binary profile by a probability threshold P_h. When the frequency of an amino acid is larger than P_h, it is converted into an integral value of 1, which means that the specified amino acid can occur in a given position of the protein sequence during evolution. Otherwise it is converted into 0. A substring of amino acid combination is then obtained by collecting the binary profile with non-zero value for each position of the protein sequences. These substrings have approximately represented the amino acids that possibly occur at a given sequence position during evolution. Figure 6-1 has shown the process of generating binary profiles.

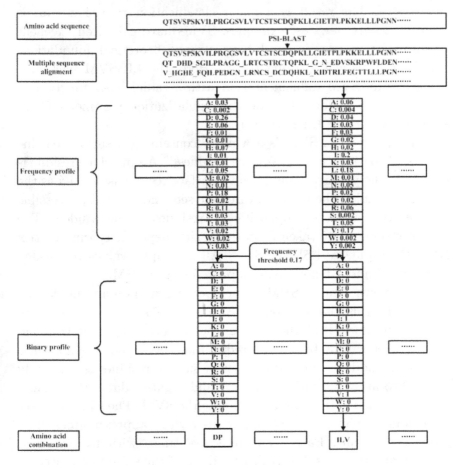

Figure 6-1　The flowchart of generating binary profiles.

The multiple sequence alignment is obtained by PSI-BLAST. The frequency profile is calculated from the multiple sequence alignment and converted to a binary profile with a frequency threshold. The substring of amino acid combination is then collected.

6.2.2.5 *Prediction*

Support Vector Machines (SVMs) are a class of supervised learning algorithms first introduced by Vapnik.[61] Given a set of labeled training vectors (positive and negative input examples), an SVM can learn a linear decision boundary to discriminate between the two classes. The result is a linear classification rule that can be used to classify new test examples. SVMs have exhibited excellent performance in practice and have strong theoretical foundations based on statistical learning theory. Here, the LIBSVM package[62] is used as an SVM implementation with a radial basis function as the kernel. The values of γ and the regularization parameter C are set to be 0.005 and 1, respectively.

The input of an SVM is a window containing a surface residue and its 12 spatially nearest surface residues.[18] An interface residue is defined as the positive sample, and a surface residue is defined as the negative sample. The input features are sequence profiles, accessible surface areas and the propensities of residues in the window. The sequence profiles are taken from the position-specific scoring matrix (PSSM) output by PSI-BLAST.[50] All the input values are scaled between -1 and 1 before being inputted to the SVM.

It is known that an SVM cannot perform well on an unbalanced dataset. In this dataset, only 27.3% of the surface residues are interface residues. If all the surface residues are used in the training, the classifier will be biased to predict that each residue is a surface residue. To address this issue, a set of surface residues is randomly selected to make the ratio of positive and negative data 1:1. Fivefold cross-validation is then used to evaluate the SVM. The whole dataset is randomly divided into five subgroups with an approximately equal number of chains. Each SVM runs five times with five different training and test sets. For each run, three of the subsets are used as the training set, one subset is used to select the optimal parameters and the last one is used as the test set.

6.2.2.6 *Performance metrics*

The following measures are used to evaluate the performances: precision, recall, accuracy, F1 and correlation coefficient (CC).

6.2.3 Binding site prediction

6.2.3.1 *Residue interface propensities*

Residue interface propensities are good indicators for binding sites and have been widely used in many studies.[9] The residue interface propensities of the four kinds of complexes are calculated from the specific dataset. A positive propensity means that the residue is abundant in the interface while a negative propensity means that the residue is abundant in the surface area.

The four kinds of complexes have similar residue interface propensities. They all show that hydrophobic residues (F, I, L, M, V) and some polar aromatic residues (W, Y, H) are favored in the interface area. The charged residue R also shows a preference for the interface area. Other polar amino acids T and E and small amino acids P and A are disfavored in the interface. The same phenomena have been observed in other studies[38] although some researchers evaluated the ASA contribution for amino acids[6, 41] while we counted them. Biophysically similar residues, such as L and I, or D and E, usually showed similar trends, indicating the reliability of the data.

There are minor differences among the four kinds of complexes. Although many amino acids show the same trend for interface area or surface area, the propensities are different for the four kinds of complexes. Furthermore, some amino acids reveal different propensities in different complexes. Amino acids Q, S and T show preferences for the hetero-complexes rather than homo-complexes. Amino acids C and L are favored in permanent complexes rather than transient ones. Ofran and Rost[49] found that the composition of all interface types differed substantially from that of SWISS-PROT.

Here, we conclude that the residue interface propensities show similar general trends and only minor differences exist among the different kinds of complexes.

6.2.3.2 *Binary profile interface propensities*

The binary profile frequencies in the interface are different from those in the surface area. These differences can be used to produce the discriminative binary profile propensities. In theory, the total number of binary profiles is extremely large (2^{20}), but in fact, only a small fraction of binary profiles appears, which is dependent on the choice of probability threshold P_h and the dataset. Based on the results of cross-validation (discussed in the subsequent section), the four kinds of complexes have different numbers of binary profiles, ranging from a hundred to several thousands. The binary profiles and their propensities in the four kinds of complexes are listed in the additional files (see additional file 1-4). Note that binary profiles with low occurrence times (<3) are ignored, since these profiles are not statistically significant and may introduce significant noise.

An increased propensity of hydrophobic residues and their combinations in the interface has been observed, such as the binary profiles FHWY and ILMV. Although some amino acids are preferred in the surface area, the combination of these amino acids with other amino acids may be preferred in the interface area, such as AEP and ST. Another special phenomenon is that some binary profiles only occur in the interface area while other binary profiles only occur in the surface area. The former results in a maximum propensity (being set as 4) and the latter results in a minimum propensity (being set as -4). Each kind of complex has many such binary profiles.

The differences in binary profile interface propensities among different complexes are significant in comparison with those of residue interface propensities. Many binary profiles show positive propensities in one complex but negative propensities in another complex. Table 6-2 summarizes the number of such binary profiles between any pair of complexes.

Table 6-2 The differences of binary profile interface propensities among the four kinds of complexes.

	Hetero-permanent[a]	Hetero-transient	Homo-permanent	Homo-transient
Hetero-permanent	—	341	378	29
Hetero-transient	261	—	893	28
Homo-permanent	267	908	—	36
Homo-transient	17	27	38	—

Note: [a]Given in the element (I, J) of the matrix are the number of binary profiles which show positive propensities in complex type I and negative propensities in complex type J.

6.2.3.3 *Comparative results with and without propensities*

The first SVM takes the profile and ASA of spatially neighboring residues as input, which are common input features used by previous studies.[18,47,63] Then we add the amino acid or binary profile interface propensities as an extra feature to evaluate whether these propensities can improve the performance or not. All the results are obtained by five-fold cross-validation.

The second SVM takes residue interface propensities as an extra feature. Table 6-3 gives the results with and without residue interface propensities. Similar performance indicates that the standard amino acid cannot provide efficient discrimination for the complicated interfaces of proteins. The results on the homo-transient complex are extremely low because there are only 5 chains in this complex. The performance of the first SVM is comparable with those of Chung *et al.*[18] They reported a precision of 0.498 and a recall of 0.568 with the same features on their 274 hetero-complexes.

The third SVM takes binary profile interface propensities as an extra feature instead of residue interface propensities. The probability threshold P_h of converting a frequency profile into a binary profile needs to be optimized. During the validation process, three sets are used to train SVM, one validation set is used to optimize the parameter and the testing set is used to give the final

Table 6-3   Comparative results with and without residue interface propensities on the four kinds of complexes.

		Precision	Recall	F1	Accuracy	CC
Hetero-permanent	Non-pro[a]	0.518	0.582	0.547	0.687	0.267
	AA-pro[b]	0.514	0.590	0.548	0.684	0.265
Hetero-transient	Non-pro	0.414	0.563	0.475	0.643	0.204
	AA-pro	0.415	0.561	0.476	0.643	0.204
Homo-permanent	Non-pro	0.463	0.607	0.526	0.687	0.288
	AA-pro	0.474	0.617	0.536	0.693	0.303
Homo-transient	Non-pro	0.206	0.463	0.279	0.691	0.136
	AA-pro	0.260	0.465	0.327	0.743	0.195

Notes: [a]The features of the SVM are the position-specific scoring matrix (PSSM) and Accessible Surface Areas (ASA); [b]Residue interface propensity is input to the SVM as an extra feature.

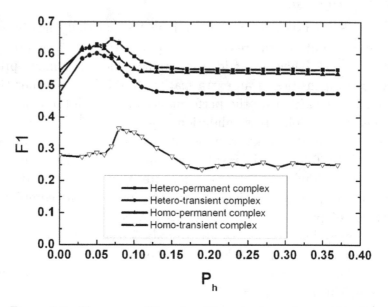

Figure 6-2   The average F1 under different values of parameter P_h.

Note: The F1 is obtained as the result of cross-validation at the validation dataset.

results. That is, we select the values of P_h that give the best results on the validation set and then such a parameter is used to test the proteins on the testing set to give the final results. The influences of P_h on the performance are illustrated in Fig. 6-2. F1 is used as

Table 6-4   Cross-validation results with binary profile interface propensities.

	P_h^a	N^b	Precision	Recall	F1	Accuracy	CC
Hetero-permanent	0.07	1558	0.599	0.700	0.644	0.735	0.396
Hetero-transient	0.05	4662	0.501	0.756	0.602	0.697	0.379
Homo-permanent	0.05	8639	0.546	0.734	0.626	0.745	0.435
Homo-transient	0.08	129	0.277	0.551	0.363	0.747	0.250

Notes: [a]The optimal probability threshold P_h of converting a frequency profile into a binary profile; [b]The number of binary profiles.

the guideline since it is a tradeoff between precision and recall. The optimal values of P_h are different for different complexes.

The results of cross-validation are then obtained with the optimal value of P_h, shown in Table 6-4. The improvement of the third SVM is significant in comparison with the other two SVMs. The F1 is improved by about 10%. According to the experimental results, we can infer that the propensities at the profile level may be more accurate than that at the amino acid level.

6.2.3.4   *Comparative results with propensities from other complexes*

An analysis of interface propensities shows that the residue interface propensities have minor differences among different complexes while the profile interface propensities differ significantly among different complexes. To validate it, the propensities from other complexes are used as an extra feature. The results are shown in Table 6-5 (residue-level) and Table 6-6 (profile-level).

As can be seen from Table 6-5, the performances are close to those seen earlier (Table 6-3), which indicates that the differences of residue interface propensities among different complexes can be negligible. The values in Table 6-6 decrease significantly in comparison with those in Table 6-4, so the profile interface propensities are sensitive to the types of complexes. In other words, the propensities at the profile level can give a more exact description of interfaces than the propensities at the residue level.

Table 6-5   Comparative results with residue interface propensities from other complexes.

Complex[a]	Propensities[b]	Precision	Recall	F1	Accuracy	CC
Hetero-permanent	Hetero-transient	0.512	0.570	0.539	0.679	0.256
	Homo-permanent	0.503	0.578	0.538	0.682	0.250
Hetero-transient	Hetero-permanent	0.419	0.568	0.482	0.646	0.212
	Homo-permanent	0.418	0.568	0.482	0.644	0.210
Homo-permanent	Hetero-permanent	0.445	0.596	0.510	0.674	0.273
Homo-transient	Hetero-permanent	0.192	0.550	0.285	0.636	0.132

Notes: [a]The complexes that the experiments are performed on; [b]The complexes that the propensities are derived from.

Table 6-6   Comparative results with binary profile interface propensities from other complexes.

Complex[a]	Propensities[b]	Precision	Recall	F1	Accuracy	CC
Hetero-permanent	Hetero-transient	0.532	0.574	0.551	0.698	0.282
Hetero-transient	Homo-permanent	0.413	0.562	0.475	0.642	0.203
Homo-permanent	Hetero-permanent	0.463	0.607	0.525	0.686	0.287
Homo-transient	Hetero-permanent	0.181	0.514	0.262	0.637	0.111

Notes: [a]The complexes that the experiments are performed on; [b]The complexes that the propensities are derived from.

6.2.3.5   *Comparison with conservation scores*

The conservation score is another widely used feature in the prediction of function sites. It indicates the importance of a residue for maintaining the structure and function of a protein.[21] Here, we compare the binary profile interface propensities with conservation scores since both of them are derived from the multiple sequence alignment of homologues. Three conservation scores are investigated including the symbol entropy score,[64] Karlin score[65] and Valdar score.[66] They are defined as follows:

$$C_{\text{entropy}} = -\sum_{i}^{K} p_i \ln p_i \times \frac{1}{\ln K} \qquad (6\text{-}5)$$

Table 6-7 Cross-validation results with conservation scores.

		Precision	Recall	F1	Accuracy	CC
Hetero-permanent	V_{entropy}	0.529	0.571	0.549	0.692	0.280
	V_{Karlin}	0.531	0.584	0.556	0.698	0.282
	V_{Valdar}	0.534	0.592	0.561	0.702	0.283
Hetero-transient	V_{entropy}	0.414	0.563	0.477	0.644	0.203
	V_{Karlin}	0.414	0.572	0.480	0.644	0.204
	V_{Valdar}	0.415	0.585	0.486	0.645	0.205
Homo-permanent	V_{entropy}	0.464	0.607	0.526	0.687	0.288
	V_{Karlin}	0.472	0.613	0.533	0.692	0.291
	V_{Valdar}	0.478	0.622	0.541	0.698	0.295
Homo-transient	V_{entropy}	0.212	0.468	0.292	0.698	0.121
	V_{Karlin}	0.226	0.478	0.307	0.710	0.127
	V_{Valdar}	0.228	0.482	0.310	0.721	0.132

$$C_{\text{Karlin}} = \sum_{i}^{N} \sum_{j>i}^{N} M(s_i, s_j) \times \frac{2}{N(N-1)} \qquad (6\text{-}6)$$

$$C_{\text{Valdar}} = \lambda \sum_{i}^{N} \sum_{j>i}^{N} w_i w_j M(s_i, s_j) \qquad (6\text{-}7)$$

Please refer to Ref. [21] for detailed calculation and comparison of these scores.

These conservation scores are used as an additional feature, and the cross-validation results are shown in Table 6-7. Overall the F1 is improved by about 2% in comparison with those without conservation scores (the first SVM).

All these conservation scores show positive correlation with binary profile interface propensities, although the Pearson correlation coefficients are small (0.017, 0.053, 0.064 for V_{entropy}, V_{Karlin} and V_{Valdar} respectively). The results show that improvement by conservation scores is much lower than that by binary profile interface propensities.

6.2.3.6 *Independent testing*

A direct comparison with other studies is difficult due to the differences in choice of dataset and definitions of surface or

Table 6-8   Results on the protein–protein docking benchmark 2.0 dataset.

Subset	No. of protein	Method[a]	Precision	Recall	F1	Accuracy	CC
Rigid body	63	AA	0.393	0.447	0.418	0.848	0.301
		BP	0.446	0.495	0.469	0.857	0.328
Medium difficult	13	AA	0.356	0.405	0.379	0.810	0.258
		BP	0.412	0.464	0.436	0.821	0.271
Difficult	8	AA	0.362	0.384	0.372	0.813	0.299
		BP	0.409	0.427	0.428	0.819	0.317
All	84	AA	0.370	0.412	0.390	0.824	0.286
		BP	0.422	0.462	0.441	0.832	0.305

Note: [a]AA, the classifiers with residue interface propensities as extra features; BP, the classifiers with binary profile interface propensities as extra features.

interface residue. Our method is tested on the protein–protein docking benchmark 2.0, which is a well-established dataset including 84 hetero-transient complexes. The proteins in hetero-transient complexes are filtered by removing the protein chains contained in the benchmark 2.0 dataset as well as their homologues. The SVMs are retrained on the filtered datasets and used to test the complexes in the benchmark 2.0 dataset. The results on different subsets (rigid-body, medium difficult and difficult sets) and the average results are shown in Table 6-8. The classifiers with binary profile interface propensities outperform those with residue interface propensities by 5% in terms of F1.

The results are better than those obtained in related works. Liang *et al.*[41] developed an empirical scoring function for binding site prediction, which is a weighted combination of energy scores, conservation scores and residue interface propensities. They achieved a precision of 0.294 and a recall of 0.305. The overall F1 was only 0.30. Their method was trained on a small dataset (only 57 proteins). Furthermore, their method was a simple combination of three features while our method is based on the discriminative model.

6.3 Gene Ontology-Based Protein Function Prediction

6.3.1 Introduction

One major component of computational function annotation is the development and use of annotation standards such as ontologies. The most widely used ontologies include Gene Ontology (GO),[67] Enzyme Commission (E.C.)[68] and MIPS Functional Catalogue (FunCat).[69] GO offers three structured ontologies that allow the description of molecular function, biological processes and cellular components. The ontology is structured as a Directed Acyclic Graph (DAG), in which child terms are instances or components of parent terms. The E.C. is a four-level hierarchy of enzyme nomenclature describing biochemical activity. The FunCat annotation scheme consists of 28 main categories. Each of the categories is organized as a hierarchical, tree-like structure. GO has been widely used for many function prediction methods,[70] the function prediction category of the biennial CASP (Critical Assessment of Techniques for Protein Structure Prediction),[71] protein subcellular location,[72] enzyme functional class[73] membrane protein type[74] and protein–protein interaction.[75] Because GO has recently become very popular and because its scheme seems to be very comprehensive, it is used here as a standard schema to develop automated methods for protein function prediction.

Over the past few decades, many methods for protein function prediction have been proposed, which can be roughly grouped into six categories[76]: sequence-based, structure-based, association-based, proteomics-experiment-based, process-based and multi-context-based methods. Since the aim of the current study is to predict protein function by using sequence information only, the sequence-based method is reviewed in a detailed manner while other methods are briefly summarized.

It is generally deemed that the homologous sequences have the same functions, which can be obtained by sequence searching methods such as BLAST[77] and PSI-BLAST.[50] However, the similarity between sequences does not mean that they are homologous.

So, some methods try to evaluate the searching results to give a relatively reliable prediction. The PFP method[78] extracted and scored GO annotations individually, and applied the function association matrix to score strongly associated pairs of annotations. It can correctly assign function using only weakly similar sequences and improves the performance by more than fivefold in comparison with the standard PSI-BLAST search. The GOPET method[79] applied a Support Vector Machine (SVM) to classify the GO annotation obtained by sequence searching methods. Igor *et al.*[80] presented an alternative method to judge whether two sequences are homologous or not. Some methods extract features from primary sequences to predict their functions, such as SVM-Prot[81] and Blast2Go.[82] Other methods predict the function of proteins from domain contents.[83] Many machine learning methods have been applied in this field, such as SVMs, neural networks, fuzzy k-nearest neighbor, probabilistic chain graphs, etc.

Due to the complexity of protein function prediction, a variety of features have been used. Structure-based methods[84] employ information from known structures, which include global structure similarity searching methods and local structure definition methods. Association-based methods[85] make use of genomic context for function prediction, such as gene order, gene fusion and phylogenetic profiles, etc. The proteomics-experiment-based methods[86] incorporate the protein–protein interaction data or the gene expression data for function prediction. The process-based methods[87] use the metabolic pathways to predict the function of uncharacterized proteins. In compensating for the limitations of each prediction method, different methods can be integrated to form a prediction system.

Although much structural and functional data have been deposited in the database, sequence information is by far the easiest retrievable source for proteins. In this study, we aim to predict protein function by using sequence composition information. Four kinds of basic building blocks of protein sequences have been investigated, including *n*-grams,[88] binary profiles,[89] PFAM domains[90] and InterPro domains,[91] most of which have been used for protein remote homology detection in our previous studies.[92] The protein sequences are mapped into high-dimensional vectors by using the occurrence frequencies of each kind of building blocks. The resulting vectors are then taken as input to a discriminative learning algorithm, such as SVM, to predict protein function defined by GO. We also use feature extraction technologies, such as Latent Semantic Analysis (LSA) and Nonnegative Matrix Factorization (NMF), to further improve the performance.

6.3.2 Building blocks of proteins

6.3.2.1 *Datasets*

The annotation subset on the PDB database is extracted from the GOA database.[93] The redundant sequences are removed with the CD-HIT package,[94] so that no two sequences in the dataset have less than 40% identity. The dataset is further filtered to discard the sequences with less than 50 residues. The final dataset contained 3738 proteins. Each node in the GO DAG follows the true path rule, that is, any protein associated with a GO term must also be associated with the ancestors of that term. For each of the GO terms, all the sequences are grouped into three sets. The positive set contains the sequences that have annotations with the specific GO term or any of its child terms. The uncertain set contains sequences that have annotation with any of its ancestor terms. The other sequences are classified into the negative set. Since most of the machine learning algorithms cannot perform well on datasets that contain a small number of samples or unbalanced samples, the GO terms that have less than 30 sequence annotations are removed. The negative samples are randomly selected so that the ratio of positive samples to negative samples is approximately equal to 1:1. This procedure yielded a total of 175 GO terms: 87 molecular function terms, 74 biological process terms and 14 cellular component terms.

6.3.2.2 *Basic building blocks of protein sequences*

In order to predict protein function from primary sequences, a suitable representation of protein sequences has to be chosen first.

In this study, each protein sequence is treated as a "document" that is composed of bag-of-X, where X can be any basic building block of protein sequences. Four kinds of basic building blocks of protein sequences have been introduced: n-grams,[88] binary profiles,[89] PFAM domains[90] and InterPro domains.[91]

n-grams: The term "n-gram" is borrowed from the field of natural language processing, which refers to n consecutive symbols (e.g. characters, words). For protein sequences, the n-grams are the set of all possible subsequences of amino acids with a fixed length of n. The number of possible n-grams in protein sequences increases exponentially with n, so the value of n is taken as 3. The total number of possible n-grams in protein sequences is 8000 (20^3), which is sufficient to predict protein function. The n-grams used here are the same as the k-spectrum for protein remote homology detection.[88] They are also very close to the signature used by Martin *et al.*[95] for protein–protein interaction prediction. The only difference between n-grams and signatures is that signatures do not consider the order of the neighboring amino acids.

Binary profiles: Binary profiles can be viewed as novel building blocks of proteins that contain evolutionary information and provide more powerful representation of protein sequences than amino acids. They have been successfully applied to many computational biology tasks, such as domain boundary prediction,[51] knowledge-based mean force potentials,[96] protein remote homology detection,[89] etc. A binary profile can be expressed by a vector with dimensions of 20, in which each element represents one kind of amino acid and can only take a value of 0 or 1. When the element takes the value of 1, it means that the corresponding amino acid can occur during evolution. Otherwise, it means that the corresponding amino acid cannot occur. A binary profile can also be expressed by a substring of amino acid combinations, which is obtained by collecting each element of the vector with non-zero value. Each combination of the 20 amino acids corresponds to a binary profile and vice versa. In the following, we will simply describe the process of generating the binary profiles.

For further details, please refer to Ref. [89]. PSI-BLAST[50] is used to generate the profiles of amino acid sequences with parameters $j = 3$ and $e = 0.001$. The search is performed against the non-redundant (NR) database from NCBI. The frequency profiles are directly obtained from the multiple sequence alignments output by PSI-BLAST, which are converted into a binary profile by a probability threshold P_h. When the frequency of an amino acid is larger than P_h, it is converted into an integral value of 1, which means that the specified amino acid can occur in a given position of the protein sequence during evolution. Otherwise it is converted into 0. In theory, the total number of binary profiles is extremely large (2^{20}), but in fact only a small number of binary profiles appear, which is dependent on the choice of probability threshold P_h and the dataset. Here, P_h is optimized on the validation set, that is, we optimally select a P_h which results in the best performance on the validation set, and this parameter is then used to test the samples on the testing set.

Domains: By focusing on limited, highly conserved regions of proteins, domains can often reveal important clues to a protein's role even if it is not globally similar to any known protein. The domains for most catalytic sites and binding sites are conserved over much wider taxonomic distances and evolutionary time than the sequences of the proteins themselves are. Thus, domains often represent functionally important regions such as catalytic sites, binding sites, protein–protein interaction sites and structural motifs.

Information regarding domains can be gathered from a well-defined database. Following previous studies, two well-known datasets are used here: the Pfam database[90] and the InterPro database.[91] In Pfam, Hidden Markov Model profiles are used to find domains in new proteins. The Pfam database comprises two parts: Pfam-A and Pfam-B. Pfam-A is manually curated, and Pfam-B is automatically generated. In this study, only Pfam-A families are used. In total, there are 2162 Pfam domains covered by the set of proteins. InterPro is an integrated resource for protein families, domains and functional sites that integrates many protein signature databases. In total, there are 3963 entries covered by the set of proteins.

6.3.2.3 *Support Vector Machine*

Support Vector Machines (SVMs) are a class of supervised learning algorithms first introduced by Vapnik.[61] Given a set of labeled training vectors (positive and negative input samples), SVMs can learn a linear decision boundary to discriminate between the two classes. The result is a linear classification rule that can be used to classify new test samples. SVMs have exhibited excellent performance in practice and have a strong theoretical foundation in statistical learning theory. SVMs have been widely used in predicting protein subcellular location, membrane protein type, protein structural class, the specificity of GalNAc-transferase, HIV protease cleavage sites in proteins, beta-turn types, protein signal sequences and their cleavage sites, alpha-turn types, catalytic triads of serine hydrolases, etc.

Here the LIBSVM package is used as the SVM implementation with a radial basis function as the kernel. In statistical prediction, the following three cross-validation methods are often used to examine a predictor for its effectiveness in practical applications: the independent dataset test, the subsampling test and the jackknife test.[97] These three methods have been widely used by investigators to examine the accuracy of various predictors. In this study, the values of kernel width γ and regularization parameter C are optimized by fivefold cross-validation. The whole dataset is randomly divided into five subgroups with an approximately equal number of samples. Each SVM runs five times with five different training and test sets. For each run, three of the subsets are used as the training set, one subset is used to select the optimal parameters (if necessary) and the remaining one is used as the test set. The search range of parameters C and γ are set as $[2^0, 2^1, \ldots, 2^{10}]$ and $[2^{-1}, 2^{-2}, \ldots, 2^{-10}]$, respectively.

6.3.2.4 *Latent semantic analysis*

Latent semantic analysis (LSA) is a theory and method for extracting and representing the contextual-usage meaning of words with statistical computation applied to a large corpus of text.[98] Here, we briefly describe the basic process of LSA. The starting point of LSA is the construction of a word-document matrix W of co-occurrences between words and documents. The elements of W can be taken as the number of times each word appears in each document; thus the dimension of W is $M \times N$, where M is the total number of words and N is the number of given documents. In specific applications, singular value decomposition is performed on the word-document matrix. Let K be the total ranks of W, then W can be decomposed into three matrices:

$$W = USV^T \tag{6-8}$$

where U is the left singular matrix with dimensions $(M \times K)$, V is the right singular matrix with dimensions $(N \times K)$ and S is the $(K \times K)$ diagonal matrix of singular values $s_1 \geq s_2 \geq \cdots s_k > 0$. One can reduce the dimensions of the solution simply by deleting the smaller singular values in the diagonal matrix. The corresponding columns of matrix U (the rows of matrix V) are also ignored. In practice only the top R $(R \ll \text{Min}(M, N))$ dimensions of which the elements in S are greater than a threshold are considered for further processing. Thus, the dimensions of matrices U, S and V are reduced to $M \times R$, $R \times R$ and $N \times R$, leading to data compression and noise removal. In this study, the above basic building blocks are treated as the "words" and the protein sequences can be viewed as the "documents". The word-document matrix is constructed by collecting the weight of each word in the documents. Then, LSA is performed on the matrix to produce the latent semantic representation vectors of protein sequences, leading to noise removal and the compact description of protein sequences. The latent semantic representation vectors are then evaluated by an SVM.

6.3.2.5 *Nonnegative matrix factorization*

Nonnegative matrix factorization is an unsupervised, parts-based learning paradigm first proposed by Lee and Seung.[99] A nonnegative matrix V with a dimensionality of $p \times n$ is decomposed into two nonnegative matrices $V = WH$, where W is a $p \times k$ matrix and H is a $k \times n$ matrix. The rank k of the factorization represents the number of latent factors in the decomposition. It is generally chosen such that $(n + p)k \ll np$, i.e., a number less than n and p. By NMF, each row (column) vector in matrix V is projected onto the basis formed by the column (row) vectors of matrix $H(W)$ and the coefficient is given by the corresponding row (column) vector of matrix $W(H)$. As a result, NMF can produce a low-dimensional approximation of the high-dimensional data. Because of its straightforward implementation, NMF has been applied in the domain of image processing and facial pattern recognition, natural language processing, Internet research, computational biology, etc.

6.3.2.6 *Performance criteria*

The following metrics are used to evaluate performance: sensitivity, specificity, accuracy and the Receiver Operator Characteristic (ROC) curve. Sensitivity measures the fraction of positive samples that are correctly predicted, and it is defined as follows:

$$\text{Sen} = \text{TP}/(\text{TP} + \text{FN}) \tag{6-9}$$

where TP is the number of true positives and FN is the number of false negatives. Specificity gives the fraction of negative samples that are correctly predicted and is defined as follows:

$$\text{Spe} = \text{TN}/(\text{TN} + \text{FP}) \tag{6-10}$$

where FP is the number of false positives and TN is the number of true negatives. The overall accuracy is defined as

$$\text{Accu} = (\text{TP} + \text{TN})/(\text{TP} + \text{TN} + \text{FP} + \text{FN}) \tag{6-11}$$

The ROC curve is plotted with true positives as a function of false positives for varying classification thresholds. A ROC score is the normalized area under the ROC curve. A score of 1 indicates perfect separation of positive samples from negative samples, whereas a score of 0 denotes that none of the sequences selected by the algorithm is positive. The ROC_{50} score is the area of the ROC curve up to 50 false positives.

6.3.3 Performance analysis

6.3.3.1 *Performance comparison of the basic building blocks*

For the SVM method based on the basic building blocks, the length of the feature vector is equal to the number of each type of building block. Each protein sequence is mapped to a high-dimensional vector by the frequency of the occurrence of each building block. These vectors are then inputted to SVM to predict whether they have the specific GO function. Table 6-9 lists the results of the methods that are based on the four kinds of building blocks. As can be seen, the n-gram achieves the lowest performance with an average accuracy of 0.71 and an average ROC score of 0.80. It is generally assumed that protein sequences can determine their structures, and the structures can further determine the function, but the sequence representation in the form of amino acids may not be suitable to predict the structure and function. So, other more informative representations should be explored. The binary profile is one such attempt that describes the sequence information at the profile level. The frequency profiles are first derived from the multiple sequence alignments, and are then converted into binary profiles by the probability threshold P_h. The influence of P_h on the accuracy is shown in Fig. 6-3. As shown in the figure, P_h has minor influence on the performance. The same phenomenon has been observed in our previous studies.[29, 36, 37] The best performance is achieved at a value of 0.27. The corresponding accuracy is 0.78, which is higher than the n-gram by 8%. Such a result indicates that the binary profile contains evolutionary information and can provide more powerful representation of protein sequences

Table 6-9   Performance comparison of the four building blocks.

Methods	Accu	Sen	Spe	ROC
n-grams	0.71	0.69	0.73	0.8
Binary profiles	0.78	0.78	0.79	0.81
PFAM domains	0.82	0.66	0.99	0.94
InterPro domains	0.87	0.76	0.97	0.93

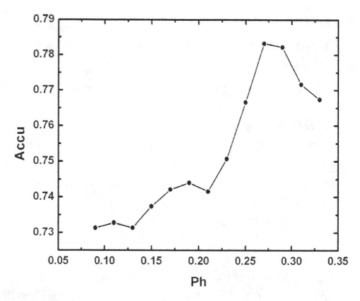

Figure 6-3   The influence of P_h on the accuracy.

than amino acids. Besides the basic amino acid or its variants, the domains can provide important clues about protein function. The PFAM domain can improve the accuracy to 0.82, while the InterPro domain can further increase the accuracy to 0.87. This is reasonable, since the InterPro database is an integration of several databases, whose entries contains more information than the PFAM domain. Domain-based methods outperform sequence-based methods, which means that the domain may be an important component for protein function.

6.3.3.2 *Performance comparison after feature extraction*

Since some of the building blocks are very large, there may be some noise data. Two feature extraction algorithms are introduced here: NMF and LSA. Both of them are based on matrix decomposition, so that the main components are extracted and the noise data can be filtered. The results of the four building blocks after NMF and LSA are listed in Tables 6-10 and 6-11. As can be seen, the performance

Table 6-10 Performance comparison after nonnegative matrix factorization.

	Accu	Sen	Spe	ROC
n-grams	0.73	0.75	0.75	0.77
Binary profiles	0.8	0.79	0.8	0.83
PFAM domains	0.81	0.66	0.95	0.92
InterPro domains	0.66	0.59	0.73	0.87

Table 6-11 Performance comparison after latent semantic analysis.

	Accu	Sen	Spe	ROC
n-grams	0.76	0.75	0.73	0.78
Binary profiles	0.79	0.78	0.8	0.82
PFAM domains	0.82	0.74	0.91	0.88
InterPro domains	0.84	0.74	0.94	0.9

of *n*-grams and binary profiles is improved by using NMF or LSA, whereas the performance of PFAM and InterPro domains is decreased after the same operation. Such a phenomenon indicates that the noise data in *n*-grams and binary profiles is more than that in the PFAM and InterPro domains. We revisit the domain vectors and find that most of the vectors are very sparse, which means that the PFAM and InterPro domains are non-redundant, so the feature extraction algorithms cannot achieve the expected performance.

6.3.3.3 *Performance difference among the GO terms*

GO provides three structured branches that describe the molecular function, biological process and cellular component, respectively. The performance of these three branches is listed in Table 6-12. As can be seen, the molecular function class is easy to predict, while the cellular component class is relatively hard to discriminate. GO is also a hierarchy DAG. The child term is more specialistic than its ancestors. The performance of the GO terms at different depths is

Table 6-12   Performance comparison among different GO types.

Type	Accu	Sen	Spe	ROC
Molecular function	0.89[a]	0.79	0.98	0.94
Biological process	0.85	0.73	0.97	0.91
Cellular component	0.83	0.73	0.94	0.92

Note: [a]Shown in the table are the average values based on InterPro domains.

Table 6-13   Performance comparison among different GO depths.

Depth	Accu	Sen	Spe	ROC
2	0.85[a]	0.73	0.96	0.93
3	0.86	0.76	0.95	0.92
4	0.87	0.76	0.97	0.93
5	0.87	0.76	0.98	0.93
6	0.87	0.75	0.98	0.93
7	0.86	0.74	0.98	0.92
8	0.87	0.79	0.95	0.93
9	0.9	0.83	0.97	0.94
10	0.96	0.91	1	0.98

Note: [a]Shown in the table are the average values based on InterPro domains.

listed in Table 6-13. As shown in the table, all the GO terms with different depths can be quite successfully predicted.

6.3.3.4 *Comparison with other studies*

Since there is no gold-standard dataset publicly available, direct comparison with other methods is not feasible. However, the reported performance can be accessed to give an indirect comparison.

The most widely used method is based on the sequence searching technique. However, the similarity between sequences does not mean that they are homologous. Thus, many researchers try to evaluate the search results to give a reliable prediction. Vinayagam *et al.*[79] developed an automated annotation system to assign functional GO terms to an unknown sequence. They defined 31 attributes for each GO term according to the sequence query results and applied a support vector machine to predict whether the given sequence has GO function or not. Their method achieved an average precision of 0.80 for 74% of all test sequences. The proposed method achieves an average accuracy of 0.71–0.87 for all test sequences. The PFP[100] method applied a function association matrix to score strongly associated pairs of annotations. It achieves more than 60% accuracy for the GO terms with depth larger than 8, while the current study obtains 87% accuracy for the GO terms with the same depth.

Domains are generally regarded as an important component for protein function. Forslund and Sonnhammer[82] presented a probabilistic model to represent the relationship between the PFAM domain content and GO terms. They achieve a sensitivity of 69% and a specificity of 99%, while the PFAM domain method in this study obtains a sensitivity of 66% and a specificity of 99%.

Protein function prediction can also be viewed as a classification problem. Sequences with unknown function can be classified into the function classes. The SVM-Prot method[80] extracted many sequence features and adopted a support vector machine to predict their function. It achieves an accuracy of 0.69–0.99 for 54 function families. The MAMMOTH method[84] adopted structure similarity as the kernel for GO-based function prediction. It achieves an average ROC score of 0.88 for 23 GO terms. The current study achieves an average accuracy of 0.87 and an average ROC score of 0.93 for 175 GO terms.

6.4 Prediction of Protein–Protein Interaction from Primary Sequences

6.4.1 Introduction

In recent years, high-throughput experimental methods for detecting protein–protein interactions, such as the two-hybrid (Y2H) screens[101] and mass spectrometry,[102] have generated many genome-scale protein interaction networks such as *Caenorhabditis elegans*,[103] *Drosophila melanogaster*,[104] *Helicobacter pylori*,[105] *H.sapiens*[106] and

Saccharomyces cerevisiae.[107] However, high throughput experiments are often associated with a high rate of false positives and false negatives.[108] The experiments are also tedious and labor-intensive. In addition, the number of possible protein interactions within one cell is enormous, which makes the experimental verification of each individual interaction impractical. Therefore, there is a continuing need for computational methods to complement the existing experimental approaches.

A number of computational methods for protein–protein interaction prediction have been developed in recent years. These methods differ in the feature sets and classification methods used for protein interaction prediction.[109] Some methods are based on genomic sequence information, such as phylogenetic profiles,[110] gene neighborhood,[111] gene fusion events[112] and correlated mRNA expression. Other methods use the primary structure information and associated physicochemical properties.[113] Protein–protein interaction data can also be extracted from the literature.[114] Many classifiers have been introduced to predict protein–protein interactions, including logistic regression,[115] Naïve Bayes,[116] decision tree,[117] K-Local hyperplane distance nearest neighbor classifiers,[118] random decision forest,[119] Support Vector Machine (SVM),[120] etc.

Even with recent improvements in proteomics and structural genomics methods, sequence information is by far the most readily retrieved source available for computational analyses.[100] Recently, advances have been made in protein–protein interaction prediction by using only sequence information (without any structural, genomic or functional information). Previous studies noted that many pairs of structural domains are overrepresented in interacting proteins and this information can be used to predict interactions.[121] Other authors have proposed Bayesian network models that use the domain or motif content of a sequence to predict interactions.[122] Such a method allows the incorporation of both "positive" and "negative" information and outperforms other attraction-only and sequence-signature models. The PIPE method[123] predicts protein–protein interactions by collecting the reoccurring short polypeptide sequences between known interacting protein pairs. However, this method is time-consuming and has a high rate of false positives. The revised method[124] significantly improves the efficiency of the original method and can be used for large-scale datasets. The correlated sequence-signatures[125] can be learned from a database of experimentally determined interacting proteins, where one protein contains one sequence-signature and its interacting partner contains another one. Such signatures have been viewed as significant markers of protein–protein interactions. Although not every protein with the one sequence-signature is expected to interact with every protein with the other sequence-signature, these identifiers can be used to direct the experimental interaction screens, significantly reducing the search in the space of protein pairs. Fang *et al.* discovered 3108 protein sequence signatures from protein–protein interaction data.[126] Approximately 94% of the sequence signatures match entries in InterPro databases.[127] Other studies have tried to predict protein–protein interactions using signature products with a sequence representation by 3mers.[95] This method uses the local sequence similarities between proteins and does not require physical or chemical information and prior knowledge of domains. Furthermore, the pairwise kernel[128] has been introduced to predict protein–protein interactions, which can integrate various data sources and provides better performance than the genome kernel.

All the sequence-based methods try to extract sequence information for protein–protein interaction prediction. However, the basic composition information has not been explored thoroughly. In this study, we aim to predict protein–protein interactions by using sequence composition information. Such composition information may contain important information about the functions of proteins and can provide clues for protein–protein interactions. Four kinds of basic building blocks of protein sequences have been investigated, including *n*-grams,[129] patterns,[130] motifs[131] and binary profiles.[53] The protein sequences are mapped into high-dimensional vectors by using the occurrence frequencies of each kind of building block. The resulting vectors are then taken as input to a discriminative learning algorithm, such as an SVM, to predict protein–protein interactions. The above building blocks have been used for protein remote homology detection in our previous studies.[53,92] Better results are obtained by using Latent Semantic Analysis (LSA), which is an efficient feature extraction technique from natural language processing.[19] Here, we also demonstrate that the use of latent semantic analysis technology can efficiently remove noise without significantly reducing performance.

6.4.2 Protein sequence vocabulary

6.4.2.1 *Dataset*

Protein–protein interaction data specific to the genome of *Saccharomyces Cerevisiae* is used because the quantity of protein–protein interaction data available for yeast far exceeds that available for any other model organism.[132] We focus on the prediction of physical interactions and use interaction data from the DIP database.[133] The "small-scale" subset is used here since it is the gold standard dataset for physical interaction.[109] Currently, it contains 3206 interaction pairs among 1628 proteins. These interaction pairs are used as positive samples. The identification of negative samples for protein–protein interactions is difficult because it is rare to find a confirmed report of noninteracting pairs. Here the negative samples are taken from the dataset generated by Qi *et al.*[109] Since SVM cannot perform well on an unbalanced dataset, negative samples are randomly selected to make the ratio of positive and negative data close to 1:1.

6.4.2.2 *Basic building blocks of protein sequences*

In order to predict protein–protein interactions from primary sequences, a suitable representation of protein sequences has to be chosen first. In this study, each protein sequence is treated as a "document" that is composed of bag-of-X, where X can be any basic building block of protein sequences. Four kinds of basic building blocks of protein sequences have been investigated, including n-grams,[129] patterns,[130] motifs[131] and binary profiles.[53]

***n-grams*:** The term "*n*-gram" is borrowed from the field of natural language processing. It refers to *n* consecutive symbols (e.g. characters, words). For protein sequences, the *n*-grams are the set of all possible subsequences of amino acids with a fixed length of *n*. The number of possible *n*-grams in protein sequences increases exponentially with *n*, so the value of *n* is taken as 3. The total number of possible *n*-grams in protein sequences are 8000 ($20^{\wedge}3$), which is sufficient to predict protein–protein interaction.

The *n*-grams used here are the same as the k-spectrum for protein remote homology detection.[129] They are also very close to the signatures used by Martin *et al.*[95] for protein–protein interaction prediction. The only difference between *n*-grams and signatures is that signatures do not consider the order of the neighboring amino acids.

***Patterns*:** During evolution, amino acid substitution is a common phenomenon. Thus the protein words can be composed of amino acids and the wildcard ('.') that can be any of the 20 amino acids. Here are some examples: E.L.K, NGF, KI...L, Q..Y.A..L. The protein words used here are the same as the patterns in biological sequence analysis. Let Σ be an alphabet; a pattern[134] is a string in $\Sigma U \Sigma$ ($\Sigma U\{'.'\})^{*}\Sigma$, that is, a string on the alphabet $\Sigma U\{'.'\}$ that starts and ends with a solid character (not a wildcard). Using patterns as the protein secondary structure words, Dong *et al.*[135] predicted the secondary structures of proteins with satisfactory results.

The TEIRESIAS[136] algorithm is used to extract patterns in protein sequences. TEIRESIAS is a deterministic algorithm that allows one to carry out pattern discovery in biological sequences, and that has been used to annotate proteins.[137] In this study, the TEIRESIAS algorithm is executed on all the training sets of protein sequences, and totally 118,049 patterns are extracted. The produced patterns contain too much redundant information and many machine learning methods cannot perform well in the high-dimensional feature space. It is highly desirable to reduce the native space by removing non-informative or redundant patterns. After an effective feature selection (chi-square selection),[138] 8000 patterns are selected as the characteristic words.

Motifs: By focusing on limited, highly conserved regions of proteins, motifs can often reveal important clues to a protein's role even if it is not globally similar to any known protein.[139] The motifs for most catalytic sites and binding sites are conserved over much wider taxonomic distances and evolutionary time than the sequences of the proteins themselves are. Thus, motifs often represent functionally important regions such as catalytic sites, binding sites, protein–protein interaction sites and structural motifs.

Several computer algorithms exist for automatically constructing a characteristic set of sequence motifs from a set of biological sequences. In this study, the MEME/MAST system version 3.0[140, 141] is used to discover motifs and search databases. MEME represents motifs as the position-dependent letter-probability matrices that describe the probability of each possible letter at each position in the pattern. MEME uses statistical modeling techniques to automatically choose the best width, number of occurrences and description for each motif. Since motifs only exist in related protein sequences, the protein sequence and its interacting partners are used to generate motifs. In total, there are 8140 motifs extracted. These motifs are referred to as motif-MEME.

Motif information can also be gathered from a well-defined database. Following previous studies,[119] the Pfam database[142] is used here, which is a protein domain family database that contains multiple sequence alignments of common domain families. In Pfam, Hidden Markov Model profiles are used to find domains in new proteins. The Pfam database consists of two parts: Pfam-A and Pfam-B. Pfam-A is manually curated, and Pfam-B is automatically generated. Both Pfam-A and Pfam-B families are used here. In total, there are 7868 Pfam domains defined by the set of proteins. These motifs are referred as motif-Pfam.

Binary profiles: Binary profiles can be viewed as novel building blocks of proteins that contain evolutionary information and provide more powerful representation of protein sequences than amino acids.

They have been successfully applied to many computational biology tasks, such as domain boundary prediction,[51] knowledge-based mean force potentials,[52] protein remote homology detection,[53] etc.

A binary profile can be expressed by a vector with dimensions of 20, in which each element represents one kind of amino acid and can only take a value of 0 or 1. When the element takes a value of 1, it means that the corresponding amino acid can occur during evolution. Otherwise, it means that the corresponding amino acid cannot occur. A binary profile can also be expressed by a substring of amino acid combination, which is obtained by collecting each element of the vector with non-zero value. Each combination of the 20 amino acids corresponds to a binary profile and vice versa. In the following, we describe the process of generating the binary profiles.

PSI-BLAST[50] is used to generate the profiles of amino acid sequences with parameters $j = 3$ and $e = 0.001$. The search is performed against the non-redundant (NR) database from NCBI. The frequency profiles are directly obtained from the multiple sequence alignments output by PSI-BLAST. The target frequency reflects the probability of the occurrence of an amino acid in a given position of the sequences. The method of target frequency calculation is similar to that implemented in PSI-BLAST.

Because the frequency profile is a matrix of frequencies for all amino acids, it cannot be directly used and needs to be converted into a binary profile by a probability threshold P_h. When the frequency of an amino acid is larger than P_h, it is converted into an integral value of 1, which means that the specified amino acid can occur at a given position of the protein sequence during evolution. Otherwise it is converted into 0. A substring of amino acid combination is then obtained by collecting the binary profile with non-zero value for each position of the protein sequences. These substrings have approximately represented the amino acids that can possibly occur at a given sequence position during evolution. Figure 6-1 shows the process of generating binary profiles.

In theory, the total number of binary profiles is extremely large (2^{20}), but in fact only a small number of binary profiles appears. This is dependent on the choice of the probability threshold P_h and the dataset. Here P_h is optimized on the validation set, that is, we optimally select a P_h which results in the best performance on the validation set and such a parameter is then used to test the samples on the testing set.

6.4.2.3 *Support Vector Machine*

Support Vector Machines (SVM) are a class of supervised learning algorithms first introduced by Vapnik.[61] Given a set of labeled training vectors (positive and negative input samples), SVM can learn a linear decision boundary to discriminate between the two classes. The result is a linear classification rule that can be used to classify new test samples. SVMs have shown excellent performance in practice and have a strong theoretical foundation of statistical learning theory. Here, the LIBSVM package[62] is used as the SVM implementation with a radial basis function as the kernel. The values of γ and regularization parameter C are set to be 0.005 and 1, respectively. Fivefold cross-validation is then used to evaluate the SVM. The whole dataset is randomly divided into five subgroups with an approximately equal number of samples. Each SVM runs five times with five different training and test sets. For each run, three of the subsets are used as the training set, one subset is used to select the optimal parameters (if necessary) and the remaining one is used as the test set.

The core component of an SVM is the kernel that measures the similarity between any two samples. The "genomic kernel"[128] can measure the similarities between two protein sequences. For protein–protein interactions, a kernel that measures two pairs of protein sequences is required. Here, we adopt the pairwise kernel $K((X_1, X_2), (X_1', X_2'))$[128] that returns the similarity between sequences X_1, X_2 and sequences X_1', X_2'

$$K((X_1, X_2), (X_1', X_2')) = K(X_1, X_1')K(X_2, X_2')$$
$$+ K(X_1, X_2')K(X_2, X_1') \quad (6\text{-}12)$$

Each protein sequence can be mapped into a high-dimensional vector by the occurrence times of each basic building block. The similarity between two pairs of proteins can be measured by the pairwise kernel.[128] Such similarities can be input to SVM to predict whether a given protein pair interacts or not. The basic hypothesis used here is that some of the interactions between proteins are mediated by a finite number of short polypeptide sequences. Such a phenomenon has also been observed by other authors.[123, 125]

6.4.2.4 *Latent semantic analysis*

Latent semantic analysis (LSA) is a theory and method for extracting and representing the contextual-usage meaning of words by statistical computation applied to a large corpus of text.[143] Here, we briefly describe the basic process of LSA.

The starting point for LSA is the construction of a word-document matrix W of co-occurrences between words and documents. The elements of W can be taken as the number of times each word appears in each document; thus the dimension of W is $M \times N$, where M is the total number of words and N is the number of given documents. To compensate for the differences in document lengths and overall counts of different words in the document collection, each word count is normalized.[143]

In the word-document matrix W, each document is expressed as a column vector. However, this representation does not recognize synonymous or related words and the dimensions are too large. In specific applications, singular value decomposition is performed on the word-document matrix. Let K be the total ranks of W, so W can be decomposed into three matrices

$$W = USV^T \tag{6-13}$$

where U is the left singular matrix with dimensions $(M \times K)$, V is the right singular matrix with dimensions $(N \times K)$ and S is the $(K \times K)$ diagonal matrix of singular values $s_1 \geq s_2 \geq \cdots s_K > 0$. One can reduce the dimensions of the solution by simply deleting the smaller singular values in the diagonal matrix. The corresponding columns of matrix U (rows of matrix V) are also ignored. In practice only the top R $(R \ll \text{Min}(M, N))$ dimensions of which the elements in S are greater than a threshold are considered for further processing. Thus, the dimensions of matrices U, S and V are reduced to $M \times R$, $R \times R$ and $N \times R$, leading to data compression and noise removal. Values of R in the range [200, 300] are typically used for information retrieval. In the present context, the best results are achieved when R takes a value around 1700.

By SVD, the column vectors of the word-document matrix W are projected onto the orthonormal basis formed by the row (column) vectors of the left singular matrix U. The coordinates of the vectors are given by the columns of SV^T. This in turn means that the column vectors Sv_j^T or, equivalently the row vectors v_jS, characterize the position of document d_j in the R-dimensional space. Each of the vectors v_jS is referred to as a document vector, uniquely associated with the document in the training set.

For a new document that is not in the training set, it is necessary to add the unseen document to the original training set and the latent semantic analysis model needs be recomputed. However, SVD is a computationally expensive process, and so performing SVD every time for a new test document is not suitable. From the mathematical properties of the matrices U, S and V, the new vector t can be approximated as follows:

$$t = dU \tag{6-14}$$

where d is the raw vector of the new document, which is similar to the columns of the matrix W.

In this study, the above basic building blocks are treated as the "words" and the protein sequences can be viewed as the "documents". The word-document matrix is constructed by collecting the weight of each word in the documents. LSA is performed on the matrix to produce the latent semantic representation vectors of protein sequences, leading to noise removal and the compact description of protein sequences. The latent semantic representation vectors are then evaluated by an SVM.

The following metrics are used to evaluate performance: sensitivity, specificity, accuracy and the Receiver Operator Characteristic (ROC) curve.

6.4.3 Prediction of protein–protein interaction

The method in this study is compared with a simple ranking method that assigns a score to a candidate interaction based on its similarity to the interacting pairs in the training set. Following the work of Ben-Hur and Noble,[128] let $l(X, X')$ denote the negative log of the E-value assigned by PSI-BLAST when searching X against X' in the context of a large database of sequences, and let $I(i, j)$ be an indicator variable for the interaction between proteins i and j. $l(X, X')$ is positive for significant matches and increases as the quality of the match increases. The score for a query (X_1, X_2) is defined as:

$$\max_{i \in p,\, j \in p} \min(l(X_1, X_i),\ l(X_2, X_j)) \qquad (6\text{-}15)$$

where P is the set of all proteins in the training set. In these experiments, we use the PSI-BLAST scores computed in the context of the nonredundant (NR) database from NCBI.

For the SVM method based on the basic building blocks, the length of the feature vector is equal to the number of each type of building block. Each protein sequence is mapped to a high-dimensional vector by the frequency of the occurrence of each building block. Two protein vectors are jointed to form an interaction vector, which is then inputted to the SVM to predict whether they interact or not. Table 6-14 gives the results of the methods that are based on the four kinds of building blocks and their combinations. As can be seen, all the SVM-based methods with basic building blocks outperform the PSI-BLAST method. There are minor differences among the different building blocks. The methods based on motifs seem to slightly outperform other methods, which indicates that the motif may be an important component of protein interactions.

For the LSA-based method, the word-document matrix is built by collecting the weight of each word in the documents. Here, each basic building block can be viewed as one kind of word. LSA is then performed on this matrix to give the latent semantic representative vectors of protein sequences. The produced vectors are then jointed to form the interaction vectors, which are inputted to SVM to predict whether they interact or not. The results are shown in Table 6-15.

Table 6-14   Comparative results of various methods.

	Sen	Spe	Accu	Roc	Roc50
PSI-BLAST	0.3371	**0.8379**	0.65912	0.6611	0.5231
n-gram	0.6471	0.7687	0.7172	0.7799	0.6511
Pattern	0.6487	0.7784	0.7133	0.7817	0.6358
Motif-MEME	0.6482	0.8040	0.7263	0.7866	0.6698
Motif-Pfam	0.6823	0.7710	0.7264	0.7916	0.6420
Binary profile	0.7066	0.6992	0.7027	0.7707	0.6261
Combination	**0.7273**	0.7733	**0.7503**	**0.8233**	**0.7003**

Table 6-15   The results of several building blocks with LSA.

	Sen	Spe	Accu	Roc	Roc50
n-gram-LSA	0.6337	0.7542	0.7068	0.7641	0.6232
Pattern-LSA	0.6378	0.7648	0.7103	0.7724	0.6397
Motif-MEME-LSA	0.6590	**0.7736**	0.7262	0.7820	0.6637
Motif-Pfam-LSA	0.6897	0.7603	0.7247	0.7881	0.6485
Binary profile-LSA	0.7124	0.7001	0.7063	0.7728	0.6195
Combination-LSA	**0.7163**	0.7647	**0.7453**	**0.8089**	**0.6939**

The LSA-based methods show a similar performance in comparison with the method without LSA. Because LSA is an efficient feature extraction technique, significant noise removal is seen and a better description of the protein sequences is obtained. The lengths of the latent semantic representative vectors are shorter than the original ones, so the prediction efficiency is significantly improved.

Figure 6-4 plots the ROC_{50} curves for several methods, which clearly demonstrates the differences between various methods. It is obvious that the PSI-BLAST method achieves the lowest performance. Among the SVM-based methods, the Motif-Pfam methods get the best performance. All the LSA-based methods have a performance that is a little lower than the corresponding SVM-based methods.

To investigate the difference between several building blocks, we count the number of samples that are correctly predicted by any two building blocks. The results are given in Table 6-16. As can be seen, consistent prediction between any two building blocks is

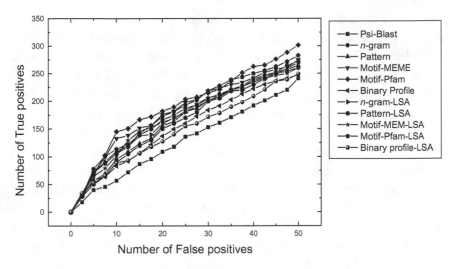

Figure 6-4　The ROC$_{50}$ curves for several methods.

Table 6-16　The percent of consistent prediction between any two building blocks.

	n-gram	Pattern	Motif-MEME	Motif-Pfam	Binary profile
n-gram	—	0.6695	0.6625	0.6834	0.6324
Pattern	0.6695	—	0.6642	0.6677	0.6239
Motif-MEME	0.6625	0.6642	—	0.6658	0.6196
Motif-Pfam	0.6834	0.6677	0.6658	—	0.6419
Binary profile	0.6324	0.6239	0.6196	0.6419	—

Note: Only the correctly predicted samples are counted.

approximately equal. There are thus no distinct differences between any two building blocks.

Since there are minor differences among the different building blocks, we check whether the combination of all the building blocks can help achieve better results. The vector of each building block is concatenated to get the final feature vector. Unfortunately the performance in this case was lower than any of the building blocks used separately (data not shown). This may be caused by the simple concatenation mechanism that results in the dimension of the final vector being as high as 74,821, and generally SVM cannot perform well when high-dimensional vectors are used as input. An additional feature selection (chi-square selection) is used and only 8000 features are selected. The results based on the new feature vectors are given in the last rows of Tables 6-14 and 6-15. Obviously, the combination method outperforms any of the building blocks. In the 8000 features, the number of n-grams, patterns, motif-MEMEs, motif-Pfams and binary profiles are 0, 2230, 2590, 1950 and 1230, respectively. An interesting phenomenon is that none of the n-grams has been selected, which indicates that their contribution to protein–protein interaction is very small in comparison with other building blocks.

Examples of non-interacting proteins are randomly chosen. To test the stability of the results with respect to the choice of negative examples, we run a set of experiments using 10 different randomly selected sets of non-interacting proteins. Predictions are based on the motif-MEME building block. The standard deviation of the resulting ROC scores is 0.08, which shows good stability.

The method presented in this study achieves a sensitivity of 63%–72%, a specificity of 70%–83% and an accuracy of 65%–75%. Such results are comparable with other protein–protein interaction prediction methods. Chen and Liu[119] adopted the random decision forest for protein–protein interaction prediction, which takes the PFam domain as features. Testing on yeast data obtained from the DIP database, they achieved a sensitivity of 79.78%, a specificity of 64.38% and an accuracy of 72.8%. Martin *et al.*[95] adopted the signature products for protein–protein interaction. Testing on the full yeast dataset, they obtained a sensitivity of 63.2%, a specificity of 71.5% and an accuracy of 69%. The PIPE method[123] is based on the sequence similarities measured by the reoccurring short polypeptide between known interacting protein pairs. Testing on the yeast dataset with small samples (100 interaction pairs and 100 non-interaction pairs), they obtained a sensitivity of 61%, a specificity of 89% and an accuracy of 75%. The PIPE2 method[124] significantly improves the efficiency of the original method and can help achieve a specificity of 99.95% with a sacrifice of sensitivity (14.6%). Guo *et al.*[144] presented the state-of-art method, which used a support vector machine combined with the auto-covariance for protein–protein interaction.

Testing on the yeast subset data obtained from the DIP database, they showed a sensitivity of 85.22%, a specificity of 87.83% and an accuracy of 86.23%. However, the negative samples are taken from the protein pairs that occupy different subcellular localizations. Such protein pairs are easy to predict since the proteins with different subcellular localizations generally do not interact. When testing on another dataset in which the negative samples are randomly chosen, they only obtained a sensitivity of 41.76%, a specificity of 62.64% and an accuracy of 58.42%. The negative samples in this study are also randomly chosen, and we got better results than those obtained by Guo *et al.*; so, our method is comparable with state-of-art methods.

Computational efficiency is an interesting factor for genome-wide prediction of protein–protein interaction. In this regard, the training times of LSA-based methods are lower than those of the SVM-based methods, but the testing times of LSA-based methods are much shorter than those of SVM-based methods. Any SVM-based method includes a vectorization step and an optimization step. The time complexity of the vectorization step of the method without LSA is $O(nml)$, where n is the number of training examples, m is the total number of building blocks and l is the length of the longest training sequence. The main bottleneck of the LSA method is the additional SVD process, which roughly takes $O(nmt)$, where t is the minimum of n and m. The optimization step of the SVM-based method takes $O(n^2 p)$, where p is the length of the latent semantic representation vector. In the SVM-based method p is equal to m, while in the LSA-based method, p is equal to R. Since $R < \text{Min}(n, m)$, the SVM optimization step of the LSA-based method is much faster than that of the SVM-based method.

The analysis presented here is based on sequences alone without using any evolutionary or structural information. Four basic building blocks of protein sequences are investigated: the n-grams, the patterns, the motifs and the binary profiles. Obviously, using structural or evolutionary information can further improve the performance of protein interaction prediction. Such evolutionary or structural information can also be used in the LSA model, so long as the structural or functional building blocks of proteins are extracted.

However, the identification of functional equivalents of "words" in protein sequences is the major hurdle in the use of natural language techniques for a variety of computational biology problems.[145] In essence, the method presented here provides fertile ground for further experimentation with building blocks that can be constructed using different properties of the amino acids and proteins.

6.5 Identifying the Missing Proteins using the Biological Language Model

6.5.1 Introduction

The Human Proteome Project (HPP)[146] was launched by the Human Proteome Organization (HUPO) in 2011, and it comprises Chromosome-centric HPP (C-HPP)[147] and Biology/Disease-Driven HPP (B/DHPP).[148] This project aims to identify as many proteins as possible with the goal of covering all human protein-encoding genes. This great goal is made possible by the cooperation between 25 international member associations.[149] The baseline metrics for the HPP contain five annually updated data resources, which are as follows[149]: the Ensembl database,[150] which provides the possible gene coding for proteins; Peptide Atlas[151] and GPMdb,[152] both of which separately screen high-confident proteins from mass spectrometry data; the Human Protein Atlas,[153] which extracts protein data using antibody-based research; and neXtProt,[154] which collects all human proteins and assigns confidence levels (PE 1–5) by protein expression evidence. Proteins at the PE1 level are identified at the protein expression level by mass spectrometry, immunohistochemistry, 3D structure and/or amino acid sequencing. The proteins at the PE2 level are detected by transcript expression but not by protein expression. At the PE3 level, there is no protein or transcript evidence, but homologies are represented in related species. Proteins at the PE4 level are speculated from gene models. Finally, the protein sequences at the PE5 level are generated from "dubious" or "uncertain" genes that seemed to have some protein-level evidence in the past, but such identifications are doubtful upon curation.

Much progress has been achieved since 2011 by the proteomics community and the HPP. On the basis of the curation of the neXtProt[155] database, currently 82% of the protein-coding genes in humans have protein expressions with high confidence. However, there are 3,564 genes at levels PE2–5 that have no or insufficient evidence of identification by any experimental methods and are thus termed "missing proteins".[155] Many of these missing proteins are hard to detect because of low abundance, poor solubility or indistinguishable peptide sequences within protein families. Such a significant amount of proteins being unaccounted for marks a significant problem in our current understanding of the human proteome and leads to particularly important questions including, e.g. whether these proteins are essential to the cell functions, and if yes, what biological roles they play in the cell and why they are not detectable by the current instruments at both transcription and translation levels. Thus, identifying the missing proteins will be a challenging task.

Previous studies have shown that there are analogies between biological sequences and natural language. In linguistics, some words and phrases can form a meaningful sentence; in biology, the tactic nucleotides denote genes, and the fixed protein sequences can determine their structure and function. Tsonis[156] discussed whether DNA is a language or not. Many linguistic approaches have been used in computational biology.[145, 157, 158] Ganapathiraju *et al.*[159] analyzed the language features of whole-genome protein sequences. Many techniques of Natural Language Processing have been used in bioinformatics, such as protein domain recognition based on language modeling,[160] dictionary-driven protein annotation,[161] protein remote homology detection by latent semantic analysis,[162–165] identification of DNA-binding proteins,[166, 167] etc.

In this section, the missing proteins in the human proteome are identified using the biological language model. Amino acid n-gram models for human and non-human protein sequences are constructed. These models are subsequently used to distinguish whether the missing proteins are natively gene-coding proteins in humans or not. The identified proteins are then analyzed by their predicted structures and functions, annotation from the neXtProt database,[154] the HGNC database[168] and other mass spectrometry datasets.[169]

6.5.2 n-gram model for gene discrimination

6.5.2.1 *Data source*

The native gene-coding proteins are downloaded from the Swiss-Prot database.[170] To construct reliable models, only the protein sequences with reviewed items are selected. In total, there are 14,565 human proteins and 70,854 non-human proteins. The redundant sequences are then filtered by using a CD-HIT program[171] with a sequence identity threshold of 90%. Finally, we get 14,189 human proteins and 59,060 non-human proteins, which are used to build the n-gram model for humans and non-humans, respectively.

"Dubious" or "uncertain" missing proteins with confidence code "PE5" are extracted from the neXtProt database[154] released on September 19, 2014. There are in total 616 proteins in this category with lengths ranging from 21 to 2252 residues. The structures of these proteins are predicted using the I-TASSER software.[172] Functions including the EC number, the GO terms and the binding sites are predicted by using the COFACTOR software.[173] Both I-TASSER and COFACTOR are run in non-homology mode where all the homologous structures identified with sequence identities greater than or equal to 30% are removed. Subcellular localization is predicted by using Hum-mPLoc.[174]

6.5.2.2 *Biological language models to discriminate the native gene-coding of human and non-human proteins*

Protein sequences are composed of 20 native amino acids, while in natural language, sentences are comprised of words. Such a similarity has drawn the attention of researchers, and the language features of DNA and protein sequences have been investigated extensively.[175–177] In this study, methods from natural language processing, especially the statistical natural language processing methods which have been successfully used to solve many of the natural language tasks,[178] are applied to identify the missing proteins. Formally, the problem of identifying missing proteins can be described as follows: given a protein $P = (a_1, a_2, \ldots, a_L)$, whether this protein is a human protein or not can be assessed by

$$P(H \mid P) > P(NH \mid P) \tag{6-16}$$

where $P(H \mid P)$ and $P(NH \mid P)$ represent the probability of this protein as being human and non-human in nature, respectively. The above equation can be converted by conditional probability formulae to

$$\frac{P(H)P(P \mid H)}{P(P)} > \frac{P(NH)P(P \mid NH)}{P(P)} \tag{6-17}$$

Since the denominator is the same, it can be ignored during the comparison. $P(H)$ and $P(NH)$ are the prior probabilities of proteins being human and non-human proteins respectively, and can be estimated from the training dataset by using maximum likelihood estimation based on the number of human and non-human proteins. By applying the conditional probability formulae repeatedly, the probability of $P(H \mid P)$ or $P(NH \mid P)$ can be decomposed into the following:

$$\begin{aligned}
P(P \mid H) &= P(a_1 \cdots a_L \mid H) \\
&= P(a_1 \mid H)P(a_2 \cdots a_L \mid H, a_1) \\
&= P(a_1 \mid H)P(a_2 \mid H, a_1)P(a_3 \cdots a_L \mid H, a_1, a_2) \\
&= P(a_1 \mid H) \sum_{i=2}^{L} P(a_i \mid a_1 \cdots a_{i-1}, H)
\end{aligned} \tag{6-18}$$

The n-gram model supposes that the occurrence of each word is only dependent on the previous $n-1$ words, so the above equation can be recalculated as

$$P(P \mid H) \approx \sum_{i=n}^{L} P(a_i \mid a_{i-n+1} \cdots a_{i-1}, H) \tag{6-19}$$

where the conditional probability can be estimated by maximum likelihood estimation

$$P(a_i \mid a_{i-n+1} \cdots a_{i-1}) = \frac{C(a_{i-n+1} \cdots a_i)}{C(a_{i-n+1} \cdots a_{i-1})} \tag{6-20}$$

where $C(a_i \cdots a_j)$ is the number of occurrences of the amino acid sequences $a_i \cdots a_j$.

The same procedure can be applied to construct the n-gram model of non-human proteins. The missing proteins can be identified by using n-gram models to assess whether they are native human proteins or not.

6.5.3 Identifying the missing proteins

Based on the n-gram models, there are 102 proteins in the neXtProt "PE5" category that have a high probability of being native human proteins. In the following sections, these proteins are analyzed by their predicted structure and function and annotations from other databases.

6.5.3.1 *Structure and function analysis of the high-probability proteins*

Since the missing proteins have not been identified by experimental methods, their structures and functions are currently unknown. In this study, the structures and functions of the high-probability proteins inferred by n-gram models are predicted using I-TASSER and COFACTOR software and the confidence scores output by the software are used to indicate the reliability of the prediction. The I-TASSER confidence score (C-score) is computed by the accuracy of the threading programs and the simulation results of the structural assembly process. The value range is between -5 and 2, with higher C-score values representing more confidence in the corresponding model, and vice-versa. A model with an I-TASSER C-score larger than -1.5 means that the structure topology is correct. The confidence score (C-score) of COFACTOR is calculated based on the confidence score of the structure prediction and the similarity between the predicted models and their native structures in the PDB. The COFACTOR C-score is normalized between 0 and 1, with a large value indicating a good prediction. Figure 6-5 shows the distribution of I-TASSER and COFACTOR C-scores of the 102 high-probability missing proteins. The number of foldable proteins (those with C-scores higher than -1.5) is less than the number of unfoldable proteins (those with C-scores lower than

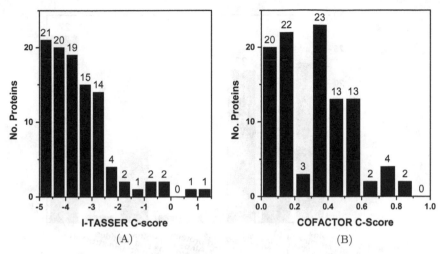

Figure 6-5   The distribution of the I-TASSER (A) and COFACTOR (B) C-scores of the identified missing proteins.

−1.5), which was also confirmed in our previous study on missing proteins.[179] The reason for this phenomenon may be that the missing proteins are not gene-coding proteins or that there is no homology template used during prediction. Based on the results of structure prediction, there are 7 foldable proteins whose I-TASSER C-scores are larger than the foldable threshold (−1.5). These proteins have good structure models with no homologous templates used during prediction, which means that they may be gene-coding proteins. Most of the COFACTOR C-scores are distributed between 0.3 and 0.6, with 8 proteins having very high COFACTOR C-scores. As shown in the figure, the COFACTOR C-score for most of the missing proteins is larger than 0.2, which indicates a good function prediction based on experience evaluation.

6.5.3.2 *Structural topology analyses of the I-TASSER models*

The SCOPe library[180] is used as the classification criterion for structure topology assessment, and it is an extended structure library integrated from the standard SCOP[181] and ASTRAL[182] databases. The structure class of the I-TASSER model is assigned as the

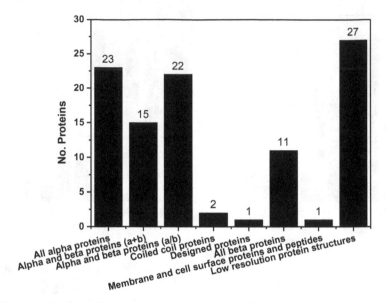

Figure 6-6   Relative frequency distribution of SCOP classes for the identified missing proteins.

corresponding structure class of the SCOPe domain which has the highest structural similarity with the model. The structure alignment program TM-align[183] is used to calculate the TM-score between the I-TASSER model and all structural domains from SCOPe. If there are multiple domains in the target model, we selected the domain that has the maximum TM-score to be the SCOPe domain. Figure 6-6 shows the distribution of the SCOPe class of the identified missing proteins. It is interesting that some missing proteins have structure topology in the "membrane and cell surface proteins and peptides" and "coiled coil proteins" classes. Such a phenomenon is reasonable since these kinds of proteins are difficult to identify by the experimental method.

6.5.3.3 *Evaluation of the function based on Gene Ontology*

The GO molecular function of the high-probability missing proteins is predicted by the COFACTOR package and the number in each

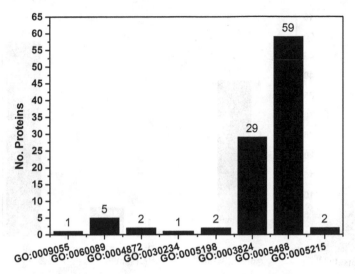

Figure 6-7 The distribution of predicted GO items from the first level of molecular function.

GO item is shown in Fig. 6-7. As shown in the figure, 13 GO terms come from the first level of GO molecular function. Most of the high-probability missing proteins have the GO functions of "binding" (GO:0005488) and "catalytic activity" (GO:0003824). However, some missing proteins may be membrane proteins since they have GO functions of "transporter activity" (GO:0005215) and "receptor activity" (GO:0004872). The results are consistent with the structural topology analysis in which there are many membrane proteins in the missing proteins.

6.5.3.4 *Comparision of subcellular localization*

Subcellular localizations of proteins are critical for their biological functions. The Hum-mPLoc 2.0 program[174] is used to predict the subcellular localizations of the high-probability missing proteins. The types of subcellular localizations and the number of proteins in each of the types are illustrated in Fig. 6-8. Most of the proteins are located in the extracellular region and in the nucleus. The missing proteins are also observed in the plasma membrane, which

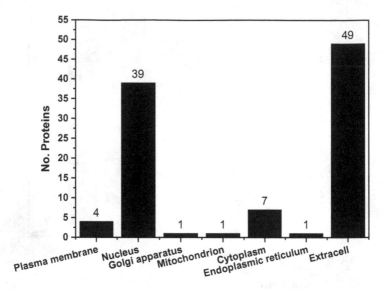

Figure 6-8   The distribution of subcellular localizations for the identified missing proteins.

is confirmed by the results from the structural topology analysis and function predictions.

6.5.3.5 *HGNC mapping analysis*

The HGNC[184] database is tasked with assigning a unique symbol and name for each gene locus from the human genome. Most of the HGNC data are manually collected and carefully checked.[184] The information from HGNC gene loci provides valuable resources to identify the missing proteins. Based on gene mapping, 71 out of the 102 high-probability missing proteins can be mapped to one or more HGNC items. We collected the corresponding gene loci types for the 71 missing proteins and counted the number of missing proteins in each loci type. The results are shown in Table 6-17. There are 9 proteins confirmed by HGNC with gene loci type "gene with protein product". There are 26 pseudogenes. Since pseudogenes are products of evolution they usually have homologous proteins. That is the reason why there are many pseudogenes in the missing proteins.

Table 6-17 The gene loci types and the number of proteins for the high-probability missing proteins after HGNC mapping.

Gene loci type	No. of missing proteins
Gene with protein product	9
Pseudogene	26
RNA, long non-coding	30
Unknown	6

6.5.3.6 *Consistence analysis with other mass spectrometry datasets*

Mass spectrometry is currently one of the most efficient methods to identify protein peptides. There is a lot of mass spectrometry data deposited in public databases, such as PeptideAtlas[185] and GPMDB.[152] The sketch of the human proteome is drawn from mass spectrometry data.[186, 187] Recently, Kim *et al.*[187] reported that about two-thirds (2535/3844) of the "missing proteins"[155] have been identified. Actually the "missing proteins" used by Kim *et al.* are those with evidence codes of "PE2", "PE3" or "PE4" in the neXtProt database. We aimed to identify the "PE5" missing proteins. Using RefSeq[188] mapping, we found that there are 41 "PE5" proteins that are also in Kim's dataset. Among these 41 missing proteins, there are 6 proteins that are foldable based on the structure prediction results in the non-homology mode. These results indicate that our findings are in good agreement with Kim *et al.*'s results.

6.6 Conclusions

In this chapter, the biological language model was used to solve several protein function problems. Different protein vocabularies were investigated including the *n*-gram, the binary profile, the frequency profile and the domains. Effective machine learning methods were adopted to explore binding site prediction, protein–protein interaction, GO function prediction and missing protein identification.

The residue interface propensities of four kinds of complexes (hetero-permanent complexes, hetero-transient complexes, homo-permanent complexes and homo-transient complexes) were collected and applied in the process of predicting the binding sites of proteins. Such propensities are improved by taking evolutionary information into consideration, which results in binary profile interface propensities. Although there are minor differences among the four kinds of complexes, the residue interface propensities cannot provide efficient differentiation between the complicated interfaces of proteins. The binary profile interface propensities can significantly improve the performance of the binding site prediction of proteins, which indicates that the propensities at the profile level are more accurate than those at the residue level.

In this chapter, an efficient method has been presented to predict the protein function from primary sequences. Four kinds of basic building blocks have been investigated to achieve this goal. The experimental results demonstrate that protein function can be inferred from sequence information. The application of SVM, NMF and LSA for protein function prediction is of great significance. There are many problems in biology that can be formulated as a classification task. Most of them, like fold prediction, tertiary structure and the functional properties of proteins, are considered to be challenging problems. Thus, these important classification tasks are potential areas for applications of machine learning techniques and can play important roles in modern proteomics. Since user-friendly and publicly accessible web servers represent the future direction for the practical development of more useful predictors [58], we shall make efforts in our future work to provide a web server for the method presented in this chapter.

We also presented an efficient method to predict protein–protein interaction. Four kinds of basic building blocks have been employed to achieve this goal. The LSA model from natural language processing was successfully introduced to filter noise and consequently better descriptions of protein sequences are obtained. The application of LSA to protein–protein interaction is of great significance. There are many problems in biology that can be formulated as a classification task. Most of them, like fold prediction, tertiary structure and the functional properties of proteins, are considered to be challenging problems. Thus, these important classification tasks are potential areas for the application of the natural language processing techniques to play important roles in modern proteomics.

Lastly, the human gene-coding proteins currently undetected were identified using biological language models. The amino acid n-gram models of human and non-human proteins were constructed. These models were then used to identify the "uncertain" missing proteins with evidence code "PE5" from the neXtProt database. The results showed that 102 high-probability proteins may be gene-coding proteins. The structure, function and subcellular localization of these proteins were then inferred using the advanced programs. The identified missing proteins were then analyzed with annotations from other databases. Without using homology templates, 7 proteins were found to have the correct structure topology with I-TASSER C-scores larger than -1.5. The predicted functions are mainly within the GO items "binding" (GO:0005488) and "catalytic activity" (GO:0003824). Nine missing proteins were confirmed by HGNC with gene loci type "gene with protein product". Six missing proteins were detected by mass spectrometry experiments. The analysis also showed that many of the unknown proteins are membrane or natively disordered proteins that are difficult to detect. The identified missing proteins need to be further validated with an experimental approach. The results in this study serve as a valuable complementary resource for the human proteome.

References

[1] Espadaler J., Querol E., Aviles F.X., Oliva B. Identification of function-associated loop motifs and application to protein function prediction. *Bioinformatics*, 2006, 22(18): 2237–2243.
[2] Zhang Z., Grigorov M.G. Similarity networks of protein binding sites. *Proteins*, 2006, 62(2): 470–478.
[3] Chelliah V., Chen L., Blundell T.L., Lovell S.C. Distinguishing structural and functional restraints in evolution in order to identify interaction sites. *J Mol Biol*, 2004, 342(5): 1487–1504.

[4] Wu X., Zhu L., Guo J., Zhang D.Y., Lin K. Prediction of yeast protein-protein interaction network: Insights from the Gene Ontology and annotations. *Nucleic Acids Res*, 2006, 34(7): 2137–2150.

[5] Venter J.C., Adams M.D., Myers E.W., Li P.W., Mural R.J., Sutton G.G., Smith H.O., Yandell M., Evans C.A., Holt R.A., Gocayne J.D., Amanatides P., Ballew R.M., Huson D.H., Wortman J.R., Zhang Q., Kodira C.D., Zheng X.H., Chen L., Skupski M., Subramanian G., Thomas P.D., Zhang J., Gabor Miklos G.L., Nelson C., Broder S., Clark A.G., Nadeau J., McKusick V.A., Zinder N., Levine A.J., Roberts R.J., Simon M., Slayman C., Hunkapiller M., Bolanos R., Delcher A., Dew I., Fasulo D., Flanigan M., Florea L., Halpern A., Hannenhalli S., Kravitz S., Levy S., Mobarry C., Reinert K., Remington K., Abu-Threideh J., Beasley E., Biddick K., Bonazzi V., Brandon R., Cargill M., Chandramouliswaran I., Charlab R., Chaturvedi K., Deng Z., Di Francesco V., Dunn P., Eilbeck K., Evangelista C., Gabrielian A.E., Gan W., Ge W., Gong F., Gu Z., Guan P., Heiman T.J., Higgins M.E., Ji R.R., Ke Z., Ketchum K.A., Lai Z., Lei Y., Li Z., Li J., Liang Y., Lin X., Lu F., Merkulov G.V., Milshina N., Moore H.M., Naik A.K., Narayan V.A., Neelam B., Nusskern D., Rusch D.B., Salzberg S., Shao W., Shue B., Sun J., Wang Z., Wang A., Wang X., Wang J., Wei M., Wides R., Xiao C., Yan C., Yao A., Ye J., Zhan M., Zhang W., Zhang H., Zhao Q., Zheng L., Zhong F., Zhong W., Zhu S., Zhao S., Gilbert D., Baumhueter S., Spier G., Carter C., Cravchik A., Woodage T., Ali F., An H., Awe A., Baldwin D., Baden H., Barnstead M., Barrow I., Beeson K., Busam D., Carver A., Center A., Cheng M.L., Curry L., Danaher S., Davenport L., Desilets R., Dietz S., Dodson K., Doup L., Ferriera S., Garg N., Gluecksmann A., Hart B., Haynes J., Haynes C., Heiner C., Hladun S., Hostin D., Houck J., Howland T., Ibegwam C., Johnson J., Kalush F., Kline L., Koduru S., Love A., Mann F., May D., McCawley S., McIntosh T., McMullen I., Moy M., Moy L., Murphy B., Nelson K., Pfannkoch C., Pratts E., Puri V., Qureshi H., Reardon M., Rodriguez R., Rogers Y.H., Romblad D., Ruhfel B., Scott R., Sitter C., Smallwood M., Stewart E., Strong R., Suh E., Thomas R., Tint N.N., Tse S., Vech C., Wang G., Wetter J., Williams S., Williams M., Windsor S., Winn-Deen E., Wolfe K., Zaveri J., Zaveri K., Abril J.F., Guigo R., Campbell M.J., Sjolander K.V., Karlak B., Kejariwal A., Mi H., Lazareva B., Hatton T., Narechania A., Diemer K., Muruganujan A., Guo N., Sato S., Bafna V., Istrail S., Lippert R., Schwartz R., Walenz B., Yooseph S., Allen D., Basu A., Baxendale J., Blick L., Caminha M., Carnes-Stine J., Caulk P., Chiang Y.H., Coyne M., Dahlke C., Mays A., Dombroski M., Donnelly M., Ely D.,

Esparham S., Fosler C., Gire H., Glanowski S., Glasser K., Glodek A., Gorokhov M., Graham K., Gropman B., Harris M., Heil J., Henderson S., Hoover J., Jennings D., Jordan C., Jordan J., Kasha J., Kagan L., Kraft C., Levitsky A., Lewis M., Liu X., Lopez J., Ma D., Majoros W., McDaniel J., Murphy S., Newman M., Nguyen T., Nguyen N., Nodell M., Pan S., Peck J., Peterson M., Rowe W., Sanders R., Scott J., Simpson M., Smith T., Sprague A., Stockwell T., Turner R., Venter E., Wang M., Wen M., Wu D., Wu M., Xia A., Zandieh A., Zhu X. The sequence of the human genome. *Science*, 2001, 291(5507): 1304–1351.

[6] Jones S., Thornton J.M. Analysis of protein-protein interaction sites using surface patches. *J Mol Biol*, 1997, 272(1): 121–132.

[7] Magliery T.J., Regan L. Sequence variation in ligand binding sites in proteins. *BMC Bioinfo*, 2005, 6: 240.

[8] Lo Conte L., Chothia C., Janin J. The atomic structure of protein–protein recognition sites. *J Mol Biol*, 1999, 285(5): 2177–2198.

[9] Bradford J.R., Westhead D.R. Improved prediction of protein-protein binding sites using a support vector machines approach. *Bioinformatics*, 2005, 21(8): 1487–1494.

[10] Nooren I.M., Thornton J.M. Structural characterisation and functional significance of transient protein–protein interactions. *J Mol Biol*, 2003, 325(5): 991–1018.

[11] Bradford J.R., Needham C.J., Bulpitt A.J., Westhead D.R. Insights into protein-protein interfaces using a Bayesian network prediction method. *J Mol Biol*, 2006, 362(2): 365–386.

[12] Chakrabarti P., Janin J. Dissecting protein-protein recognition sites. *Proteins*, 2002, 47(3): 334–343.

[13] Pils B., Copley R.R., Schultz J. Variation in structural location and amino acid conservation of functional sites in protein domain families. *BMC Bioinfo*, 2005, 6: 210.

[14] Lichtarge O., Bourne H.R., Cohen F.E. An evolutionary trace method defines binding surfaces common to protein families. *J Mol Biol*, 1996, 257(2): 342–358.

[15] Morgan D.H., Kristensen D.M., Mittelman D., Lichtarge O. ET viewer: An application for predicting and visualizing functional sites in protein structures. *Bioinformatics*, 2006, 22(16): 2049–2050.

[16] Yao H., Kristensen D.M., Mihalek I., Sowa M.E., Shaw C., Kimmel M., Kavraki L., Lichtarge O. An accurate, sensitive, and scalable method to identify functional sites in protein structures. *J Mol Biol*, 2003, 326(1): 255–261.

[17] Yao H., Mihalek I., Lichtarge O. Rank information: A structure-independent measure of evolutionary trace quality that improves

identification of protein functional sites. *Proteins*, 2006, 65(1): 111–123.

[18] Chung J.L., Wang W., Bourne P.E. Exploiting sequence and structure homologs to identify protein-protein binding sites. *Proteins*, 2006, 62(3): 630–640.

[19] Cheng G., Qian B., Samudrala R., Baker D. Improvement in protein functional site prediction by distinguishing structural and functional constraints on protein family evolution using computational design. *Nucleic Acids Res*, 2005, 33(18): 5861–5867.

[20] Panchenko A.R., Kondrashov F., Bryant S. Prediction of functional sites by analysis of sequence and structure conservation. *Prot Sci*, 2004, 13(4): 884–892.

[21] Valdar W.S. Scoring residue conservation. *Proteins*, 2002, 48(2): 227–241.

[22] La D., Sutch B., Livesay D.R. Predicting protein functional sites with phylogenetic motifs. *Proteins*, 2005, 58(2): 309–320.

[23] Kim Y., Subramaniam S. Locally defined protein phylogenetic profiles reveal previously missed protein interactions and functional relationships. *Proteins*, 2006, 62(4): 1115–1124.

[24] Liu A.H., Zhang X., Stolovitzky G.A., Califano A., Firestein S.J. Motif-based construction of a functional map for mammalian olfactory receptors. *Genomics*, 2003, 81(5): 443–456.

[25] Wang B., Chen P., Huang D.S., Li J.J., Lok T.M., Lyu M.R. Predicting protein interaction sites from residue spatial sequence profile and evolution rate. *FEBS Lett*, 2006, 580(2): 380–384.

[26] Yan C., Dobbs D., Honavar V. A two-stage classifier for identification of protein-protein interface residues. *Bioinformatics*, 2004, 20(Suppl 1): I371–I378.

[27] Bordner A.J., Abagyan R. REVCOM: a robust Bayesian method for evolutionary rate estimation. *Bioinformatics*, 2005, 21(10): 2315–2321.

[28] Thibert B., Bredesen D.E., Del Rio G. Improved prediction of critical residues for protein function based on network and phylogenetic analyses. *BMC Bioinfo*, 2005, 6(1): 213.

[29] Zhou H.X., Shan Y. Prediction of protein interaction sites from sequence profile and residue neighbor list. *Proteins*, 2001, 44(3): 336–343.

[30] Meiler J., Baker D. ROSETTALIGAND: Protein-small molecule docking with full side-chain flexibility. *Proteins*, 2006, 65(3): 538–548.

[31] Osterberg F., Morris G.M., Sanner M.F., Olson A.J., Goodsell D.S. Automated docking to multiple target structures: Incorporation of

protein mobility and structural water heterogeneity in Auto-Dock. *Proteins*, 2002, 46: 34–40.

[32] Laurie A.T., Jackson R.M. Q-SiteFinder: an energy-based method for the prediction of protein-ligand binding sites. *Bioinformatics*, 2005, 21(9): 1908–1916.

[33] Zhang C., Liu S., Zhu Q., Zhou Y. A knowledge-based energy function for protein-ligand, protein-protein, and protein-DNA complexes. *J Med Chem*, 2005, 48(7): 2325–2335.

[34] Torrance J.W., Bartlett G.J., Porter C.T., Thornton J.M. Using a library of structural templates to recognise catalytic sites and explore their evolution in homologous families. *J Mol Biol*, 2005, 347(3): 565–581.

[35] Ivanisenko V.A., Pintus S.S., Grigorovich D.A., Kolchanov N.A. PDBSite: A database of the 3D structure of protein functional sites. *Nucleic Acids Res*, 2005, 33(Database issue): D183–D187.

[36] Wilczynski B., Hvidsten T.R., Kryshtafovych A., Tiuryn J., Komorowski J., Fidelis K. Using local gene expression similarities to discover regulatory binding site modules. *BMC Bioinfo*, 2006, 7: 505.

[37] Snyder K.A., Feldman H.J., Dumontier M., Salama J.J., Hogue C.W. Domain-based small molecule binding site annotation. *BMC Bioinfo*, 2006, 7: 152.

[38] Neuvirth H., Raz R., Schreiber G. ProMate: A structure based prediction program to identify the location of protein-protein binding sites. *J Mol Biol*, 2004, 338(1): 181–199.

[39] Res I., Mihalek I., Lichtarge O. An evolution based classifier for prediction of protein interfaces without using protein structures. *Bioinformatics*, 2005, 21(10): 2496–2501.

[40] Yan C., Terribilini M., Wu F., Jernigan R.L., Dobbs D., Honavar V. Predicting DNA-binding sites of proteins from amino acid sequence. *BMC Bioinfo*, 2006, 7: 262.

[41] Liang S., Zhang C., Liu S., Zhou Y. Protein binding site prediction using an empirical scoring function. *Nucleic Acids Res*, 2006, 34(13): 3698–3707.

[42] Rossi A., Marti-Renom M.A., Sali A. Localization of binding sites in protein structures by optimization of a composite scoring function. *Prot Sci*, 15(10): 2366–2380.

[43] Down T., Leong B., Hubbard T.J. A machine learning strategy to identify candidate binding sites in human protein-coding sequence. *BMC Bioinfo*, 2006, 7: 419.

[44] Deng H., Chen G., Yang W., Yang J.J. Predicting calcium-binding sites in proteins — A graph theory and geometry approach. *Proteins*, 2006, 64(1): 34–42.

[45] Chen H., Zhou H.X. Prediction of interface residues in protein-protein complexes by a consensus neural network method: Test against NMR data. *Proteins*, 2005, 61(1): 21–35.

[46] Dubey A., Realff M.J., Lee J.H., Bommarius A.S. Support vector machines for learning to identify the critical positions of a protein. *J Theor Biol*, 2005, 234(3): 351–361.

[47] Koike A., Takagi T. Prediction of protein-protein interaction sites using support vector machines. *Prot Eng Des Sel*, 2004, 17(2): 165–173.

[48] Li M.H., Lin L., Wang X.L., Liu T. Protein-protein interaction site prediction based on conditional random fields. *Bioinformatics*, 2007, 23(5): 597–604.

[49] Ofran Y., Rost B. Analysing six types of protein-protein interfaces. *J Mol Biol*, 2003, 325(2): 377–387.

[50] Altschul S.F., Madden T.L., Schaffer A.A., Zhang J.H., Zhang Z., Miller W., Lipman D.J. Gapped Blast and Psi-blast: A new generation of protein database search programs. *Nucleic Acids Res*, 1997, 25(17): 3389–3402.

[51] Dong Q.W., Wang X.L., Lin L., Xu Z.M. Domain boundary prediction based on profile domain linker propensity index. *Comput Biol Chem*, 2006, 30(2): 127–133.

[52] Dong Q., Wang X., Lin L. Novel knowledge-based mean force potential at the profile level. *BMC Bioinfo*, 2006, 7: 324.

[53] Dong Q., Wang X., Lin L. Protein remote homology detection based on binary profiles. *Lecture Notes in Computer Science*. In the *1st International Conference on Bioinformatics Research and Development* (BIRD 2007), 2007, 4414: 212–223.

[54] Kouranov A., Xie L., de la Cruz J., Chen L., Westbrook J., Bourne P.E., Berman H.M. The RCSB PDB information portal for structural genomics. *Nucleic Acids Res*, 2006, 34(Database issue): D302–D305.

[55] Bordner A.J., Abagyan R. Statistical analysis and prediction of protein-protein interfaces. *Proteins*, 2005, 60(3): 353–366.

[56] Henrick K., Thornton J.M. PQS: A protein quaternary structure file server. *Trends Biochem Sci*, 1998, 23(9): 358–361.

[57] Nooren I.M., Thornton J.M. Diversity of protein-protein interactions. *Embo J*, 2003, 22(14): 3486–3492.

[58] Wu C.H., Apweiler R., Bairoch A., Natale D.A., Barker W.C., Boeckmann B., Ferro S., Gasteiger E., Huang H., Lopez R., Magrane M., Martin M.J., Mazumder R., O'Donovan C., Redaschi N.,

Suzek B. The Universal Protein Resource (UniProt): An expanding universe of protein information. *Nucleic Acids Res*, 2006, 34(Database issue): D187–D191.

[59] Xenarios I., Salwinski L., Duan X.J., Higney P., Kim S.M., Eisenberg D. DIP, the Database of Interacting Proteins: A research tool for studying cellular networks of protein interactions. *Nucleic Acids Res*, 2002, 30(1): 303–305.

[60] Kabsch W., Sander C. Dictionary of secondary structure in proteins: Pattern recognition of hydrogenbonded and geometrical features. *Biopolymers*, 1983, 22(12): 2577–2637.

[61] Vapnik V.N. *Statistical Learning Theory*. 1998. New York, NY: Wiley.

[62] Chang C.C., Lin C.J. LIBSVM: a library for support vector machines. 2001. Software available at http://www.csie.ntu.edu.tw/~cjlin/libsvm.

[63] Ofran Y., Rost B. Predicted protein-protein interaction sites from local sequence information. *FEBS Lett*, 2003, 544(1–3): 236–239.

[64] Sander C., Schneider R. Database of homology-derived protein structures and the structural meaning of sequence alignment. *Proteins*, 1991, 9(1): 56–68.

[65] Karlin S., Brocchieri L. Evolutionary conservation of RecA genes in relation to protein structure and function. *J Bacteriol*, 1996, 178(7): 1881–1894.

[66] Valdar W.S., Thornton J.M. Protein-protein interfaces: Analysis of amino acid conservation in homodimers. *Proteins*, 2001, 42(1): 108–124.

[67] Harris M.A., Clark J., Ireland A., Lomax J., Ashburner M., Foulger R., Eilbeck K., Lewis S., Marshall B., Mungall C., Richter J., Rubin G.M., Blake J.A., Bult C., Dolan M., Drabkin H., Eppig J.T., Hill D.P., Ni L., Ringwald M., Balakrishnan R., Cherry J.M., Christie K.R., Costanzo M.C., Dwight S.S., Engel S., Fisk D.G., Hirschman J.E., Hong E.L., Nash R.S., Sethuraman A., Theesfeld C.L., Botstein D., Dolinski K., Feierbach B., Berardini T., Mundodi S., Rhee S.Y., Apweiler R., Barrell D., Camon E., Dimmer E., Lee V., Chisholm R., Gaudet P., Kibbe W., Kishore R., Schwarz E.M., Sternberg P., Gwinn M., Hannick L., Wortman J., Berriman M., Wood V., de la Cruz N., Tonellato P., Jaiswal P., Seigfried T., White R. The Gene Ontology (GO) database and informatics resource. *Nucleic Acids Res*, 2004, 32(Database issue): D258–D261.

[68] Nomenclature committee of the international union of biochemistry and molecular biology (NC-IUBMB), Enzyme Supplement 5 (1999). *Eur J Biochem*, 1999, 264(2): 610–650.

[69] Ruepp A., Zollner A., Maier D., Albermann K., Hani J., Mokrejs M., Tetko I., Guldener U., Mannhaupt G., Munsterkotter M., Mewes H.W. The FunCat, a functional annotation scheme for systematic classification of proteins from whole genomes. *Nucleic Acids Res*, 2004, 32(18): 5539–5545.

[70] Gupta K., Sehgal V., Levchenko A. A method for probabilistic mapping between protein structure and function taxonomies through cross training. *BMC Struct Biol*, 2008, 8: 40.

[71] Moult J., Fidelis K., Kryshtafovych A., Rost B., Hubbard T., Tramontano A. Critical assessment of methods of protein structure prediction-Round VII. *Proteins*, 2007, 69(Suppl 8): 3–9.

[72] Shen H.B., Yang J., Chou K.C. Euk-PLoc: An ensemble classifier for large-scale eukaryotic protein subcellular location prediction. *Amino Acids*, 2007, 33(1): 57–67.

[73] Chou K.C., Cai Y.D. Using GO-PseAA predictor to predict enzyme sub-class. *Biochem Biophys Res Commun*, 2004, 325(2): 506–509.

[74] Chou K.C., Cai Y.D. Using GO-PseAA predictor to identify membrane proteins and their types. *Biochem Biophys Res Commun*, 2005, 327(3): 845–847.

[75] Chou K.C., Cai Y.D. Predicting protein-protein interactions from sequences in a hybridization space. *J Proteome Res*, 2006, 5(2): 316–322.

[76] Hawkins T., Kihara D. Function prediction of uncharacterized proteins. *J Bioinform Comput Biol*, 2007, 5(1): 1–30.

[77] Altschul S.F., Gish W., Miller W., Myers E.W., Lipman D.J. Basic local alignment search tool. *J Mol Biol*, 1990, 215(3): 403–410.

[78] Hawkins T., Chitale M., Luban S., Kihara D. PFP: Automated prediction of gene ontology functional annotations with confidence scores using protein sequence data. *Proteins*, 2009, 74(3): 566–582.

[79] Vinayagam A., Konig R., Moormann J., Schubert F., Eils R., Glatting K.H., Suhai S. Applying support vector machines for gene ontology based gene function prediction. *BMC Bioinfo*, 2004, 5: 116.

[80] Tetko I.V., Rodchenkov I.V., Walter M.C., Rattei T., Mewes H.W. Beyond the 'best' match: Machine learning annotation of protein sequences by integration of different sources of information. *Bioinformatics*, 2008, 24(5): 621–628.

[81] Cai C.Z., Han L.Y., Ji Z.L., Chen X., Chen Y.Z. SVM-Prot: Web-based support vector machine software for functional classification of a protein from its primary sequence. *Nucleic Acids Res*, 2003, 31(13): 3692–3697.

[82] Götz S., García-Gómez J.M., Terol J., Williams T.D., Nagaraj S.H., Nueda M.J., Robles M., Talón M., Dopazo J., Conesa A. High-throughput functional annotation and data mining with the Blast2GO suite. *Nucleic Acids Res*, 2008, 36(10): 3420–3435.

[83] Forslund K., Sonnhammer E.L. Predicting protein function from domain content. *Bioinformatics*, 2008, 24(15): 1681–1687.

[84] Qiu J., Hue M., Ben-Hur A., Vert J.P., Noble W.S. A structural alignment kernel for protein structures. *Bioinformatics*, 2007, 23(9): 1090–1098.

[85] Wu H., Su Z., Mao F., Olman V., Xu Y. Prediction of functional modules based on comparative genome analysis and Gene Ontology application. *Nucleic Acids Res*, 2005, 33(9): 2822–2837.

[86] Baudot A., Martin D., Mouren P., Chevenet F., Guenoche A., Jacq B., Brun C. PRODISTIN Web Site: A tool for the functional classification of proteins from interaction networks. *Bioinformatics*, 2006, 22(2): 248–250.

[87] Green M.L., Karp P.D. A Bayesian method for identifying missing enzymes in predicted metabolic pathway databases. *BMC Bioinfo*, 2004, 5: 76.

[88] Leslie C., Eskin E., Noble W.S. The spectrum kernel: A string kernel for SVM protein classification in *Biocomputing 2002*. Singapore: World Scientific, pp. 564–575.

[89] Dong Q.W., Wang X.L., Lin L. Protein remote homology detection based on binary profiles. *Lecture Notes in Computer Science*. In the *1st International Conference on Bioinformatics Research and Development*, BIRD 2007. 2007, 4414: 212–223.

[90] Bateman A., Coin L., Durbin R., Finn R.D., Hollich V., Griffiths-Jones S., Khanna A., Marshall M., Moxon S., Sonnhammer E.L., Studholme D.J., Yeats C., Eddy S.R. The Pfam protein families database. *Nucleic Acids Res*, 2004, 32(Database issue): D138–D141.

[91] Mulder N.J., Apweiler R., Attwood T.K., Bairoch A., Bateman A., Binns D., Bork P., Buillard V., Cerutti L., Copley R., Courcelle E., Das U., Daugherty L., Dibley M., Finn R., Fleischmann W., Gough J., Haft D., Hulo N., Hunter S., Kahn D., Kanapin A., Kejariwal A., Labarga A., Langendijk-Genevaux P.S., Lonsdale D., Lopez R., Letunic I., Madera M., Maslen J., McAnulla C., McDowall J., Mistry J., Mitchell A., Nikolskaya A.N., Orchard S., Orengo C., Petryszak R., Selengut J.D., Sigrist C.J., Thomas P.D., Valentin F., Wilson D., Wu C.H., Yeats C. New developments in the InterPro database. *Nucleic Acids Res*, 2007, 35(Database issue): D224–D228.

[92] Dong Q.W., Wang X.L., Lin L. Application of latent semantic analysis to protein remote homology detection. *Bioinformatics*, 2006, 22(3): 285–290.

[93] Camon E., Magrane M., Barrell D., Emily Dimmer V.L., Maslen J., Binns D., Harte N., Lopez R., Apweiler R. The Gene Ontology Annotation (GOA) Database: Sharing knowledge in Uniprot with Gene Ontology. *Nucleic Acids Res*, 2004, 32(Database issue): D262–D266.

[94] Li W., Godzik A. Cd-hit: a fast program for clustering and comparing large sets of protein or nucleotide sequences. *Bioinformatics*, 2006, 22(13): 1658–1659.

[95] Martin S., Roe D., Faulon J.-L. Predicting protein-protein interactions using signature products. *Bioinformatics*, 2005, 21(2): 218–226.

[96] Dong Q.W., Wang X.L., Lin L. Novel knowledge-based mean force potential at the profile level. *BMC Bioinfo*, 2006, 7: 324.

[97] Chou K.C., Shen H.B. Recent progress in protein subcellular location prediction. *Anal Biochem*, 2007, 370(1): 1–16.

[98] Landauer T.K., Foltz P.W., Laham D. Introduction to latent semantic analysis. *Discourse Proc*, 1998, 25(2&3): 259–284.

[99] Lee D.D., Seung S.H. Learning the parts of objects by nonnegative matrix factorization. *Nature*, 1999, 401(6755): 788–791.

[100] Hawkins T., Luban S., Kihara D. Enhanced automated function prediction using distantly related sequences and contextual association by PFP. *Prot Sci*, 2006, 15(6): 1550–1556.

[101] Uetz P., Giot L., Cagney G., Mansfield T.A., Judson R.S., Knight J.R., Lockshon D., Narayan V., Srinivasan M., Pochart P., Qureshi-Emili A., Li Y., Godwin B., Conover D., Kalbfleisch T., Vijayadamodar G., Yang M., Johnston M., Fields S., Rothberg J.M. A comprehensive analysis of protein-protein interactions in *Saccharomyces cerevisiae*. *Nature*, 2000, 403(6770): 623–627.

[102] Ho Y., Gruhler A., Heilbut A., Bader G.D., Moore L., Adams S.L., Millar A., Taylor P., Bennett K., Boutilier K., Yang L., Wolting C., Donaldson I., Schandorff S., Shewnarane J., Vo M., Taggart J., Goudreault M., Muskat B., Alfarano C., Dewar D., Lin Z., Michalickova K., Willems A.R., Sassi H., Nielsen P.A., Rasmussen K.J., Andersen J.R., Johansen L.E., Hansen L.H., Jespersen H., Podtelejnikov A., Nielsen E., Crawford J., Poulsen V., Sorensen B.D., Matthiesen J., Hendrickson R.C., Gleeson F., Pawson T., Moran M.F., Durocher D., Mann M., Hogue C.W., Figeys D., Tyers M. Systematic identification of protein complexes in Saccharomyces cerevisiae by mass spectrometry. *Nature*, 2002, 415(6868): 180–183.

[103] Li S., Armstrong C.M., Bertin N., Ge H., Milstein S., Boxem M., Vidalain P.O., Han J.D., Chesneau A., Hao T., Goldberg D.S., Li N., Martinez M., Rual J.F., Lamesch P., Xu L., Tewari M., Wong S.L., Zhang L.V., Berriz G.F., Jacotot L., Vaglio P., Reboul J., Hirozane-Kishikawa T., Li Q., Gabel H.W., Elewa A., Baumgartner B., Rose D.J., Yu H., Bosak S., Sequerra R., Fraser A., Mango S.E., Saxton W.M., Strome S., Van Den Heuvel S., Piano F., Vandenhaute J., Sardet C., Gerstein M., Doucette-Stamm L., Gunsalus K.C., Harper J.W., Cusick M.E., Roth F.P., Hill D.E., Vidal M. A map of the interactome network of the metazoan *C. elegans*. *Science*, 2004, 303(5657): 540–543.

[104] Giot L., Bader J.S., Brouwer C., Chaudhuri A., Kuang B., Li Y., Hao Y.L., Ooi C.E., Godwin B., Vitols E., Vijayadamodar G., Pochart P., Machineni H., Welsh M., Kong Y., Zerhusen B., Malcolm R., Varrone Z., Collis A., Minto M., Burgess S., McDaniel L., Stimpson E., Spriggs F., Williams J., Neurath K., Ioime N., Agee M., Voss E., Furtak K., Renzulli R., Aanensen N., Carrolla S., Bickelhaupt E., Lazovatsky Y., DaSilva A., Zhong J., Stanyon C.A., Finley R.L., Jr., White K.P., Braverman M., Jarvie T., Gold S., Leach M., Knight J., Shimkets R.A., McKenna M.P., Chant J., Rothberg J.M. A protein interaction map of *Drosophila melanogaster*. *Science*, 2003, 302(5651): 1727–1736.

[105] Rain J.C., Selig L., De Reuse H., Battaglia V., Reverdy C., Simon S., Lenzen G., Petel F., Wojcik J., Schachter V., Chemama Y., Labigne A., Legrain P. The protein-protein interaction map of *Helicobacter pylori*. *Nature*, 2001, 409(6817): 211–215.

[106] Rual J.F., Venkatesan K., Hao T., Hirozane-Kishikawa T., Dricot A., Li N., Berriz G.F., Gibbons F.D., Dreze M., Ayivi-Guedehoussou N., Klitgord N., Simon C., Boxem M., Milstein S., Rosenberg J., Goldberg D.S., Zhang L.V., Wong S.L., Franklin G., Li S., Albala J.S., Lim J., Fraughton C., Llamosas E., Cevik S., Bex C., Lamesch P., Sikorski R.S., Vandenhaute J., Zoghbi H.Y., Smolyar A., Bosak S., Sequerra R., Doucette-Stamm L., Cusick M.E., Hill D.E., Roth F.P., Vidal M. Towards a proteome-scale map of the human protein-protein interaction network. *Nature*, 2005, 437(7062): 1173–1178.

[107] Ito T., Chiba T., Ozawa R., Yoshida M., Hattori M., Sakaki Y. A comprehensive two-hybrid analysis to explore the yeast protein interactome. *Proc Natl Acad Sci USA*, 2001, 98(8): 4569–4574.

[108] von Mering C., Krause R., Snel B., Cornell M., Oliver S.G., Fields S., Bork P. Comparative assessment of large-scale data sets of protein-protein interactions. *Nature*, 2002, 417(6887): 399–403.

[109] Qi Y., Bar-Joseph Z., Klein-Seetharaman J. Evaluation of different biological data and computational classification methods for use in protein interaction prediction. *Proteins*, 2006, 63(3): 490–500.

[110] Pazos F., Valencia A. Similarity of phylogenetic trees as indicator of protein-protein interaction. *Prot Eng*, 2001, 14(9): 609–614.

[111] Yanai I., Mellor J.C., DeLisi C. Identifying functional links between genes using conserved chromosomal proximity. *Trends Genet*, 2002, 18(4): 176–179.

[112] Enright A.J., Iliopoulos I., Kyrpides N.C., Ouzounis C.A. Protein interaction maps for complete genomes based on gene fusion events. *Nature*, 1999, 402(6757): 86–90.

[113] Bock J.R., Gough D.A. Predicting protein–protein interactions from primary structure. *Bioinformatics*, 2001, 17(5): 455–460.

[114] Cooper J.W., Kershenbaum A. Discovery of protein-protein interactions using a combination of linguistic, statistical and graphical information. *BMC Bioinfo*, 2005, 6(1): 143.

[115] Bader J.S., Chaudhuri A., Rothberg J.M., Chant J. Gaining confidence in high-throughput protein interaction networks. *Nat Biotechnol*, 2004, 22(1): 78–85.

[116] Jansen R., Yu H., Greenbaum D., Kluger Y., Krogan N.J., Chung S., Emili A., Snyder M., Greenblatt J.F., Gerstein M. A Bayesian networks approach for predicting protein–protein interactions from genomic data. *Science*, 2003, 302(5644): 449–453.

[117] Zhang L.V., Wong S.L., King O.D., Roth F.P. Predicting co-complexed protein pairs using genomic and proteomic data integration. *BMC Bioinfo*, 2004, 5: 38.

[118] Nanni L., Lumini A. An ensemble of K-local hyperplanes for predicting protein-protein interactions. *Bioinformatics*, 2006, 22(10): 1207–1210.

[119] Chen X.W., Liu M. Prediction of protein-protein interactions using random decision forest framework. *Bioinformatics*, 2005, 21(24): 4394–4400.

[120] Dohkan S., Koike A., Takagi T. Prediction of protein-protein interactions using support vector machines. In *Proceedings of the Fourth IEEE Symposium on Bioinformatics and Bioengineering (BIBE)*, Taichung, Taiwan. 2004, pp. 576–583.

[121] Deng M., Mehta S., Sun F., Chen T. Inferring domain-domain interactions from protein-protein interactions. *Genome Res*, 2002, 12(10): 1540–1548.

[122] Gomez S.M., Noble W.S., Rzhetsky A. Learning to predict protein-protein interactions from protein sequences. *Bioinformatics*, 2003, 19(15): 1875–1881.

[123] Pitre S., Dehne F., Chan A., Cheetham J., Duong A., Emili A., Gebbia M., Greenblatt J., Jessulat M., Krogan N., Luo X., Golshani A. PIPE: a protein-protein interaction prediction engine based on the re-occurring short polypeptide sequences between known interacting protein pairs. *BMC Bioinfo*, 2006, 7: 365.

[124] Pitre S., North C., Alamgir M., Jessulat M., Chan A., Luo X., Green J.R., Dumontier M., Dehne F., Golshani A. Global investigation of protein-protein interactions in yeast Saccharomyces cerevisiae using re-occurring short polypeptide sequences. *Nucleic Acids Res*, 2008, 36(13): 4286–4294.

[125] Sprinzak E., Margalit H. Correlated sequence-signatures as markers of protein-protein interaction. *J Mol Biol*, 2001, 311(4): 681–692.

[126] Fang J., Haasl R.J., Dong Y., Lushington G.H. Discover protein sequence signatures from protein-protein interaction data. *BMC Bioinfo*, 2005, 6: 277.

[127] Mulder N.J., Apweiler R., Attwood T.K., Bairoch A., Bateman A., Binns D., Bork P., Buillard V., Cerutti L., Copley R., Courcelle E., Das U., Daugherty L., Dibley M., Finn R., Fleischmann W., Gough J., Haft D., Hulo N., Hunter S., Kahn D., Kanapin A., Kejariwal A., Labarga A., Langendijk-Genevaux P.S., Lonsdale D., Lopez R., Letunic I., Madera M., Maslen J., McAnulla C., McDowall J., Mistry J., Mitchell A., Nikolskaya A.N., Orchard S., Orengo C., Petryszak R., Selengut J.D., Sigrist C.J., Thomas P.D., Valentin F., Wilson D., Wu C.H., Yeats C. New developments in the InterPro database. *Nucleic Acids Res*, 2007, 35(Database issue): D224–D228.

[128] Ben-Hur A., Noble W.S. Kernel methods for predicting protein-protein interactions. *Bioinformatics*, 2005, 21(Suppl 1): i38–i46.

[129] Leslie C., Eskin E., Noble W.S. The spectrum kernel: A string kernel for SVM protein classification. In *Proceedings of the Pacific Symposium on Biocomputing*, 2002, Singapore: World Scientific, pp. 564–575.

[130] Dong Q., Lin L., Wang X., Li M. A pattern-based SVM for protein remote homology detection. In *Proceedings of the Fourth IEEE International Conference on Machine Learning and Cybernetics*, Guangzhou, China. 2005, pp. 3363–3368.

[131] Ben-Hur A., Brutlag D. Remote homology detection: A motif based approach. *Bioinformatics*, 2003, 19(Suppl 1): i26–i33.

[132] Han D.S., Kim H.S., Jang W.H., Lee. PreSPI: A domain combination based prediction system for protein-protein interaction. *Nucleic Acids Res*, 2004, 32(21): 6312–6320.

[133] Salwinski L., Miller C.S., Smith A.J., Pettit F.K., Bowie J.U., Eisenberg D. The Database of Interacting Proteins: 2004 update.

Nucleic Acids Res, 2004, 32(Database issue): D449–D451.

[134] Pisanti N., Crochemore M., Grossi R., Sagot M.F. A Basis for Repeated Motifs in Pattern Discovery and Text Mining. 2002, Juillet: IGM 2002-10, pp. 268–285.

[135] Dong Q.W., Wang X.L., Lin L., Guan Y., Zhao J. A Seqlet-based maximum entropy Markov approach for protein secondary structure prediction. *Science in China Ser. C Life Sciences*, 2005, 48(1): 87–96.

[136] Rigoutsos I., Floratos A. Combinatorial pattern discovery in biological sequences: The TEIRESIAS algorithm. *Bioinformatics*, 1998, 14(1): 55–67.

[137] Rigoutsos I., Huynh T., Floratos A., Parida L., Platt D. Dictionary-driven protein annotation. *Nucleic Acids Res*, 2002, 30(17): 3901–3916.

[138] Yang Y., Pedersen J.A. A comparative study on feature selection in text categorization. In *Proceedings of 14th International Conference on Machine Learning*, San Francisco, USA. 1997, pp. 412–420.

[139] Nevill-Manning C.G., Wu T.D., Brutlag D.L. Highly specific protein sequence motifs for genome analysis. *Proc Natl Acad Sci USA*, 1998, 95(11): 5865–5871.

[140] Bailey T.L., Elkan C. Fitting a mixture model by expectation maximization to discover motifs in biopolymers. In *Proceedings of the Second International Conference on Intelligent Systems for Molecular Biology*, Menlo Park, California. 1994, pp. 28–36.

[141] Bailey T.L., Gribskov M. Combining evidence using p-values: Application to sequence homology searches. *Bioinformatics*, 1998, 14(1): 48–54.

[142] Bateman A., Coin L., Durbin R., Finn R.D., Hollich V., Griffiths-Jones S., Khanna A., Marshall M., Moxon S., Sonnhammer E.L., Studholme D.J., Yeats C., Eddy S.R. The Pfam protein families database. *Nucleic Acids Res*, 2004, 32(Database issue): D138–D141.

[143] Landauer T.K., Foltz P.W., Laham D. Introduction to Latent Semantic Analysis. *Discourse Proc*, 1998, 25(2&3): 259–284.

[144] Guo Y., Yu L., Wen Z., Li M. Using support vector machine combined with auto covariance to predict protein-protein interactions from protein sequences. *Nucleic Acids Res*, 2008, 36(9): 3025–3030.

[145] Ganapathiraju M., Balakrishnan N., Reddy R., Klein-Seetharaman J. Computational biology and language. ambient intelligence for scientific discovery. *LNAI*, 2005, 3345: 25–47.

[146] Legrain P., Aebersold R., Archakov A., Bairoch A., Bala K., Beretta L., Bergeron J., Borchers C.H., Corthals G.L., Costello C.E., Deutsch E.W., Domon B., Hancock W., He F., Hochstrasser D., Marko-Varga G., Salekdeh G.H., Sechi S., Snyder M., Srivastava S.,

Uhlen M., Wu C.H., Yamamoto T., Paik Y.K., Omenn G.S. The human proteome project: Current state and future direction. *Mol Cell Proteomics*, 2011, 10(7): M111 009993.

[147] Paik Y.K., Jeong S.K., Omenn G.S., Uhlen M., Hanash S., Cho S.Y., Lee H.J., Na K., Choi E.Y., Yan F., Zhang F., Zhang Y., Snyder M., Cheng Y., Chen R., Marko-Varga G., Deutsch E.W., Kim H., Kwon J.Y., Aebersold R., Bairoch A., Taylor A.D., Kim K.Y., Lee E.Y., Hochstrasser D., Legrain P., Hancock W.S. The Chromosome-Centric Human Proteome Project for cataloging proteins encoded in the genome. *Nat Biotechnol*, 2012, 30(3): 221–223.

[148] Aebersold R., Bader G.D., Edwards A.M., van Eyk J.E., Kussmann M., Qin J., Omenn G.S. The biology/disease-driven human proteome project (B/D-HPP): Enabling protein research for the life sciences community. *J Proteome Res*, 2013, 12(1): 23–27.

[149] Marko-Varga G., Omenn G.S., Paik Y.K., Hancock W.S. A first step toward completion of a genome-wide characterization of the human proteome. *J Proteome Res*, 2013, 12(1): 1–5.

[150] Flicek P., Amode M.R., Barrell D., Beal K., Billis K., Brent S., Carvalho-Silva D., Clapham P., Coates G., Fitzgerald S., Gil L., Giron C.G., Gordon L., Hourlier T., Hunt S., Johnson N., Juettemann T., Kahari A.K., Keenan S., Kulesha E., Martin F.J., Maurel T., McLaren W.M., Murphy D.N., Nag R., Overduin B., Pignatelli M., Pritchard B., Pritchard E., Riat H.S., Ruffier M., Sheppard D., Taylor K., Thormann A., Trevanion S.J., Vullo A., Wilder S.P., Wilson M., Zadissa A., Aken B.L., Birney E., Cunningham F., Harrow J., Herrero J., Hubbard T.J., Kinsella R., Muffato M., Parker A., Spudich G., Yates A., Zerbino D.R., Searle S.M. Ensembl 2014. *Nucleic Acids Res*, 2014, 42(Database issue): D749–D755.

[151] Farrah T., Deutsch E.W., Hoopmann M.R., Hallows J.L., Sun Z., Huang C.Y., Moritz R.L. The state of the human proteome in 2012 as viewed through PeptideAtlas. *J Proteome Res*, 2013, 12(1): 162–171.

[152] Craig R., Cortens J.P., Beavis R.C. Open source system for analyzing, validating, and storing protein identification data. *J Proteome Res*, 2004, 3(6): 1234–1242.

[153] Uhlen M., Oksvold P., Fagerberg L., Lundberg E., Jonasson K., Forsberg M., Zwahlen M., Kampf C., Wester K., Hober S., Wernerus H., Bjorling L., Ponten F. Towards a knowledge-based Human Protein Atlas. *Nat Biotechnol*, 2010, 28(12): 1248–1250.

[154] Lane L., Argoud-Puy G., Britan A., Cusin I., Duek P.D., Evalet O., Gateau A., Gaudet P., Gleizes A., Masselot A., Zwahlen C., Bairoch A. neXtProt: a knowledge platform for human proteins. *Nucleic Acids Res*, 2012, 40(Database issue): D76–D83.

[155] Lane L., Bairoch A., Beavis R.C., Deutsch E.W., Gaudet P., Lundberg E., Omenn G.S. Metrics for the Human Proteome Project 2013–2014 and strategies for finding missing proteins. *J Proteome Res*, 2014, 13(1): 15–20.

[156] Tsonis A.A., Elsner J.B., Tsonis P.A. Is DNA a language? *J Theor Biol*, 1997, 184(1): 25–29.

[157] Dyrka W., Nebel J.C. A stochastic context free grammar based framework for analysis of protein sequences. *BMC Bioinfo*, 2009, 10: 323.

[158] Searls D.B. Linguistic approaches to biological sequences. *Comput Appl Biosci*, 1997, 13(4): 333–344.

[159] Ganapathiraju M., Weisser D., Rosenfeld R., Carbonell J., Reddy R., Klein-Seetharaman J. Comparative n-gram analysis of whole-genome protein sequences. In *Proceedings of the Second International Conference on Human Language Technology Research*, Morgan Kaufmann Publishers Inc., 2002, pp. 76–81.

[160] Coin L., Bateman A., Durbin R. Enhanced protein domain discovery by using language modeling techniques from speech recognition. *Proc Natl Acad Sci USA*, 2003, 100(8): 4516–4520.

[161] Rigoutsos I., Huynh T., Floratos A., Parida L., Platt D. Dictionary-driven protein annotation. *Nucleic Acids Res*, 2002, 30(17): 3901–3916.

[162] Dong Q.-W., Wang X.-L., Lin L. Application of latent semantic analysis to protein remote homology detection. *Bioinformatics*, 2006, 22(3): 285–290.

[163] Liu B., Wang X., Lin L., Dong Q. A discriminative method for protein remote homology detection and fold recognition combining Top-n-grams and latent semantic analysis. *BMC Bioinfo*, 2008, 9: 510.

[164] Liu B., Xu J., Zou Q., Xu R., Wang X., Chen Q. Using distances between Top-n-gram and residue pairs for protein remote homology detection. *BMC Bioinfo*, 2014, 15(Suppl 2): S3.

[165] Liu B., Zhang D., Xu R., Xu J., Wang X., Chen Q., Dong Q., Chou K.C. Combining evolutionary information extracted from frequency profiles with sequence-based kernels for protein remote homology detection. *Bioinformatics*, 2014, 30(4): 472–479.

[166] Liu B., Xu J., Fan S., Xu R., Zhou J., Wang X. PseDNA-Pro: DNA-binding protein identification by combining Chou's PseAAC and physicochemical distance transformation. *Mol Info*, 2015, 34(1): 8, 17.

[167] Liu B., Xu J., Lan X., Xu R., Zhou J., Wang X., Chou K.C. iDNA-Prot|dis: identifying DNA-binding proteins by incorporating amino acid distance-pairs and reduced alphabet profile into the general pseudo amino acid composition. *PloS One*, 2014, 9(9): e106691.

[168] Gray K.A., Yates B., Seal R.L., Wright M.W., Bruford E.A. Genenames. org: The HGNC resources in 2015. *Nucleic Acids Res*, 2015, 43(D1): D1079–D1085.

[169] Kim M.-S., Pinto S.M., Getnet D., Nirujogi R.S., Manda S.S., Chaerkady R., Madugundu A.K., Kelkar D.S., Isserlin R., Jain S. A draft map of the human proteome. *Nature*, 2014, 509(7502): 575–581.

[170] Consortium U. UniProt: A hub for protein information. *Nucleic Acids Res*, 2014: gku989.

[171] Fu L., Niu B., Zhu Z., Wu S., Li W. CD-HIT: Accelerated for clustering the next-generation sequencing data. *Bioinformatics*, 2012, 28(23): 3150–3152.

[172] Roy A., Kucukural A., Zhang Y. I-TASSER: A unified platform for automated protein structure and function prediction. *Nat Protoc*, 2010, 5(4): 725–738.

[173] Roy A., Yang J., Zhang Y. COFACTOR: An accurate comparative algorithm for structure-based protein function annotation. *Nucleic Acids Res*, 2012, 40(Web Server issue): W471–W477.

[174] Shen H.B., Chou K.C. A top-down approach to enhance the power of predicting human protein subcellular localization: Hum-mPLoc 2.0. *Anal Biochem*, 2009, 394(2): 269 274.

[175] Liu B., Liu F., Fang L., Wang X., Chou K.C. repDNA: A Python package to generate various modes of feature vectors for DNA sequences by incorporating user-defined physicochemical properties and sequence-order effects. *Bioinformatics*, 2015, 31(8): 1307–1309.

[176] Liu B., Liu F., Wang X., Chen J., Fang L., Chou K.C. Pse-in-One: a web server for generating various modes of pseudo components of DNA, RNA, and protein sequences. *Nucleic Acids Res*, 2015.

[177] Liu B., Liu F., Fang L., Wang X., Chou K.C. repRNA: A web server for generating various feature vectors of RNA sequences. *Mol Genet Genomics*, 2015.

[178] Hristea F.T. Statistical Natural Language Processing, in *International Encyclopedia of Statistical Science*. 2011, Springer. pp. 1452–1453.

[179] Dong Q., Menon R., Omenn G.S., Zhang Y. Structural bioinformatics inspection of neXtProt PE5 proteins in the human proteome. *J Proteome Res*, 2015, 14(9): 3750–3761.

[180] Fox N.K., Brenner S.E., Chandonia J.-M. SCOPe: Structural Classification of Proteins — extended, integrating SCOP and ASTRAL data and classification of new structures. *Nucleic Acids Res*, 2014, 42(D1): D304–D309.

[181] Murzin A.G., Brenner S.E., Hubbard T., Chothia C. SCOP: A structural classification of proteins database for the investigation of sequences and structures. *J Mol Biol*, 1995, 247(4): 536–540.

[182] Chandonia J.M., Hon G., Walker N.S., Lo Conte L., Koehl P., Levitt M., Brenner S.E. The ASTRAL Compendium in 2004. *Nucleic Acids Res*, 2004, 32(Database issue): D189–D192.

[183] Zhang Y., Skolnick J. TM-align: A protein structure alignment algorithm based on the TM-score. *Nucleic Acids Res*, 2005, 33(7): 2302–2309.

[184] Gray K.A., Yates B., Seal R.L., Wright M.W., Bruford E.A. Genenames.org: The HGNC resources in 2015. *Nucleic Acids Res*, 2014.

[185] Desiere F., Deutsch E.W., King N.L., Nesvizhskii A.I., Mallick P., Eng J., Chen S., Eddes J., Loevenich S.N., Aebersold R. The PeptideAtlas project. *Nucleic Acids Res*, 2006, 34(Database issue): D655–D658.

[186] Wilhelm M., Schlegl J., Hahne H., Moghaddas Gholami A., Lieberenz M., Savitski M.M., Ziegler E., Butzmann L., Gessulat S., Marx H., Mathieson T., Lemeer S., Schnatbaum K., Reimer U., Wenschuh H., Mollenhauer M., Slotta-Huspenina J., Boese J.H., Bantscheff M., Gerstmair A., Faerber F., Kuster B. Mass-spectrometry-based draft of the human proteome. *Nature*, 2014, 509(7502): 582–587.

[187] Kim M.S., Pinto S.M., Getnet D., Nirujogi R.S., Manda S.S., Chaerkady R., Madugundu A.K., Kelkar D.S., Isserlin R., Jain S., Thomas J.K., Muthusamy B., Leal-Rojas P., Kumar P., Sahasrabuddhe N.A., Balakrishnan L., Advani J., George B., Renuse S., Selvan L.D., Patil A.H., Nanjappa V., Radhakrishnan A., Prasad S., Subbannayya T., Raju R., Kumar M., Sreenivasamurthy S.K., Marimuthu A., Sathe G.J., Chavan S., Datta K.K., Subbannayya Y., Sahu A., Yelamanchi S.D., Jayaram S., Rajagopalan P., Sharma J., Murthy K.R., Syed N., Goel R., Khan A.A., Ahmad S., Dey G., Mudgal K., Chatterjee A., Huang T.C., Zhong J., Wu X., Shaw P.G., Freed D., Zahari M.S., Mukherjee K.K., Shankar S., Mahadevan A., Lam H., Mitchell C.J., Shankar S.K., Satishchandra P., Schroeder J.T., Sirdeshmukh R., Maitra A., Leach S.D., Drake C.G., Halushka M.K., Prasad T.S., Hruban R.H., Kerr C.L., Bader G.D., Iacobuzio-Donahue C.A., Gowda H., Pandey A. A draft map of the human proteome. *Nature*, 2014, 509(7502): 575–581.

[188] Pruitt K.D., Brown G.R., Hiatt S.M., Thibaud-Nissen F., Astashyn A., Ermolaeva O., Farrell C.M., Hart J., Landrum M.J., McGarvey K.M., Murphy M.R., O'Leary N.A., Pujar S., Rajput B., Rangwala S.H., Riddick L.D., Shkeda A., Sun H., Tamez P., Tully R.E., Wallin C., Webb D., Weber J., Wu W., DiCuccio M., Kitts P., Maglott D.R., Murphy T.D., Ostell J.M. RefSeq: An update on mammalian reference sequences. *Nucleic Acids Res*, 2014, 42(Database issue): D756–D763.

Chapter 7

Summary and Future Perspectives

In the field of bioinformatics, the study of the structure and function of proteins is undoubtedly the most challenging problem. Although researchers have made unremitting efforts, they are still far from reaching the ultimate goal.

With the maturity of protein primary structure sequencing technology, the amount of genomic and proteomic sequence data is increasing, alongside the growth of structural and functional data, making computing methods and information technology extremely useful in the field. Based on the n-gram statistical analysis of the genomic protein sequence, and on the basis of verifying the linguistic characteristics of the whole genome protein sequence, the technology of the biological language model is introduced into bioinformatics in this book. In order to promote the development of protein sequence–structure–function mapping, new computational methods are used to predict the structure and function of proteins, simplify the model of protein structure and function prediction, and improve the accuracy of protein structure and function prediction. The main research results of this book include the following aspects:

1. The n-gram and linguistic features of whole genome protein sequences were analyzed. We found that there exists Zipf's law in whole genome protein sequences, and the Shannon n-gram entropy analysis shows that the natural genome proteins are different from the artificial proteins.

2. We systematically investigated the basic building blocks of the biological language model, i.e. the amino acid encoding schemes. These basic protein units were benchmarked and compared with the protein secondary structure prediction and protein fold recognition task. Similar to the distributed representation in natural language processing, the distributed representations of amino acids or n-gram amino acids have potential power for use in many protein-level research tasks.

3. The Latent Semantic Analysis and the Auto-Cross Covariance transformation methods were introduced for protein remote homology detection. Several basic building units of protein sequences were explored. Testing on the SCOP 1.53 and SCOP 1.67 dataset showed that the results are better than other existing methods.

4. The biological language model was used to solve several issues of protein structure prediction including protein structure prediction, protein domain boundaries, protein local structures and knowledge-based potential energy functions. The Profile Domain Linker propensity Index (PDLI), which contains the evolutionary information of profiles, was proposed for domain linker prediction. A structural alphabet for protein structures was also proposed. Novel nonlinear potentials were implemented as well.

5. The biological language model was used to solve several protein function problems. Different protein vocabularies were investigated including the n-gram, the binary profile, the frequency profile and the domains. Effective machine learning methods were adopted to explore binding site prediction, protein–protein interaction, GO function prediction and missing protein identification.

In this book, the above research prospects were assessed and only minor results were achieved. In order to make better use of the biological language model to solve bioinformatics problems, we believe that the following aspects should be further studied:

1. In this book, the binary profile was a simplification of the frequency profile. A single probability threshold was used to

determine whether the corresponding amino acids appeared in the binary profile. However, the frequency of different amino acids varies greatly. It is impossible to capture the homologous information accurately by using the binary profile. We can consider further refinement of the binary profile, for example, the formation of an N-ary profile — containing evolutionary information — which will be widely used in many problems of protein structure and function prediction.

2. Mining the equivalent words in protein sequences. It is well known that a protein sequence determines its structure, and that its structure is closely related to its function. However, it is difficult to find the relationship between amino acids and protein structure, namely the so-called "second genetic code". Therefore, protein sequences can be expressed in other ways in order to find the mapping relationship between basic sequences and structures.

3. Developing the biological language model. The emergence of a large number of corpuses has promoted the development of computational linguistics. Similarly, with the emergence of a large number of protein sequences, structures and functional data, statistical modeling methods can be applied to this field. However, due to the complexity of protein structure, it will be difficult to accurately construct a protein folding model. More complex and effective methods are necessary to handle those tasks.

4. The application of the biological language model in proteome-based functional research. A protein is not an isolated individual in an organism. Its function is affected by the environment as well as by other proteins. A protein can be regarded as a basic unit. The interaction between proteins can be simulated by natural language processing technology, so that the function of proteins can be studied at a higher level.

Index

East China Normal University Scientific Reports
Subseries on Data Science and Engineering

Published (continued from page ii)

CPSIA information can be obtained
at www.ICGtesting.com
Printed in the USA
BVHW062059280620
582418BV00015B/349